Strategies
For
Persuasive
Communication

Ronald L. Applbaum
Karl W. E. Anatol
California State University,
Long Beach

CHARLES E. MERRILL PUBLISHING COMPANY
A Bell & Howell Company
Columbus, Ohio

To
Our Wives
Susan and Peggy
the truly successful persuaders

Published by
Charles E. Merrill Publishing Company
A Bell & Howell Company
Columbus, Ohio 43216

ISBN: 0-675-08803-8

Library of Congress Catalog Card Number: 74-75147

2 3 4 5 6 7 — 78 77

Printed in the United States of America

Contents

Contents

Preface

Webster's *New World Dictionary* defines a preface as a statement preliminary or introductory to a book, telling its subject, purpose, and plan. Its primary function is informational; however, it is just as concerned with persuading teachers and students that the text offers the approach and materials necessary to accomplish their desired course or individual objectives.

It is somewhat coincidental that a book which attempts to provide its readers with an understanding of the persuasive process as it operates should attempt to persuade you to read the text. However, we will not attempt to persuade you to a certain course of action in regard to persuasion, but alert you to the strategies that may provide the basis for successful persuasive attempts.

The text is not prescriptive in nature. We will not tell you how to develop or present a persuasive communication. However, we do present guidelines or propositions drawn from research at the end of chapters 2 through 7 which suggest key concepts and factors that are relevant to successful persuasive communication. In chapters 8 through 10 we show how persuasion operates in real situations—product advertising, courtroom, and classroom.

We would like to acknowledge "Scotty" Davidson and Louise Rogers for their secretarial assistance and William Irvin for gathering research materials used in the text.

part one

An
Introduction

1

An Orientation to Persuasion

Most people go through life unaware of the complex of events occurring around them, of environmental pressures, of rapid technological change, of people and groups who influence their very existence. Civilized people need to know not only what their environment is like, but how they are influenced by it. Today, this is not an easy task even for the most intelligent and aware for we live in the age of a communication explosion. We are asked to cope with a proliferation of information that at times exceeds our human potential, and we are forced to utilize mammoth amounts of data in making decisions whether or not we understand their ultimate implications or consequences.

The average consumer is potentially exposed to 1,500 ads per day. The shopper in the supermarket may be exposed to 6,000 items from which he will purchase only a small proportion. New products are vying for consumer attention every day. The number of influence attempts that are made upon us to purchase consumer products is seemingly unlimited.

In 1973 it was estimated that the American public spent, on the average, six hours a day in front of the television. We are subjected not only to the never-ending number of commercials, but also to media's definition and interpretation of the news. It is impossible for the media, radio, television, newspapers, and magazines, to provide us with all the information or all the news that occurs within a twenty-four hour time span. Television, for example, has begun devoting more and more time to the news to provide a more comprehensive treatment of daily events, but it can still only present a capsulated form of any one occurrence. As the media decides what will be covered and discarded, it distorts perception of the event. Consequently, our decisions on daily issues are biased by the coverage of the media. The media becomes an even more important influencing agent when it becomes the only access we have to the information we need to make our decisions ranging from electing a president to supporting a local bond drive.

During election years, we are confronted with television, radio, newspapers, pamphlets, and door-to-door canvassers selling their product —the candidate for public office. These campaigns contribute to the demise as well as the rise of a politician. The advent of new technologies adapted to modern political campaigns has changed the democratic character of our election process. The frequency of elections on national, state, and local levels has made many individuals tired of political harangues, the faces of politicians beaming from billboards, mailboxes overloaded with brightly colored brochures, "paid political advertisements" preempting favorite television programming, and canvassers disrupting the serenity of the weekend, extolling the virtues of their candidate. The appeal of the candidate in the local arena has become a performance; as with any actor's performance, it is staged for the benefit of the listening audience.

Just as Americans have substituted political elections for revolutions by force, so we have substituted courtroom debate for private war. The main business of the law is the trial and decision of specific disputes. Throughout this country people are summoned to sit on juries to make these decisions. The medium of the law is language; and the lawyer's success or failure may depend largely on his skill and precision in using the language to influence the judge or jury. The jury may be inundated with legalistic jargon, the layman's brain overloaded to the point where his mental fuse burns out. And yet, he is faced with the reality of deciding the validity, guilt, or innocence of a particular event, person, or group on the basis of the presented information.

Man is, to a great extent, the product of his environment. His ability to cope with the constant bombardment of new information as it attempts to influence his ideas and feelings will determine whether his decisions reflect an intelligent and rational process. Think back to decisions you have had to make within the last week: Should I use Bufferin or aspirin for my headache? Should I accept the ideas of my professor as reflecting the correct point of view? Should I purchase Shell or Gulf gasoline? Should I go to see a Chaplin film festival or listen to a Bach concert in the college auditorium? We all recognize that these decisions are not entirely our own. They are the products of certain pressures exerted upon us from the environment—culture, groups, individuals with whom we associate, the media, and so on. We probably understand this fundamental fact. However, it is important that we have the insight to recognize the extent of these influences and how they affect our behavior in different situations. An understanding of the types of influence that are made upon us and their effect on our behavior is the primary goal of this text.

A Model of Persuasive Communication

As we present our model of the persuasive process, keep in mind that no model is ideal or complete. This model is a reflection of our particular interests and biases. However, the model enables us to illustrate the forms and elements of persuasion so we can see more clearly how they operate within the persuasive act. Figure 1-1 illustrates our model of persuasion. This model also illustrates the basic organizational format of the text.

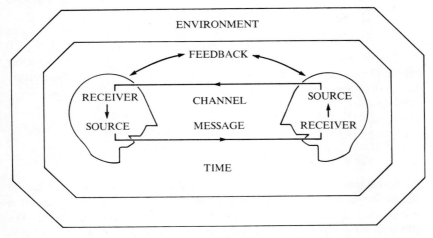

FIGURE 1-1. A Model of Persuasive Communication

The act of persuasion involves a specific period of time and at least two individuals. Any act of persuasion occurs within a specific environmental setting. The environment might be:

1. an advertising campaign;
2. a political campaign;
3. a law court;
4. a classroom;
5. a home.

These are the external boundaries of the persuasive process. Internally, our model includes four primary elements: source, receiver, message, and channel.

A *source* is the individual or group that initiates the communication, a sender or speaker who uses verbal and/or nonverbal means of communicating. For example:

1. wife
2. employer
3. book

4. teacher
5. fraternity
6. broadcaster

The source is the element of the process that attempts to produce the persuasive effect.

A *receiver* is the individual or group that is the target of the source's communication. The source is acting to produce a change in the receiver's attitudes, values, and/or behavior. For example:

1. audience
2. group of friends

3. television viewer
4. student

A *message* is the information transmitted between source and receiver. There are two basic types of messages: nonverbal and verbal. Nonverbal messages include:

1. facial expressions
2. bodily gestures
3. use of space
4. eye contact

5. vocal sounds
6. use of time
7. fashion

All transmission of information between source and receiver without the use of words is nonverbal. The verbal messages are the products of a translation of the source's communication into a language code. We will generally use the English language as the basis for our verbal messages in this country. The organization, content, arrangement of language, and manner of delivering the code will all affect the ultimate persuasive act. The source may select one piece of information to transmit and reject another, he may repeat evidence, or he may summarize. Each source makes certain decisions regarding the transmission and selection of messages that will best achieve his persuasive intent.

The receiver determines the ultimate success of the persuasive effort of the source and his message. The impact of the persuasive transaction depends on the willingness of the receiver to respond to both the source and his message. If the receiver refuses to perceive a source or listen to his message, the persuasive act can never be successful.

A *channel* is the vehicle by which the message passes between the source and receiver. For example:

Message medium	Channel
sound	airwaves
visual	light waves

We should recognize that most communication entails the use of more than one channel at a time. For example, when we are watching a television program, we are receiving messages that are both visual and oral and, therefore, the messages are transmitted over airwaves and light waves. In addition, the television transmission is being carried to our television set from the broadcast studio by the means of electro-magnetic waves.

Feedback, in our model, refers to the return process in communication whereby the source can tell how a message is interpreted. Does the receiver say, "Yes, I agree with your argument," as we attempt to persuade him? Does he shake his head from side to side showing disagreement? Does the editor of a newspaper receive letters protesting a recent editorial? Does the television switchboard light up following "Meet the Press"? Does the audience wildly applaud its favorite candidate's remarks? In answering each of these questions, we are concerned with the feedback that a receiver transmits to the source of the communication. The successful persuader attends to feedback and modifies his message in light of what he sees and hears from his receivers.

All the elements of our model are interrelated. None exists as a distinct entity in the persuasive process. Let us now examine some of the more important interrelationships between the various components of our model.

The *source-receiver* relationship is determined by the purpose of the persuasive act. For example, in a senatorial campaign, the source (candidate) communicates to his receivers (constituents) with the intent of gaining votes. The manager will communicate to the lineworker with the intent of increasing morale or company productivity. Their relationship is determined by the change in attitudes, values, and/or behavior the source seeks from the receiver.

The *source-environment* relationship refers to the effect of social, political, and cultural variables on the source in a particular persuasive situation. The presidential candidate will react quite differently when speaking before the public over television than in an arena containing five thousand screaming supporters. The lawyer will approach a jury quite differently from Madison Avenue advertisers in attempting to sell a product to a specific demographic area in our country. The source's actions will be directly affected by the environment in which the persuasive act occurs.

The *receiver-environment* relationship refers to the effect of social, political, and cultural variables on the psychological sets of the receiver. The situation presents conditions that are external to the communication, but which affect what the receiver will listen to and ultimately accept. A student may accept the information a teacher communicates in the classroom only when that information directly relates to the objectives of the course. If the course is in biology, attempts by the teacher to influence the students' political views might fall short of the source's expectations. The environment could dictate which persuasive attempts would be successful or unsuccessful. The relationship exists between receiver-environment only to the extent that the receiver internalizes the environment.

The *receiver-message* relationship refers to the effect a communicative act has upon the receiver. The organization and order of speech materials, presentation of those materials, and so on will all affect the receiver's perception of the persuasive act and its ultimate effect upon the receiver. A potential voter may desire that a source's message present the important political issues in a clear and coherent pattern. If the message does not reach the expectations desired by the receiver, he may not be influenced to vote for the candidate. In turn, the receiver's perception of the appropriate message will be influenced by the environment in which the persuasive act occurs.

We are concerned with a pattern of interrelationships between source, receiver, message, and environment. Collectively, the pattern of relationships between elements of our model will determine the success of the persuasive effort. We must recognize the interdependence of these relationships. The primary element in any specific persuasive situation will be determined by the pattern of relationships. We are suggesting that in certain situations the primary agent for activating persuasion might be the message. In other situations it might be the source or environment. No one element is always the determining agent of persuasion. Persuasion occurs in a system. No dimension operates or exists as an isolated entity or part. A change in any element will result in changes throughout the system. Viewing persuasion as a system suggests that no single element can actually be understood in isolation. However, an understanding of each element is necessary to understand the total system.

We now should recognize that the persuasive system is extremely complex. For one thing, all elements are interacting simultaneously. Second, the elements are constantly changing while interacting.

A Definition of Persuasion

A definition of any concept attempts to determine or set down certain characteristics and limits of what the term means or has meant. If only one set of characteristics or limits existed for previous definitions of persuasion, our task would be simple. However, persuasion has a number of different definitions and limitations. In developing our own definition, we might begin by searching for specific characteristics of the persuasive act. Let us examine several persuasive situations.

1. It is Saturday night, a boy has been studying all day, and yet he hasn't begun work on a paper due on Monday. The paper's grade is determined in part by its being on time. His girlfriend calls on the phone. She suggests that he relax in her apartment tonight. He decides to spend the evening with her.

2. "My fellow Americans, let me make one thing perfectly clear. If you vote for me, I promise to make the water in this country fit for human consumption. A vote for me is a vote for clean water and clean government." The majority of listeners run out the next day and vote for the candidate.

3. A young lawyer approaches the jury. He summarizes his case, makes numerous references to famous individuals and their thinking on similar problems, and asks the jury to favor his client, the defendant. The jury meets for one hour and finds the defendant not guilty.

4. You turn on the television. A young man who has won seven gold medals in the previous Olympics suggests that it is important to drink milk regularly. An announcer asks, "If Mark can drink milk, shouldn't you?" You quickly change the channel to watch the local basketball game, run to the refrigerator for a cold beer, and relax on the living room couch.

5. A father admonishes his son's behavior toward some guests. The son apologizes, but suggests that his behavior was not meant to malign the visitors. The father realizes that his judgment may have been made in haste and suggests that the entire matter be forgotten.

In these five situations, what conclusions can be drawn regarding characteristics and limits to the act of communication we call persuasion?

First, *all situations involved symbolic communication* — that is, the transmission and reception of verbal and/or nonverbal cues. The lawyer, for example, sends out to the jury certain words in combination with factors of voice quality, reinforced or contradicted by his gestures, postures, and facial expressions. Symbols stand for other things, but bear no relationship to them. The word source is not the actual source but serves as a symbol of the initiator of a communication. A *sign*, on the other hand, bears a real relationship to the thing for which it stands. The twitching of a communicator's hands when talking may be a sign of his nervousness. Here there is a real rather than an arbitrary relationship between the thing (nervousness) and the sign (twitching of the hands). A sign, then, is a nonsymbolic representation of a thing for which it stands. Human interaction entails both symbolic and nonsymbolic cues. However, the primary vehicle for human communication is the symbolic interchange between individuals. Human communication involves verbal and nonverbal symbols. Verbal symbols are the words like "car" or "Bob," which refer to specific objects and people, or "anger," "hate," which refer to internal feelings. Verbal symbols can be either oral or written. Nonverbal symbols are all symbolic behaviors, except verbal ones, that a source or receiver performs in a persuasive situation. For example, a receiver frowns, slouches in his chair, and shakes his head from side to side in response to a source's message.

Because a symbol is an arbitrary designation for some object, concept, or thing, the idea held by the communicator and the idea transmitted to the receiver may not be the same; thoughts behind a communicator's message and the thoughts of a receiver as he interprets the message can never be identical. The linkage between source and receiver is not direct, mechanical, or totally predictable. As Colin Cherry (1961) expressed it, "If I push a man into the lake, he inevitably goes in; if I tell him to jump in, he may do one of a thousand things."

If the father, when admonishing his son's behavior, raises his hand as if to strike the child, the persuasive situation has involved both symbolic (the admonition) and nonsymbolic (raising the hand to strike) interaction. The raising of the hand is a sign of the father's anger toward the son's behavior. In this case, the sign may indicate the intensity of the feeling expressed symbolically by the admonition. In a persuasive situation the interaction between source and receiver will be influenced by both symbolic and nonsymbolic communication.

Second, *persuasion is a complex process.* When the girl calls her boyfriend, her persuasive effort began prior to the telephone call. Her telephone message, the ideas, organization or arguments, and methods used to persuade her boyfriend are affected by the immediate communication situation and all previous persuasive attempts. The boy's acceptance of her invitation is based primarily on the present communication, but influenced by all past experiences and future expectations. All communication is a process. It is a circular, symbolic interaction in which each communicator affects the behavior of the other. Everything that occurs within the context of a communicative effort is dynamic, ongoing, and continuous. When we say communication and, therefore, persuasion is a process, we mean it has no beginning, end, or fixed sequence of events. It is ever-changing. These changes are irreversible, continuous, and unrepeatable. When we communicate certain words to another, they can never be unspoken.

Third, *most communicators seek to elicit a specific response from their listener(s).* The girlfriend wanted her boyfriend to come to her apartment, the candidate sought the listener's votes, the commercial was attempting to gain additional milk drinkers, the lawyer hoped that the jury would respond with a not-guilty verdict, and the father requested an apology for his son's behavior.

We are not suggesting that people do not unconsciously seek specific responses or will not unintentionally persuade another person. In some communication situations, the listener is exposed to communications that are not intended for him. When we hear a friend at a cocktail party telling a group the merits of buying a Buick over a Ford, we may decide to buy the Buick. As we walk down a school corridor, we might hear a fellow student suggest a cold beer at the local tavern. The idea appears to have merit so we immediately leave campus for some liquid refreshment. However, in most persuasive situations, the source consciously or intentionally attempts to elicit a specific response. In this text, we will concentrate on those situations in which one individual *deliberately* attempts to elicit a specific behavior from another individual or group.

Fourth, *the role of communicator may switch in the persuasive situation.* In situation five, the father was the source attemping to elicit an apology. However, when the son attempted to explain the real meaning of his behavior, he became the source and his father the receiver. Both father and son were persuader and persuadee. These roles alternated, rather than occurred simultaneously.

Fifth, *most persuasive situations involve at least two individuals or groups* — boyfriend-girlfriend, candidate-potential voters, TV commercial-television audience, father-son and lawyer-jury. There are those instances, however, when an individual may persuade himself to a specific course of action. For example, let's say that we have two tickets. One ticket is for a musical in the college auditorium and the second ticket is for an NCAA basketball playoff game. We might deliberate the advantages of both events and persuade ourselves to attend the basketball game over the musical.

Sixth, *persuasion occurs in all daily communication.* We are alternately persuading or being persuaded. We are targets of persuasion in our conversation with family, friends, co-workers, and when listening to radio or television. In turn, we are constantly attempting to elicit specific responses from our family, friends, or co-workers.

Seventh, *attempts at persuasion are not always successful.* If we fail to begin drinking milk after listening to the TV commercial, the intended response has not been achieved. Even if we initially ran out and began drinking milk, only to quit one week later, the persuasive message has had only limited success. At other times, we may not respond as the communicator wishes at the time he so desires. His initial persuasive attempt may have little or no effect. However, when we reflect upon his arguments some time later we may decide to change our beliefs and actions because we now see value in the source's position.

Eighth, *the persuader and persuadee are responding to external and internal forces.* The boy who must decide whether to go to the girlfriend's apartment is concerned with the external pressures of his classroom assignment and the internal psychological pressures to share her company.

Persuasion is a complex process of communication by which one individual or group elicits (intentionally or unintentionally) by nonverbal and/or verbal means a specific response from another individual or group.

There are some who believe that persuasion is not involved in all communication situations in which behavior is influenced by a set of stimuli (Bettinghaus 1973). However, it is our belief that all communication situations are persuasive. When the police association requests support for its widow and orphan fund, we are persuaded to give money. When supermarkets place advertisements in a newspaper, they are attempting to sell their products. There are less obvious persuasive attempts, however. When a teacher describes a model of communication, he may be suggesting to the students that they accept this model when describing the communication process. When we walk down a street and say hello to a friend and he responds, we are attempting to elicit either a similar behavioral response or influence the individual's perception of our self. Even though the last two examples are not always considered persuasion, the goal of the communicative effort conforms to our definition of persuasion. Any time an individual communicates, he is attempting to produce a specific response from the other. He may or may not be successful, but the original intent was persuasive in nature.

Bettinghaus (1968) has also differentiated between persuasion and compliance. Let's say a teacher tells a student, "I don't care whether you want to write your paper that way or not. That is the way you'll do it." He is concerned with compliance behavior, that is, attempting to produce a specific behavioral response regardless of the individual's feelings or thoughts. We believe that compliance is a product of persuasion. Persuasion is concerned with eliciting changes of attitude, cognition, value and/or behavior. If the communicator's desired response to his communication is a change in an individual's overt behavior, and only the behavior of the receiver changes, he has still elicited the desired behavior. A change in cognitions is not necessary for persuasion to take place. However, many times a modification of behavior will lead to a change in beliefs.

An additional limitation usually placed on a definition of persuasion is the exclusion of all physical or psychological demands, whether actual or implied (Schiedel 1967). Those who accept this limitation suggest that persuasion reflects *choice* on the part of the listener; that is, the listener must be able to choose whether he will accept or reject the persuasive effort. We suggest that implied coercion is in reality a very valid type of persuasion. If your boss suggests that you do things his way or be fired and you conform to his expectations, you have been persuaded. He has elicited the desired response from you. Unfortunately, since the time of Aristotle, rhetoricians — those who attempt to study and apply the various strategies of persuasion to oral communication — have tended to categorize coercion as bad or inherently unethical and, therefore, distinct from persuasion. As Simons (1972) suggests, rhetoricians have assumed that persuasion and coercion are not only separable but antithetical. The trouble with this distinction is that the persuasion-coercion dichotomy does not apply in reality. The source who threatens the listener with death unless he accepts his position has still given the listener a choice. However, the alternatives, death or acceptance of a position, may not be equally distasteful.

Overview

We have divided this text into three separate, but interrelated parts. Part two, which contains chapters 2 through 3, is concerned with the nature of attitudes and theories of attitude change. Part three, which contains chapters 4 through 7, deals with the nature of four elements of our persuasive model — source, receiver, channel, and message. Part four, containing chapters 8 through 10, will emphasize the practical application of persuasive strategies in education, law, and product advertising.

Before we proceed to the next chapter, let us examine a short overview of the remaining nine chapters.

Chapter 2. An examination of the characteristics and components of attitudes. A comparison and contrast between attitudes, opinions, beliefs, and values.

Chapter 3. An examination of several theoretical orientations derived from learning theories, consistency theories, functional theories, social comparison and inoculation theory.

Chapter 4. An examination of the source's role in the persuasive process. Three major areas are investigated: (1) source credibility; (2) source-receiver similarity; and (3) power.

Chapter 5. An examination of the message's role in the persuasive process. Three major areas are investigated: (1) form of the message; (2) content of the message; and (3) presentation of the message.

Chapter 6. An examination of the channel's role in the persuasive process. Three major areas are investigated: (1) the effects of the mass media; (2) the relevance of reference or interest groups to the overall process of persuasion; and (3) the value and comparative effectiveness of "face-to-face" or dyadic communication.

Chapter 7. An examination of the receiver's role in the persuasive process. Ten receiver variables — self-esteem, anxiety and insecurity, Machiavellianism, authoritarianism, dogmatism, ego-defensiveness, cognitive style, intelligence, age, and sex — are investigated.

Chapter 8. An examination of the nature and definition of product advertising. Five areas are investigated: (1) key psychological targets to be
deployed; (2) specific objectives and methods of achievement; (3) types
of appeals utilized; (4) creative mix; and (5) effective use of headlines,
illustrations, and color.

Chapter 9. An examination of the persuasive process operating in the
courtroom. Three courtroom variables are investigated: (1) the lawyer;
(2) the jury; and (3) the message.

Chapter 10. An examination of the classroom as a persuasive environment. Three areas are investigated: (1) the teacher; (2) the message;
and (3) classroom control.

Each chapter concludes with a set of propositions emphasizing the
application of the chapter's content to the persuasive process, and a set
of annotated readings for those who wish to investigate the chapter's
content in greater depth.

Additional Readings

Anderson, K. E. *Persuasion Theory and Practice.* Boston: Allyn and Bacon,
    1971, pp. 1-40. An examination of the persuasive process and its role
    in today's society.

Bettinghaus, E. P. *Persuasive Communication.* 2d. ed. New York: Holt,
    Rinehart, and Winston, 1973, pp. 7-27. A clear explanation of the rela-
    tionship between communication and persuasion.

Scheidel, T. M. *Persuasive Speaking.* Glenview, Ill.: Scott, Foresman, 1967,
    pp. 3-17. A short, clear overview of classical rhetorical contributions to
    the study of persuasion.

part two

Attitudes: Psychological Constructs

2

The Nature of
Attitudes

Attitude is perhaps the most widely studied concept in communication and social psychology. Even in our everyday traffic with others, there is a persistent involvement with attitudes. We want to know how our friends feel toward us. The auto salesman wants to know how the prospective customer feels about a particular model or how he feels concerning cost of purchase. The instructor wants to know how students feel toward him and the subject matter. The student is concerned with the feelings of the instructor toward him. Managers attempt to assess the feelings of workers toward their jobs, and workers attempt to discover what impressions they make on management. The politician's major concern is whether citizens will vote for him; he seeks the assistance of campaign managers who try to predict outcomes by measuring voter attitudes. Attitudes are important to all of us as long as choices must be made, and relationships cultivated. In the never-ending battle for the mind, attitudes are the most strategic targets.

What is an attitude? A precise definition is difficult because the concept overlaps with other kinds of psychological concepts, and it is in this area of overlap that some clarification must first be attempted. As early as 1935, Gordon Allport defined an attitude as *"A mental and neural state of readiness, organized through experience, exerting a directive or dynamic influence upon the individual's response to all objects and situations with which it is related."* Krech and Crutchfield (1948) defined an attitude as "an enduring organization of motivational, emotional, perceptual, and cognitive processes with respect to some aspect of the individual's world." These definitions view an attitude as a *hypothetical construct.* A hypothetical construct is "an entity or process that is inferred as actually existing . . . and as giving rise to measurable phenomena" (English and English 1958). Let us examine some of the crucial characteristics and components of attitudes as have been defined by Allport (1935) and Krech and Crutchfield (1948).

Characteristics of Attitudes

Attitudes Have an Object

To say that "Jack has a positive attitude" offers incomplete information. It would be more helpful to say that Jack has a positive attitude toward trade with Red China, or women's liberation, or planned parenthood, or blacks, and so on. Given this information, we should be able to estimate how Jack might behave or act in certain situations. We would expect Jack to speak in favor of trade with Red China in a discussion on this particular issue, or to recommend that his friends support only those political candidates who endorse a "trade with Red China" policy. In short, Jack's attitude toward trade with Red China (the attitude object) influences his behavior with reference to that particular issue. Attitude objects may be specific, such as a particular item or commodity which may be involved in trade with Red China. Or the object may be general, such as pertains to *all* issues of trade. Attitude objects may consist of abstractions such as loyalty, vice, morality, capitalism, corruption, law and order. Or the attitude object may be a person, a social class of people, or social institutions.

Attitudes Have Direction, Degree, Intensity

Attitudes are characterized by an *orientation* toward objects. There are varying degrees and intensity of orientation. Opinion surveys or questionnaires and audience analyses, when conducted, usually attempt to measure the direction, degree, and intensity of attitudes.

The direction of an attitude indicates association or disassociation with an issue or proposal, like or dislike of a given object, and so on.

We should recall that Allport speaks of an attitude as exerting a directive or dynamic influence upon an individual's response. Let us consider anti-Semitism, for instance. The attitude determines the target—Jews; consequently, the individual will act or react with hostility or aggression toward Jews.

In addition to assessing direction, there is a possibility of assessing *degree*. How much does an individual dislike Jews? Is his dislike of such degree that he would not fraternize or associate with a Jew? Or is his dislike so great that he would firebomb the home of a Jew? A measure of degree may be generally obtained by questions that ask *how* favorable or unfavorable a person feels toward an attitude object.

Intensity tells us something about the level of conviction with which an attitude is held. In order to measure intensity, we may use such indices as galvanic skin response, heart rates, pupil dilation measures, and so on.

Attitudes Are Learned

Attitudes develop through direct or indirect experience with an object or person. Direct experience is perhaps the most important contributor to attitude formation. A white individual who has been trapped on a street in the midst of a ghetto riot would most likely develop a dislike or negative attitude toward riots or perhaps even toward a protesting minority group. However, the effects of indirect experiences on attitude development should not be minimized. Merely watching a riot on TV or hearing someone else's story of being endangered by gun-fire during a riot may be sufficient to foster a negative attitude. Several attitudes that we hold are influenced by indirect experience relayed to us by others. It is possible for us to hold strong or highly intense attitudes—positive or negative—toward objects and persons we have never actually encountered. Thus, we, as students of communication, must be concerned with the effect of both direct and indirect experience on attitude formation and attitude change.

Attitudes Are Stable and Enduring

The definition by Krech and Crutchfield notes this characteristic. We should recognize that attitudes are not momentary or "fickle" states; neither are they absolute, rigid, or permanent. That they are sometimes difficult to change, and that they sometimes *do* change gives ample evidence that attitudes range between two extremes. McDavid and Harari (1968) point out that "the very fact that attitudes are products of accumulated experience implies directly that as long as the organism is able to accumulate further experience with an object, his attitude toward that object will be subject to some degree of change." On the other hand, the longer the actual experience with an attitude object is, the less likely is the chance that an attitude will be changed by an encounter with a *single* new experience. Our task, as persuaders, would be to assess how stable different attitudes are, and thereby know how to tailor our presentations or whether persuasion is indeed possible. The more persistent an individual's experience with an attitude object, the less likely would it be that his attitude may be changed by a single message presentation.

So far we have discussed an attitude from a macroscopic or "whole" point of view. We have considered an attitude in terms of a large unit or construct containing certain characteristics of object orientation, directiveness, and stability. Let us look at attitude from a different point of view by studying three components of an attitude: the *cognitive,* the *affective,* and the *behavioral or conative.* This trichotomy suggested in Krech and Crutchfield's (1948) definition pertains largely to man's knowing, feeling, and acting activities. Let us discuss each component separately.

Components of Attitudes

The *cognitive component* has to do with beliefs about an object, including evaluative beliefs—that is, good or bad, appropriate or inappropriate. Triandis (1971) discusses the cognitive component in terms of "idea" formation. He writes:

> A cognitive component, that is, the *idea* which is generally some category used by humans in thinking. Categories are inferred from consistencies in responses to discriminably different stimuli. The category *cars* can be inferred, for example, by determining that people make similar responses to Fords, Chevrolets, etc., and other stimuli that they are capable of discriminating. Statements (belief-utterances) of the form "cars are. . . ." "cars have. . . ." are also parts of this component.

A close examination of the cognitive or "knowledge" component of an attitude should reveal to us how it is quite easy to form inaccurate beliefs. It has been conceded that, as human beings, we are incapable of recognizing the infinite number of differences that distinguish one object from another, or one person from another. While we pay lip service to the notion that "no two things are alike," we tend to treat these discriminable, nonidentical entities as though they are indeed alike. What happens is that man uses the most economical way of categorizing stimuli in order to achieve simple ways of responding to his environment. After all, it's simpler and more economical to "perceive" all snakes as poisonous than to carefully examine the shape of the head of each snake encountered before coming to a conclusion or taking some line of action. Unfortunately, we tend to deal with our fellow-man in much the same way. We concede that categorizing is valuable to our survival, but it involves, as Allport (1954) and Bruner (1958) point out, a great loss of information.

Our use of language plays a key role in categorization. Language provides terms for a particular category; through language we can point to "the young bi-ped ambling along a road" and respond with the term "boy." However, our language is sometimes too weak to pack a maximum of attributes into a single term and we consequently fall into the trap of stereotyping. Consider such terms as "traitor," "criminal," "snow," "wicked woman," "underpriviledged kids"—what must they mean to different people! The cognitive component is, then, a strategic target in persuasive communication. Sometimes, the major task for a persuader consists of moving the receiver, listener, or audience into a more precise alignment with the "facts" or "true" nature of a circumstance.

The *affective component* has to do with likes or dislikes. It is related to the cognitive component in that it is the emotion which changes the idea. The cognitive component outlines the stimulus, "child-molester"; the affective component charges or motivates our feeling toward the term, "child-molester." The measures of *direction* and *intensity,* which we discussed earlier, are vital to the study of the affective component. When someone says, "I'm opposed to a guaranteed minimum wage for every eligible citizen of the United States," he has given voice to an affective response to the stimulus of a government-granted minimum wage by indicating a direction of feeling. And when he adds, "I feel darn strongly about it," he is indicating an index of the intensity of his feelings. According to Triandis (1971, p. 3), "if a person 'feels good' or 'feels bad' when he thinks about a category (child-molester, for instance), we would say that he has a positive or negative affect toward the members of this category."

Some interesting speculation concerning the dynamic of the affective component has been going on among communicologists and social psychologists. Triandis (1971), for example, conjectures that when a

category has formed, it soon becomes associated with pleasant or unpleasant states. That is like saying that we often tyrannize information
or knowledge with an attitude. In other words, we are not so much
knowledge-seeking beings as we are feeling-seeking beings. We discover
a notion and concurrently become affected toward that notion. We must
realize, of course, that our feelings or affects are dictated largely by our
prior experience—direct or indirect—with a particular category. If past
experiences were pleasant, we feel favorable; if unpleasant, we feel
unfavorable.

Peak (1955) views the relationship between category and affect
in terms of *utility*. She suggests that our attitude toward a particular
object depends on the instrumental relation between objects and goals.
We have positive affects toward objects that aid us in reaching our goals,
and negative affects toward objects that prevent us from reaching our
goals. Rosenberg (1956), Carlson (1956), and to some extent, Fishbein
(1961) utilized an arbitrary equation to explain this utility principle.
Consider, "graduate education," for example. An individual may see it
as being related to some undesirable outcomes (for example, too much
study) as well as to certain desirable outcomes (for example, better status
in a job market). That individual's affect toward the category "graduate
education" will be determined by his perceptions of the probabilities of
a connection between "graduate education" and various outcomes, and
also the "satisfaction" score which is associated with each outcome. The
formula for determining affect is stated as follows:

$$A = P_1 E_1 + P_2 E_2 + \ldots + P_n E_n$$

That is, the affect toward the attitude object (A) is determined by the
probabilities (P) of the outcomes that are important (P_1, P_2, . . ., P_n) to
the individual, and the evaluation (E) which he attaches to each of the
outcomes.

Fishbein (1961) amplifies the *utility* formula by taking into consideration the individual's "beliefs" (B) about the object, and the individual's evaluative (E) aspect of the beliefs. Here is his formulation:

If a person believes that there is a high probability (for example,
+3 on a −3 to +3 scale) that a black would be *musically gifted,* and
he (the individual) values that particular talent very much (for example,
+5 on a −5 to +5 scale), then his *affect* would be $(+3) \times (+5) = 15$.

By this formulation, then, one could assess the affect scores that
pertain to different situations, and perhaps on the basis of comparison
predict an attitude or behavior.

The *behavioral or conative component* deals with the action tendency. This component includes the readiness to behave in a particular way associated with an attitude, but does not predict the actual behavior itself. The behavioral component refers to a *predisposition to action.*

We are carefully drawing this distinction between overt or actual action and tendency to action because of the impress exerted by external social and physical conditions. An individual may have a positive attitude toward integrated housing, but because of group pressure he may join a boycott against a black family moving into his neighborhood. Also, we should realize that some attitudes have more "action structure or potential" than others. When we discuss a functional theory of attitude formation in the next chapter we will notice that certain functions can be served merely by holding an attitude, and that no action is necessary or expected.

A reliable index of the behavioral or conative component would be derived, of course, from observing how a person behaves. However, the paper and pencil questionnaire is the most commonly used method to find out how the person says he would act regarding a given category or attitude object. For instance, one way of finding out the attitude of citizens toward a liberal orientation on the marijuana laws would be to ask: "Would you vote for or against legalizing the sale of marijuana in the United States?" However, if the respondent says "No," we still have no justification for stating that he has a negative attitude toward liberal stances on the marijuana issue. It is quite possible that he is afraid of coming out in favor of the issue. As Triandis (1971) puts it: "A positive emotion will not *necessarily* lead to norms of approach, and a negative emotion will not *necessarily* lead to a hostile norm." Several studies (Bastides and Van den Berghe 1957; Triandis, Vassilou and Nassiakou 1968) report correlations of approximately +.60 between *behavior* and *behavioral intentions.* Under normal situations, consistency among the three components—cognitive, affective, behavioral—is the general rule.

We should now summarize our discussion on the three components of an attitude by placing these components into a theoretical interrelating scheme or framework.

In a given situation, a person selects some of the available stimuli and neglects others. He then sorts or catalogs the selected stimuli in certain ways, and reacts to these selected stimuli affectively and by behavioral intentions which later appear as behavior under "proper" social, environmental, or physical conditions. Our ability to predict between stimulus and outcome is determined by the attitude in terms of three components each of which lends itself to observable or measur-

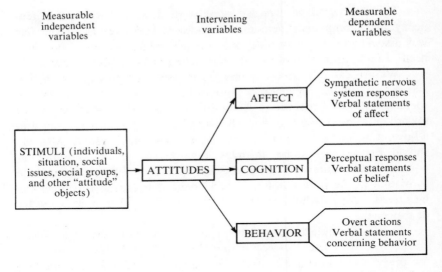

FIGURE 2-1. A Schematic Conception of Attitudes (after Rosenberg and Hovland 1960)

able effects. Rosenberg and Hovland (1960) schematize the situation as shown in figure 2-1.

Krech, Crutchfield and Ballachey (1962) suggest that attitudes tend to differ in their impact on actions according to three primary characteristics:

1. the nature of the three components: cognition, affect, and behavioral tendency;

2. the nature of the attitude system or systems brought into use by a particular situation;

3. the nature of the total constellation, cluster, or overall pattern of the individual's attitude in general.

Some commentators, such as Zimbardo and Ebbesen (1969), Watson and Johnson (1972), Sherif, Sherif and Nebergall (1965), contend that the study of the nature of attitudes from the standpoint of both characteristics and components is instructive only to a certain point. The study of the characteristics and components of attitudes does not necessarily tell us how attitudes might be changed. The dynamics of attitude change will be explained in the next chapter. For the moment, let us "tidy up" our understanding of what an attitude is by differentiating it from opinions, beliefs, and values.

Attitudes Versus Opinions, Beliefs and Values

Jones and Gerard (1967) define attitudes as the implication of combining a *belief* with a relevant *value,* and suggest that attitudes may be changed by changing either the underlying belief or the underlying value. What, then, is a *belief*? What is a *value*?

A *belief* expresses the relations between two cognitive categories when neither defines the other. Most commonly held beliefs concern the associated characteristics of an object. Thus, a statement that lions are dangerous is a belief associating the characteristic "dangerous" to the object "lion." Or, a statement that God is alive associates the characteristic "alive" with the subject "God" and, therefore, is a belief.

A *value* is a frame of reference applied by a person to assess the goodness of an object, situation, or behavior. Values express a relationship between a person's emotional feelings and particular cognitive categories. When a person states, "stealing is wrong," he is expressing a value as he is attaching feelings (wrongness) to the category "stealing." Anything that a person approaches, desires, or espouses reflects a positive value, anything that he avoids, dislikes, or deplores reflects a negative value (Watson and Johnson 1972, p. 224). Rokeach (1966) contends that individuals hold many more attitudes than values. A grown person probably has tens of thousands of beliefs, hundreds of attitudes, but only dozens of values.

Katz and Stotland (1959) make a fine distinction between attitudes and values in their discussion of value systems. They view attitudes as pertaining to a single object, whereas value systems are orientations toward whole classes. The attitudes that we hold are generally organized into a value system. For instance, if liberality is a central value in our value system we would be inclined (generally) to have favorable attitudes toward welfare, women's liberation, labor unions, etc.

Finally, what distinction can we draw between an attitude and an opinion? Hovland, Janis and Kelley (1953) define *opinion* from a stimulus–response standpoint: "(opinions are) verbal answers that an individual gives in response to stimulus situations in which some general question is raised." They see an intimate relationship between an opinion and an attitude. "While the term opinion will be used to designate a broad class of anticipations and exceptions, the term 'attitude' will be used exclusively for those implicit responses which are oriented toward approaching or avoiding a given object, person, group, or symbol." Rokeach (1968) puts it more tersely; he states: "An opinion is defined as a verbal expression of some belief, attitude or value." Secord and Backman (1964) offer perhaps one of the most controversial definitions of an opinion in relationship with attitudes. They write:

> Brief mention should be made of a distinction commonly made between attitude and *opinion*. An opinion is a belief that one holds about some object in his environment. It differs from attitude in being relatively free of emotion—it lacks the affective component central to attitude. The cognitive component or element of knowledge is prominent in opinion: it may take the form of a factual statement about the environment. For example, a man may believe that the earth is spherical, or that women drivers are less capable than men. If to him these are matters of fact, they are regarded as opinions or beliefs. They lack the affective component common to attitudes.

Notice that Secord and Backman suggest no difference between an opinion and a belief. Lindesmith and Strauss (1956) describe an opinion as the overall expression from which an attitude is inferred. Campbell (1947) regards opinion as the observable dependent variable and attitude as the intervening variable.

Definitions are numerous, and the conflict grows. McGuire (1969) describes the controversy well: "Perhaps more effort has been expended to distinguish attitudes from opinions than from any other construct." Indeed, we seem faced with a situation involving names in search of a distinction, rather than a distinction in search of a terminology.

Controversies notwithstanding, attitudes remain the most strategic target in the path of persuasion. A communicator's interest in attitudes derives from his need to predict persuasibility on the basis of his knowledge of the variables that intervene between message impact and audience response to that message. If listeners, readers, or viewers are favorably inclined toward an issue or a product, the persuader should be able to construct messages designed to maintain or consolidate the existing favorable attitude. If the audience is perceived to be hostile toward the issue or product, messages should be designed to change the attitude. This task is not easy; hence the information in the remaining chapters of this textbook. Finally, if the issue or product is new to the audience, then the creation or formation of an attitude (a favorable one!) would be the persuader's major task.

Propositions

1. An attitude may be defined as "a mental and neural state of readiness, organized through experience, exerting a directive or dynamic influence upon the individual's response to all objects and situations with which it is related."

2. An attitude may be further defined in terms of a number of characteristics.
   2a. An attitude is generally focused on an object, situation, event, issue, or person.
   2b. An attitude is characterized by direction, degree, and intensity.
   2c. An attitude is a learned response.
   2d. An attitude is generally stable and enduring.

3. An attitude consists of three fundamental components: cognitive, affective, behavioral.
   3a. The cognitive component consists of the type, quantity, and quality of knowledge or beliefs one possesses concerning an attitude object.
   3b. The affective component consists of the type, quantity and quality of feelings or emotions one experiences concerning an attitude object.
   3c. The behavioral component consists of the "action," or "predisposition to action" tendencies.

4. Attitudes tend to differ in their impact on actions because of or according to three primary characteristics.
   4a. The nature of the cognitive, affective, and behavioral components will determine the kind of action taken.
   4b. The nature of the individual's "attitude system" will determine behavior or action in a particular situation.
   4c. The nature of the total cluster or overall pattern of the individual's attitude will also determine the course of action.

5. For the sake of definition and analysis, attitudes should be distinguished from opinions, beliefs, and values.
   5a. Attitudes are the implicit responses which are oriented toward approaching or avoiding a given object, person, group, or symbol.
   5b. Opinions are verbal statements or answers offered by individuals in response to stimulus situations in which some general question is raised.
   5c. A belief expresses the relationship between two cognitive elements; e.g. "lion" and "dangerous."

5d. A value is a frame of reference applied by a person to assess the goodness of an object, situation, or behavior.

Additional Readings

Jahoda, Marie and Neil Warren. *Attitudes*. Baltimore, Maryland: Penguin Books Inc., 1966. This book provides a series of readings on various facets of the study of attitudes. The first section, "The Concept of Attitude," reports the viewpoints of five major theorists. Their arguments and points of difference make for stimulating reading.

Rokeach, Milton. *Beliefs, Attitudes, and Values*. San Francisco: Josey-Bass Inc., 1969. Chapter 5 contains an excellent discussion on the nature of attitudes, and proceeds to set up some ways of perceiving the differences between the concepts of "attitude" and "behavior." Chapter 6 should also be helpful to the student who wishes to explore the matter in greater depth. It touches upon problems involved in attempts to understand how attitudes and attitude change may affect behavior.

Secord, Paul and Carl Backman. *Social Psychology*. New York: McGraw-Hill, 1964. Pages 97-108 are suggested for a simple yet thorough discussion of the nature of attitudes, and also for a brief description of various scales used to measure attitudes and attitude change.

3

Theories of
Attitude Change

We need to see how the entire scheme of attitudes fits into the process of persuasion. In order to do this, we should look at a few theoretical orientations derived from learning theories, consistency theories, functional theories, social comparison, and inoculation theory. First, let us try to gain some understanding of the nature and function of theory in the study of persuasion and attitude change.

The Nature and Function of Theory

Theory is a way of explaining things, but it goes further than mere explanation. Deutsch and Krauss (1965) state: "Theories are intellectual tools for organizing data in such a way that one can make inferences or logical transitions from one set of data to another; they serve as guides to investigation, explanation, organization, and discovery of observable facts." Kaplan (1964) adds, "theory will appear as the device for interpreting, criticizing, and unifying established laws, modifying them to fit the data unanticipated in their formulation, and guiding the enterprise of discovering new and more powerful generalizations."

We see that theory serves a unifying function by pulling together the descriptive and explanatory statements that we formulate as we approach understanding. Theory also serves as a guide to investigations by supplying us with general statements from which we derive concepts, known as constructs, and hypotheses. *Constructs* are usually theoretical, because we rarely have direct evidence that they do exist. Attitude is such a construct, for we have no concrete or direct evidence of a physical state called attitude. We observe it indirectly or by inference from its effects. Some other constructs of which we shall speak in this book are intelligence, ego-involvement, open-mindedness, cognitions, dissonance, credibility, and dogmatism.

Hypotheses are statements that predict the effect of one variable on another; for example, the effect of message organization (variable 1) upon attitudes (variable 2). Hypotheses utilize constructs and provide a way to investigate and explain specific behaviors in terms of theory. Hypotheses can be directly derived from theory, and provide ways of testing the validity of that theory.

Constructs and hypotheses in turn lead us to experimentation, which includes observation, description, and verification. This interrelationship is illustrated in figure 3-1. The elements in this diagram interact in an ongoing process of theory building. Theory is formulated, tested, refined, and retested in a continuous search for theory that truly explains human communicative behaviors.

How do we use theories in persuasion research? Why do we need them? Why can't we simply investigate and analyze without them? We shall answer the last two questions first. The use of theory gives us a scheme for interpreting and understanding the results of a study. Miller (1964) points out that theory has great value in giving cohesion and

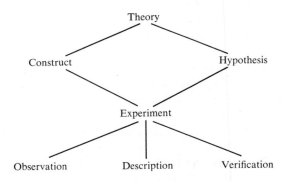

FIGURE 3-1.   Relationship of Theory to Scientific Investigation

direction to quantitative research in communication, and ensures that our finding will have wider application, from which general laws can be discovered. Theory also provides a framework for asking pertinent questions.

How can theory be used in a manner that helps us? Let us take, for example, Festinger's theory of cognitive dissonance. We will discuss it in detail later, but let us simply pull out a couple of constructs just for the sake of explanation.

The theory states that when an individual suffers conflicting or inconsistent cognitions (dissonance), the result is psychological disturbance, and an attempt or drive to reconcile these cognitions by creating a state of consistency (consonance).

The theory gives us the constructs "dissonance" and "consonance," which help explain human behavior. If our audience's attitude does change, we can explain this change as an attempt to reduce dissonance and achieve consonance. The theory (in this case, the theory of cognitive dissonance), allows us to derive testable hypotheses about dissonance that are directly related to attitude structure and to attitude and opinion change. Dissonance theory suggests that if an individual listens to a persuasive message that runs counter to his beliefs, he may develop a more favorable attitude toward this position. This may sound like a "revolutionary" hypothesis, but let us observe how dissonance theory leads us toward such a conclusion. We stated earlier that when a person is confronted with two conflicting or inconsistent cognitions, he finds himself in the psychologically uncomfortable state of dissonance, and that he will be driven to seek comfort by resolving that dissonance. What he might do, when faced with dissonance, is narrow the gap between his beliefs and the speaker's position. This, of course, is not the way every individual behaves; however, when such a behavior does occur, there is also a theory to explain why.

With this brief explanation of the nature and usefulness of theory, let us review a few of the theories that have assisted students and researchers to better understand the process of persuasion and attitude change. We shall outline the basic principles of learning theory approaches, cognitive theory approaches, the social judgment-involvement approach, social influence approach, and the functional approach.

Learning Theory Approaches

If attitudes are *learned* responses, it should follow that the methods which are utilized in several "learning situations" may also be used effectively to create and change attitudes. We shall discuss two basic methods which may be subsumed under the general headings of *classical conditioning* and *operant conditioning.*

Classical Conditioning

Classical conditioning operates on the principle of stimulus generalization which hypothesizes that when a certain response follows a particular stimulus, such a response will be likely to occur even when another but similar stimulus or one resembling it is presented to the subject.

Staats (1967, 1968) suggests that all attitudes are acquired through classical conditioning. Using the principle of stimulus generalization, for instance, one could subject a person to electric shocks and loud, harsh sounds in order to evoke a negative emotional response, but one would also discover that words accompanied by electric shocks and loud, harsh sounds will also evoke negative emotional responses (Staats, Staats, and Crawford 1962). In short, new stimuli (or conditioned stimuli or CS) — in this case, words — are effective in creating the same negative, emotional response, when they are associated with an old stimulus or the unconditioned stimulus, or UCS — in this case, electric shock.

We can take the principle one step further. If a word, as we have just explained, can become powerful enough to produce a negative, emotional response (because of its association with an earlier stimulus, or some significant event), it is possible that another word or symbol could be utilized to create the same negative emotional response. Of course, we should remember that it must be associated with the original stimulus, or CS. As Watson and Johnson (1972) explain, "If, for example, through classical conditioning the word 'dangerous' has been paired with painful stimuli to evoke negative emotional responses; and another word 'noxious' is paired with 'dangerous,' the negative emotional responses conditioned to the word 'dangerous' will transfer to the word 'noxious' and in the future, 'noxious' will also elicit a negative emotional response." This phenomenon is known as "higher-order conditioning." The response that we generally make toward the contents of a bottle bearing the symbol of a skull and crossed bones is typical of this higher-order conditioning. Prejudice is also a response born of classical conditioning. Now, if this response is learned through classical conditioning, how do we change it? In order to bring about change, we must use a procedure known as *counter-conditioning.*

Counter-conditioning is achieved by pairing a stimulus which evokes a negative emotional response with a stimulus which evokes a positive emotional response. This process will condition the positive response to the negative stimulus as long as the positive stimulus elicits more powerful responses than the negative stimulus. Here is an example: If the negative stimulus "black person" is paired with a stimulus "highly-decorated war hero," or "famous brain surgeon," or "talented musician," and so on, in the future, the stimulus "black person" will elicit a positive emotional response. It must be noted again, however, that the new stimulus—"war hero," etc.—must be powerful enough to distract from the individual's peroccupation with "black person." The movie "Guess Who's Coming to Dinner" demonstrated the principle of counter-conditioning quite well.

Litcher and Johnson (1968) tested the method of counter-conditioning on white elementary school children. The children in the experimental group used readers which included middle-class characters from several ethnic groups. The children in the control group used readers depicting only white characters. They had ascertained before the study that all the children had negative attitudes toward blacks. However, after both groups had used the separate readers for four months, they discovered that the children who had used the multi-ethnic readers depicting blacks of comparable status with whites (middle class) later responded more favorably to blacks than did the white children who did not use multiethnic readers.

The implications of this study should be clear to us—it is possible to use curriculum materials as a conditioning agent in order to effect attitude change. But there are yet other ways to effect change under the terms of learning theory. We may utilize *operant conditioning*.

Operant Conditioning

Operant conditioning derives from a *response reinforcement* principle which states that responses become more enduring the more they are associated with rewards.

Operant conditioning hypothesizes that attitudes which are rewarded are more likely to be developed and maintained. For example, if a negative attitude toward a political issue is likely to bring us reinforcement from a group to which we belong (say, the Conservative Republicans of America), then we will tend to develop attitudes which will prolong that reinforcement. Of course, the converse could be applied. That is, if a positive attitude toward another issue evokes reinforcement, we will then continue to cultivate that positive attitude. In debate situations, Scott (1957, 1959) found that winners changed their attitudes in the direction advocated in their speech, while losers did not. Winning was the reinforcement or the operant conditioner which enforced attitude change.

Much of the work conducted by Carl Hovland and his associates in The Yale Communciation and Attitude Change Program revolved around the testing of learning theory hypotheses. Hovland, Janis and Kelley (1953) have outlined much of this research in a book entitled *Communcation and Persuasion*. They suggest that the "recommended opinion" which the communicator presents in a persuasive message is one of the key elements in the attitude learning situation. Either explicitly or implicitly, a persuader must present a stimulus which evokes a need to answer in the listener or reader.

> When exposed to the recommended opinion, a member of the audience is assumed to react with at least two distinct responses. He thinks of his own answer to the question, and also of the answer suggested by the communicator. The first response results from the previously established verbal habit constituting the individual's original opinion; the second response is assumed to result from a general aspect of verbal behavior, namely, the acquired tendency to repeat to oneself communications to which one is attending. Hence, a major effect of the persuasive communication lies in stimulating the individual to think both of his initial opinion and the new opinion recommended in the communication. (p. 11)

The idea that attitude change and opinion change depend on an individual's "rehearsing" or "practicing" a mental and verbal response is a key factor in any stimulus-response theory of attitude change and attitude formation. We shall see this same principle of "rehearsal" at work when we discuss McGuire's inoculation approach in the following section of this chapter.

One other fundamental feature in the work of Hovland, Janis and Kelley deals with the effect of "incentives." Incentives, of course, play a significant role in the process of operant conditioning. Hovland, Janis and Kelley claim that:

> Practice, which is so important for memorizing verbal material in educational or training situations, is not sufficient for bringing about the acceptance of a new opinion. We assume that acceptance is contingent upon incentives, and that in order to change an opinion it is necessary to create greater incentives for making the new implicit response than for making the old one. (p. 11)

They stress that more than a mere learning of a response is necessary; it is also necessary that the subject or target-person have some motivation for choosing that particular response to the attitude question in preference to other available responses. This motivation will be influenced by (1) "the observable characteristics of the perceived source of the communication"; (2) "the setting in which the person is exposed to the communication; including, for example, the way in which the other members of the audience respond during the presentation"; (3) the communication stimuli, including content elements such as "arguments" or "appeals."

Even though many commentators argue justifiably that the work conducted by Hovland, Janis and Kelley does not constitute theory as we have defined it, it is generally conceded that the research conducted in the Yale Program was outstanding. What is important is that they were able to isolate certain key variables and stimulate a wide-ranging program of research.

The principles of motivation, incentives, and practice also play a fundamental role in the inoculation approach. Its concerns, however, are unlike those of the other theories that we review in this chapter. Inoculation theory suggests a method for inducing resistance against persuasion or for strengthening already existing attitudes.

Inoculation Approach

In 1961, William J. McGuire and a group of fellow social psychologists launched a series of research experiments under the assumptions of a *Theory of Inoculation*. McGuire's inoculation approach is analogous to the process used in immunization against certain types of diseases. In the biological situation, a person is made resistant to some attacking virus by exposure to a weakened dose of the virus in order to stimulate his defenses against any massive viral attack. Note, however, that the inoculating dosage is not strong enough itself to cause the disease.

Another way of creating resistance against a disease could be achieved through supportive therapy such as vitamins, tonic, plenty of sleep, and so on. The problem here is that such supportive therapy, though useful, is not as effective as immunization by inoculation.

By analogy, a person may be enabled to build up some sort of defense against arguments that oppose a particular belief that he holds if he is provided with arguments that *support* his beliefs. However, this method (supportive) may turn out to be less effective than would the inoculation process suggested by McGuire. Through the inoculation process, a person is exposed to small doses of arguments that others may subsequently use to dissuade him from his belief. In short, an inoculating, or *refutational defense,* should prove more effective than a *supportive defense.*

Most of McGuire's experimentation in inoculation utilized cultural truisms. Cultural truisms are beliefs so universally shared that the person holding the belief does not perceive such beliefs to be susceptible to attack. One such truism might be: "Mental illness is not contagious." Surprisingly, a person may be unable to conjure up many supporting arguments if his belief were indeed challenged. This inability to counter-argue may be due to the fact that he had previously never felt any need to justify such a belief, and consequently has never had any practice in doing so. McGuire's research demonstrated, quite convincingly, that beliefs in certain cultural truisms *do* prove vulnerable in the face of attack. An inoculation technique which supplies the person with counter-arguments should enable him to defend those truisms.

The person's assumption that his belief will not be attacked, at least "not by any one in his right mind," contributes largely to vulnerability. A sense of complacency develops. Therefore, the first step in the inoculation schedule would be to unsettle that assumption by convincing the person that the truism could indeed be challenged and overcome. The person is exposed to counter-arguments. Remember, however, that the counter-arguments should be mildly threatening (a weakened dose of the virus), so that the person feels that he has a reasonable chance of arguing against the counter-arguments, and will be motivated to conjure up the necessary rebuttals. Studies which compared the effectiveness of refutational or inoculating defenses with supportive defenses showed that *refutational defenses produce greater resistance to later attacks than do supportive defenses.*

It seems also, from research evidence, that a combination of both a supportive and a refutational defense produces an even more powerful method for safeguarding beliefs from destructive attacks. And an even stronger resistance is created if, in advance of the inoculation, the person is *forewarned* about an attack (McGuire and Papageorgis 1962). Apparently, the mere knowledge of an impending threat motivates a person to make sure that he is putting the defenses to good use. He rehearses "good" arguments, and he may even go a step further in scouting out a few of his own.

So, we have seen two theoretical orientations of differing purpose under the terms of a learning theory approach. Classical and operant conditioning are utilized mainly to influence attitude change, while inoculation theory is used solely to confirm or strengthen already existing beliefs and (hopefully) attitudes. We now turn to a brief discussion of cognitive theory approaches.

Cognitive Consistency Approaches

There are several consistency theories. These theories assume that cognitions (perceiving, believing, thinking, imagining, and so on) about some person or event tend to be organized or structured into a meaningful whole. This organization gives structure, meaning, and stability to our daily experience. Sometimes, new information tends to disrupt the cognitive organization; and because it is difficult to tolerate this state of affairs, a state of tension develops, which in turn drives us to attempt to reduce the disharmony and inconsistency. We often attempt this reduction by striving to restore balance, harmony, and consistency between the various cognitive elements. The "drive for consistency" has been studied by social scientists for a long time; but it is only within the last fifteen years, beginning mainly from the pioneer work of Fritz Heidler (1946, 1958), that the principle of consistency has been given consistent theoretical treatment.

We will examine three consistency theories in this chapter; namely the congruity hypothesis (Osgood and Tannenbaum 1955), the balance approach (Rosenberg and Abelson 1960), and the dissonance approach (Festinger 1957). We believe that these three theories include most of the major principles of the general idea of balance.

The Principle of Congruity

Osgood and Tannenbaum (1955) developed a theory of attitude change representing a special application of the balance concept. Their congruity model approaches the study of the effects of persuasive communication by focusing on the links between *sources* toward which one has an attitude and *objects* toward which one has an attitude. Osgood and Tannenbaum substitute the term "congruity" for balance and maintain that we strive toward congruity among our attitudes and cognitions.

Here's how the congruity hypothesis operates: Suppose that you feel very strongly negative about *The Nazi Newsletter* and you have somewhat positive but rather weak attitudes concerning off-shore oil drilling. Then one day, you read the following headlines: THE NAZI

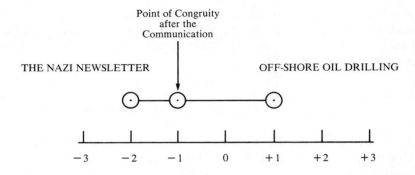

FIGURE 3-2.   Cognitive Shifts According to the Congruity Model

NEWSLETTER IS IN FAVOR OF OFF-SHORE OIL DRILLING. How will you
feel about this communication?

According to Osgood and Tannenbaum (1955), your attitude toward
this communication will fall somewhere between your attitude toward
the source, *Nazi Newsletter,* and the object, off-shore oil drilling. However, since your attitude toward the newspaper is stronger than your
attitude toward off-shore drilling, you should find that your attitude
toward the headlines or communication will fall closer to your attitude
toward the newspaper than toward off-shore oil drilling. Figure 3-2
depicts the outcome.

Let us look at the formula which is used to calculate and predict
the amount of shift or movement toward congruity. Our feeling (affect)
toward the source is represented by the symbol a_1; our affect toward
the object by the symbol a_2. Suppose that we rated the source *Nazi
Newsletter* as -2 on the scale that ranged from $+3$ (good) to -3
(bad), and the object off-shore oil drilling as $+1$ on the same scale.

In order to understand the operations of the principle, we need
two kinds of symbols: (1) the *absolute* scale value of both the source
and the object (here, we omit the signs), thus we have $|a_1| = 2$, and
$|a_2| = 1$; and (2) P, which is the pressure toward congruity, i.e. the
unit difference between source and object. We need one more symbol,
AC, which represents change. The change toward the source is AC_1,
and the change toward the object is AC_2. Here is the complete formula.

$$AC_1 = \frac{|a_2|}{|a_1| + |a_2|} \, P_{\text{source}}$$

and

$$AC_2 = \frac{|a_1|}{|a_1| + |a_2|} \, P_{object}$$

Let us substitute the values:

$$AC_1 = \frac{1}{1 + 2} \, (+3) = 1$$

$$AC_2 = \frac{2}{1 + 2} \, (-3) = -2$$

We see, then, that the change in our feeling toward the *Nazi Newsletter* is just one unit from -2 to -1 on the scale. (See figure 3-2.) The change in our feeling toward off-shore oil drilling is two units from $+1$ to -1 on the scale. Overall, the (-1) position on the scale represents our new placement of affect or feeling toward both source and object. In short, we have induced congruity.

One fundamental notion in the congruity hypothesis is that the feeling that is more polarized or extreme changes least. We can see that this is the case in our example, for our feeling toward the *Nazi Newsletter* changed less than our feeling toward off-shore oil drilling.

Affective-Cognitive Consistency Theory

Affective-cognitive consistency theory is generally associated with the names of Rosenberg and Abelson (Rosenberg 1953, 1956, 1960a, 1960b, 1960c; Abelson and Rosenberg 1958; Rosenberg and Abelson 1960). The theory concentrates on what happens within the individual in relation to the affective and cognitive components. We may recall that the affective component refers to the feeling state; however, when Rosenberg speaks of the cognitive component, he speaks not only of beliefs about the attitudinal object but also beliefs about its relationship to the individual's other values. The theory contends that attitudes are related to central values, and offers a framework for describing correlations between the nature and strength of the feelings towards the attitudinal object on the one hand, with the beliefs and perceptions associated with it on the other. Rosenberg and Abelson (1960) state:

Strong and stable positive affect (feeling) towards a given object should be associated with beliefs that it leads to the attainment of a number of important values, while strong, negative affect should be associated with beliefs that the object tends to block the attainment of important values. Similarly, moderate positive or negative affects should be associated with beliefs that relate the attitude object, either to less important values, or, if to important values, then with less confidence about the relationships between these values and the attitude object. (p. 18)

In general, Rosenberg argues that when affect and cognition are inconsistent or in conflict, something has to give. Thus, if a person changes his cognitive component after listening to a message, there will be a tendency for him to change his affective component as well. The converse is also likely; that is, an experience that changes a person's affect or feelings about the attitude object may also bring about a change in his cognitions.

Because there is a drive toward balance or consistency between feelings and/or beliefs, it would follow from Rosenberg and Abelson's approach that attitudes can be modified by changing either the affective and/or cognitive components. If a situation arises that produces a change in either beliefs or feelings (which in turn leads to a degree of inconsistency which exceeds the individual's level of tolerance), there will be a tendency to change the remaining component. There will be a push toward reorganization until either consistency is reached or the inconsistency that cannot be reconciled is pushed into some sort of psychological twilight zone of unawareness.

Obviously, attitude change does not always occur as a consequence of cognitive-affective inconsistency. Granted, a psychological pressure will be set in motion; however, there are several escape ploys that may be utilized, one of which is to push the issue into a zone of unawareness. Or it may happen that, when a person is exposed to a communication, distinctions are made among them, and his affect may not change. Triandis (1971) explains this cognitive restructuring with the following example:

A person who dislikes blacks when hearing of some good deeds performed by certain blacks, may make the distinction between "good blacks" and "most blacks" and will continue feeling negatively about "most blacks"; since there is little cognitive change, there is no affective change. Or a person may have a positive experience that changes his affect toward blacks but that has only a small affect on his cognitions because the cognitions are "reinterpreted." For example, previously blacks were bad and loud, and loud was associated with being obnoxious. After the positive experience, blacks are now good, although they are still loud, only now loud is associated with "swinging," "fun to have around," etc. In other words, it is possible for one component to change without producing a change in the other but, in general, when one component changes the other does also. (p. 73)

Whatever the mode of cognitive restructuring, it would appear that the act itself may quite possibly "soften" the individual to the extent that a complete attitude change (with both cognitive and affective components in balance) may occur later through some communication or new pleasant experiences.

We stated earlier that the affective-cognitive consistency theory suggests that attitudes are related to central values. That is, *positive* feelings about the object of an attitude are associated with beliefs that it leads to the achievement of important values, while *negative* feelings toward an object suggest that the object is an obstacle to the attainment of those values. This relationship between attitudes and values is very important as a target in persuasion.

As Triandis (1971) puts it: "If A is the attitude object and B is a value, and if there is an implicative relationship involving these elements, the subject's affect toward A depends on the strength of this value and the strength of the implicative relationship."

Carlson (1956) conducted an experiment demonstrating the attitudes-value relationship and its potential as a persuasion target. The experimental manipulations involved an attempt to demonstrate that allowing blacks to move into white neighborhoods would facilitate the attainment of four values: American prestige in other countries, protection of property values, equal opportunity for personal development, and being experienced, broadminded, and worldly-wise. The results supported this idea. In short, the persuasive attempt to link an attitude to values did succeed in creating a new attitude (attitude-change), a new cognitive component, and a different affect.

As far as the impact of all persuasive communication, we may say (on the assumptions of the affective-cognitive consistency model): Such communications "will be accepted by the person (or at least will be seen by him as pleasant and persuasive even if the attitudes are not changed) to the degree that they help to resolve cognitive imbalances" (Cohen 1964).

Basically, the affective-cognitive consistency approach focuses on internal consistency, to the neglect of behavior elements and various other factors which do facilitate or impede attitude change. We feel, however, that *this* model (which represents the gist of most balance theories) and the model of cognitive dissonance which will be discussed next give us more to work with than does Osgood and Tannenbaum's congruity hypothesis.

Cognitive Dissonance Theory

Dissonance theory (Festinger 1957; Brehm and Cohen 1962; Aronson 1968) is concerned with the psychological inconsistencies between what people know and how they act and how they deal with these inconsistencies. The cognitive dissonance theory states that two cognitive elements are in a *dissonant* relationship if, considering these two alone, the obverse from one element follows from the other. Cognitive elements are defined as bits of knowledge or opinions and beliefs about oneself, about one's behavior, and about one's environment. Two cognitive elements may be: "The knowledge that I smoke," and "The knowledge that smoking causes cancer." Or, "The knowledge that I claim to be generous and charitable," and "The knowledge that I did not contribute to the March of Dimes campaign." The existence of cognitive dissonance gives rise to pressures to reduce it in order to achieve consonance or consistency between the cognitive elements.

The dissonance model is relevant to the study of attitude change, particularly with respect to situations of *forced compliance*. The forced compliance situation usually involves the necessity of having to choose between doing something we would not do voluntarily or not doing it at all. To ensure that we do it, some type of pressure or force is brought to bear upon us. This pressure is usually in the form of a threat of punishment for noncompliance and promise of a reward for compliance. A typical situation is the case of the school principal who is opposed to school integration but is told by federal officials that he should integrate his school promptly. If the principal complies, he experiences dissonance created by these two inconsistent cognitions: (1) I am against letting blacks into my school, and (2) I have allowed blacks to enroll in my school.

Now, here is the crucial point in the relationship between persuasion and attitude change. The offer of reward or the threat of punishment reduces the dissonance by providing the individual a chance to find consistency. If the federal government were to give the principal seventy thousand dollars in education funds as a reward for compliance, or if it were to threaten him with a stiff jail sentence for noncompliance, his dissonance would be reduced because he would have been given more arguments or cognitive elements to help make his behavior consistent. Once he has performed the behavior, he could easily justify that behavior with such statements as: "Hell, it was easy to integrate my school for seventy thousand bucks," or "Man, I had to integrate—or those bastards would have iced me away!" In such circumstances, we could not say realistically that a genuine attitude change toward integration had taken place. So what's the catch? The catch is for the persuader to set up situations in which dissonance increases rather than reduces, as was the case in our example.

Let us see how the principle works. The less pressure exerted upon us to do something undesirable, the greater is our dissonance. To the extent that we cannot reduce dissonance by distorting or denying our inconsistent behavior, then we will have to change our attitudes so that they are more consistent with our behavior. Theoretically, the greatest attitude change will occur when the pressure exerted is the minimum necessary to get us to perform the act. So, the principal whose compliance is elicited rather than forced should show more dissonance on his commitment. When little pressure is applied to the principal and he supports a position he opposes, he feels more dissonance because he cannot create new cognitive elements consistent with his behavior.

Festinger and Carlsmith (1959) conducted a study which is now considered classical as a test of the forced compliance derivation of dissonance theory. Subjects were given a boring and repetitive task without reward, which they fulfilled because the experimenter, through his prestige and veiled threats, forced them to comply. After the task was completed, the subjects were asked to act in deception and tell others the task had actually been very enjoyable. In the study, some subjects received a relatively large reward, some received a relatively small reward, and some received no reward. At the end of the experiment, subjects were asked to rate how enjoyable the original task had been. Of the three groups, the low-rewarded group indicated greatest enjoyment of the task. Dissonance theory offers this explanation: the larger the reward received, the less dissonance is experienced by the individual, and the smaller the subsequent opinion change.

In summary we could say: (1) The more compelling the reasons for doing what goes against your values, the less the dissonance. (2) The fewer the supports or excuses, or rewards, or punishments for doing it, the greater the dissonance, the greater the pressure to reduce it and, assuming irrevocable commitment, the greater the change of attitude.

Unlike many other approaches discussed in this chapter, the cognitive dissonance approach deals very little with complications of motivational, perceptual, and emotional processes. The model is simple—

too simple, according to some critics. Chapanis and Chapanis (1964)—
the most devastating critics of the theory—maintain that it is not realistic
to reduce complex social situations to two simple dissonant statements.

> We cannot go into the details of full criticism, however the
> interested reader should consult Chapanis and Chapanis, 1964;
> M. J. Rosenberg, 1965a, 1966; Elms, 1967; Bem, 1965, 1967. The
> defense by dissonance theorists may be found in Brehm, 1965;
> Aronson, 1966; Linder, Cooper and Jones, 1967. For a fuller dis-
> cussion of dissonance theory, the reader may consult Abelson,
> Aronson, McGuire, Newcomb, Rosenberg, and Tannenbaum
> (1968) and Kiesler, Collins, and Miller (1969).

This concludes our discussion of the representative balance or
consistency theories. In the remaining section we will discuss a few of
the principles of *the social judgment-involvement* approach which examines what makes up an attitude, how we change that attitude, and
what variables affect the attitudinal structure, and the *functional* approach to the study of attitudes, which emphasizes the functions which
attitudes perform for the personality, the motivational base of those
attitudes, and the conditions which facilitate attitude change.

The Social Judgment-Involvement Approach

The social judgment-involvement approach, also known as social judgment theory, originated with Hovland and Sherif (1952). In keeping
with the orientation of this approach, Sherif and Sherif (1967) defined
an attitude as a learned set of categories used by individuals for positive
or negative evaluations of incoming stimuli. For example, a person with
an attitude toward abortion has learned to evaluate incoming messages
about it by placing them in one of several categories. The messages that
agree with his attitudes might be placed in a negative category. Sherif,
Sherif, and Nebergall (1965) suggest that an individual has three basic
categories or *latitudes* in which he places incoming messages. These
latitudes are: (1) latitude of acceptance, (2) latitude of rejection, and
(3) latitude of noncommitment.

The latitude of acceptance consists of the position that is most
acceptable to an individual plus all other acceptable positions or statements relative to his attitude. If an individual loves the Miami Dolphins
(these are football players, not sea mammals!), his most acceptable
position might be that the Dolphins are the greatest team in professional

football. But there are other statements such as "the Dolphins have the best defensive line," "they have one of the top five quarterbacks in the league," or "they have a good wide receiver," which are totally acceptable to him. Such statements, messages, or positions form the latitude of acceptance.

The latitude of rejection consists of the position that is most objectionable to an individual plus all other objectionable positions or statements relative to his attitude. To the Dolphin fan in our example, the most objectionable position might be that the Dolphins are the worst team in professional football. Statements that "the Dolphins are vastly overrated," "the Dolphins choke in the big games," "the Dolphins have never really faced good competition," are regarded as objectionable and form the latitude of rejection.

The latitude of noncommitment consists of statements or positions that the individual neither accepts nor rejects. These are the statements or positions about which the individual does not have enough information, or does not add any importance or concern to them. Again using the Dolphin devotee as an example, a statement that the Dolphins will probably change their type of football shoes in five years cannot be evaluated with the available information, or may be too inconsequential to think about.

Attitude change, according to the social judgment approach, is manifested by a change in a person's latitudes on a particular attitude. Since attitudes are enduring states, if a person should possess the same or consistent latitude makeup over a considerable period of time, or if one should confront a person with a series of statements about an object toward which he has an attitude, he will place these statements in his latitudes of acceptance, rejection, or noncommitment.

Of course, adding new statements or positions to the latitudes does not guarantee attitude change, since all people are not equally susceptible to attitude change on the same issue. One important factor in receptivity is *ego-involvement*. Ego-involvement refers to the significance or salience of an issue to an individual—the extent to which he is "caught up" in the issue. Our ego-involvement varies from one issue to another.

Sherif, Sherif, and Nebergall (1965) draw three conclusions about a person's susceptibility to attitude change:

1. The more ego-involved a person is, the more difficult it would be to change his attitudes. Individuals who are highly ego-involved in an issue tend to have small latitudes of acceptance and noncommitment and large latitudes of rejection.

2. Individuals who are moderately or lowly ego-involved in an issue tend to be more susceptible to persuasion on that issue. The mod-

erately ego-involved individual has moderately large latitudes of acceptance and noncommitment and a small latitude of rejection. The person with low ego-involvement has large latitudes of acceptance and noncommitment and a very small latitude of rejection.

3. Most issues have a number of sides, however, most highly ego-involved individuals tend to see only their side as being right. They reject all other explanations. The less ego-involved the person, the more willing he is to look at the issue from as many sides as possible.

The social judgment-involvement approach identifies two kinds of cognitive distortions typically made by individuals who are highly involved in an issue. These distortions are assimilation and contrast. *Assimilation* occurs when statements that are rather close to the person's own position are perceived as being more similar to that person's position than they really are. *Contrast* occurs when statements that are different from the person's own position are seen as being more different than they really are. Assimilation facilitates persuasion; contrast hinders it.

Selock (1967) conducted research which described the two distortions—assimilation and contrast—rather well. He administered Newcomb's political-economic conservatism scale to a sample of subjects and then asked the subjects to judge whether twenty-one persons or political groups were "conservative" or "radical," using an eleven-point scale. He found that extreme conservatives differed from extreme radicals in the way that they judged these attitude objects. For example, the more radical the person, the more he tended to place Dr. Martin Luther King on the conservative side of the eleven-point scale. Similarly, the more conservative the subject, the more he tended to see the Ku Klux Klan as a "moderate" organization. Assimilation facilitates persuasion; contrast hinders it.

The Functional Approach

One of the most interesting attempts to understand the reasons people hold the attitudes they do and the needs which are fulfilled by them has been devised by Katz (1960). According to Katz, the functions which attitudes perform for the personality can be grouped under four headings: (1) instrumental, adjustive, or utilitarian; (2) ego-defensive; (3) value-expressive; and (4) knowledge.

The *instrumental, adjustive,* or *utilitarian* function implies that as we attempt to maximize the rewards and minimize the punishments or penalties meted out by our environments, we tend to develop favorable or unfavorable attitudes relative to objects and persons which we associate with satisfaction and dissatisfaction, reward and punishment, approval and disapproval. In short, we develop favorable attitudes toward those things in our environment which are associated with satisfaction.

The *ego-defensive* function enables us to protect ourselves from acknowledging certain unacceptable truths about ourselves and certain harsh realities in our external world. Attitudes serving the ego-defensive function proceed from within the person, from internal conflict and insecurity, and function like defense mechanisms. Prejudiced attitudes, for example, help to sustain the individual's self-concept by maintaining a sense of superiority over others. While such ego-defensive attitudes can be adaptive, and offer temporary relief for a short time, they are likely to handicap the person in his social relations over a long period of time.

The *value-expressive* function enables us to give positive expression to our central values, and also enables us to portray the kind of persons we perceive ourselves to be.

The *knowledge* function is served by those attitudes which help us to understand and give meaning to situations which may not be instantly meaningful to us. We prefer certainty, consistency, and stability to uncertainty, instability and ambiguity. We need standards and frames of reference for understanding our world, and attitudes supply us with such standards. Sometimes these standards are constructed imprecisely and with very scant information. Stereotypes, for instance, represent one such imprecise frame of reference—they may not give us an accurate picture of the world as it really is. The point is, however, that they serve a purpose.

If we know *why* a person holds the attitudes he does, we may be in a better position to change them (see table 3-1). The functional approach to attitude change suggests that the conditions for change vary by the type of attitude.

Changing Utilitarian Attitudes

An attitude formed to serve a utilitarian function can be changed (1) if it no longer leads to satisfaction, (2) if the acceptance of another attitude can be shown to be more instrumental to need satisfaction, or (3) if the individual's level of aspiration has changed.

The listener or receiver may be aware that his present point of view is not personally rewarding and may, as a result, be persuaded to change his attitudinal orientation toward an alternative point of view. New ideas or orientations may possess certain self-gratifying advantages which can be shown to be more conclusive to need satisfaction.

TABLE 3-1. Determinants of Attitude Formation, Arousal, and Change in Relation to Type of Function

Function	Origin and Dynamics	Arousal Conditions	Change Conditions
Adjustment	Utility of attitu-dinal object in need satisfaction; maxi-mizing external rewards and minimizing punishments	1. Activation of needs 2. Salience of cues associated with need satisfaction	1. Need depri-vation 2. Creation of new needs and new levels of aspira-tion 3. Shifting rewards and punishments 4. Emphasis on new and better paths for need satisfaction
Ego defense	Protecting against internal conflicts and external dangers	1. Posing of threats 2. Appeals to hatred and re-pressed impulses 3. Rise in frustra-tions 4. Use of authori-tarian suggestion	1. Removal of threats 2. Catharsis 3. Development of self-insight
Value expression	Maintaining self-identity; en-hancing favorable self-image; self-expression and self-determination	1. Salience of cues associated with values 2. Appeals to indi-vidual to reassert self-image 3. Ambiguities which threaten self-concept	1. Some degree of dissatisfaction with self 2. Greater appro-priateness of new attitude for the self 3. Control of all environmental supports to undermine old values
Knowledge	Need for under-standing for meaningful cogni-tive organization, for consistency and clarity	1. Reinstatement of cues associated with old problem or of old problem itself	1. Ambiguity created by new information or change in environment 2. More meaning-ful information about problems

Source: Excerpted from D. Katz, "The Functional Approach to the Study of Attitudes," *Public Opinion Quarterly* 24 (1960) : 163-204, by permission.

Changing Ego-Defensive Attitudes

Attitudes serving the ego-defensive function are not changed easily; quite frequently change can only be induced through clinical and psycho-analytic treatments.

Three basic factors, however, can help change ego-defensive attitudes. In the first place, the removal of threat is a necessary, though
not a sufficient, condition. The permissive and even supportive atmosphere which the therapist attempts to create for his patients is a special
instance of the removal of threat. Where the ego-defensive behavior of
the delinquent is supported by his group, the social worker must gain a
measure of group acceptance so as not to be perceived as a threat by
the individual group members. An objective, matter-of-fact approach can
serve to remove threat, especially in situations where people are accustomed to emotional appeals. Humor can also be used to establish a
nonthreatening atmosphere, but it should not be directed against the
audience or even against the problem. Cooper and Jahoda (1947)
attempted to change prejudiced attitudes by ridicule, in the form of
cartoons which made Mr. Biggott seem silly, especially when he rejected a blood transfusion which did not come from "100 percent
Americans." Instead of changing their attitudes, the subjects in this
experiment found ways of evading the meaning of the cartoons.

In the second place, catharsis or the ventilation of feelings can
help to set the stage for attitude change. Mention has already been made
of the building up of tension owing to the lack of discharge of inhibited
impulses. When emotional tension is at a high level the individual will
respond defensively and resist attempts to change him. Hence, providing
him with opportunities to blow off steam may often be necessary before
attempting a serious discussion of new possibilities of behavior. Again,
humor can serve this purpose.

There are many practical problems in the use of catharsis, however, because of its complex relationship to other variables. In his review
of the experimental work on the expression of hostility, Berkowitz (1958)
reports more findings supporting than contradicting the catharsis hypothesis, but there is no clear agreement about the mechanisms involved.
Under certain circumstances, permitting emotional outbursts can act as
a reward. In a gripe session to allow individuals to express their complaints, group members can reinforce one another's negative attitudes.
Unless there are positive forces in the situation which lead to a serious
consideration of the problem, the gripe session may have boomerang
effects. The technique often employed is to keep the group in session
long enough for the malcontents to get talked out so that more sober
voices can be heard. Catharsis may function at two levels. It can operate
to release or drain off energy of the moment, as in the above description.
It can also serve to bring to the surface something of the nature of the
conflict affecting the individual. So long as his impulses are repressed

and carefully disguised, the individual has little chance of gaining even rudimentary insight into himself.

In the third place, ego-defensive behavior can be altered as the individual acquires insight into his own mechanisms of defense. Information about the nature of the problem in the external world will not affect him. Information about his own functioning may have an influence, if presented without threat, and if the defenses do not go too deep into the personality. In other words, only prolonged therapy can help the psychologically sick person. Many normal people, however, employ ego defenses about which they have some degree of awareness, though generally not at a time of the expression of such defenses. The frustrations of a tough day at work may result in an authoritarian father displacing his aggression that night on his family by yelling at his wife or striking his youngsters. Afterward he may recognize the cause of his behavior. Not all defensive behavior, then, is so deeply rooted in the personality as to be inaccessible to awareness and insight. Therefore, procedures for arousing self-insight can be utilized to change behavior, even in mass communications. The importance of ego-defensive attitudes to persuaders is not in terms of trying to change them, but in avoiding communication which elicits or provokes them.

Changing Value-Expressive Attitudes

The advertising and marketing industry frequently utilize value-expressive attitudes as their main targets. The marketing persuader ties product attitudes directly to the expression of value-oriented needs. Value-expressive attitudes can be changed when a person is dissatisfied with his self-image and wants to demonstrate a more self-enhancing one. Katz (1960) suggests two basic approaches to effecting attitude change. Again, two conditions are relevant in changing value-expressive attitudes.

First, some degree of dissatisfaction with one's self-concept or its associated values is the opening wedge for fundamental change. The complacent person, smugly satisfied with all aspects of himself, is immune to attempts to change his values. Dissatisfaction with the self can result from failures or from the inadequacy of one's values in preserving a favorable image of oneself in a changing world. The man with pacifist values may have become dissatisfied with himself during a period of fascist expansion and terror. Once there is a crack in the individual's central belief systems, it can be exploited by appropriately directed influences. The techniques of brain washing employed by the Chinese Communists, both on prisoners of war in Korea and in the thought reform of Chinese intellectuals, were essentially procedures for changing value systems.

Second, dissatisfaction with old attitudes as inappropriate to one's values can also lead to change. In fact, people are much less likely to find their values uncongenial than they are to find some of their attitudes inappropriate to their values. The discomfort with one's old attitudes may stem from new experiences or from the suggestions of other people. Senator Vandenburg, as an enlightened conservative, changed his attitudes on foreign relations from an isolationist to an internationalist position when critical events in our history suggested change. The influences exerted upon people are often in the direction of showing the inappropriateness of their present ways of expressing their values. Union leaders attempt to show that good union men should not vote on the old personal basis of rewarding friends and punishing enemies but should instead demand party responsibility for a program.

Changing Knowledge Function Attitudes

Attitudes serving the knowledge function can change when a person discovers that the attitudes do not provide a meaningful or accurate picture of "things as they really are." Change may be induced by providing the person with new information inputs which show his existing store of knowledge to be inaccurate, incomplete, or misleading. The main consideration, however, is that the persuader must find ways to overcome the person's tendency to avoid information that conflicts with his existing attitudes.

In summary, functional theory suggests that we cannot proceed to change attitudes until we have an assessment of the functions served for the individuals we want to change. Since it is possible that the same attitude serves different functions for different persons, it is difficult to utilize blanket strategies in persuasion. Thus it would appear that Katz's functional approach is more suited to dyadic or one-to-one situations than typical audience situations.

Propositions

Several theoretical orientations or approaches may be used in studying how attitudes are formed, and how to change them. A few of the theories or approaches discussed are: (1) learning theories (classical conditioning, operant conditioning, the inoculation approach); (2) the principle of congruity; (3) affective-cognitive consistency theory; (4) cognitive-dissonance theory; (5) social judgment-involvement approach; and (6) the functional approach.

Learning Theory Approaches

1. Attitudes are learned responses, and the methods, such as classical and operant conditions, normally utilized in "learning situations" may also be used to create and change attitudes.
   1a. When a certain attitudinal response follows a particular stimulus, such an attitude will be likely to occur even when another but similar stimulus is presented to an individual.
   1b. When a new stimulus is repeatedly paired or associated with another stimulus that automatically elicits a certain response, the new one alone gradually becomes capable of exciting or eliciting the same or similar response.

2. Attitudinal responses learned through the kinds of conditioning suggested in 1a and 1b may be changed through a process of counter-conditioning.
   2a. A negative stimulus (e.g. "black man") when paired repeatedly with a positive stimulus (e.g. "war hero") will eventually lead to a positive attitudinal response.
   2b. Attitudes which are rewarded are more likely to be developed and maintained.

The Inoculation Approach

3. An individual may be able to build up defenses against attacks on his belief if he is previously supplied with supportive arguments or if he is previously exposed to threatening or refutational arguments.
   3a. Refutational (inoculating) defenses produce greater resistance to later attacks than do supportive defenses.
   3b. The combination of both a supportive and a refutational defense produces an even stronger resistance to later attack against an individual's belief.
   3c. Forewarning an individual of an impending attack, when combined with refutational and supportive defenses, will produce an even greater resistance against counter-persuasion.

The Principle of Congruity

4. When two attitude objects (for example, a source and an issue) of differing evaluation on an attitude scale are linked with an assertion,

there is a tendency for the evaluation of each to shift toward a point of equilibrium or congruity. (For example, if the President of the United States praised an avowed enemy of the country, there would be a tendency for the "enemy" to be evaluated more highly and for the President to be evaluated less highly.

   4a. When two objects of judgment are associated with an assertion, the resulting pressure produces movement toward a point of equilibrium.

   4b. Both objects of judgment do not change equally in evaluation.

   4c. The more polarized object of evaluation changes proportionately less than the less polarized object of evaluation, i.e. change is inversely proportional to the degree of polarization.

Affective-Cognitive Consistency Theory

5. The affective-cognitive consistency theory concentrates on what happens within an individual as he strives to maintain consistency between the affective and cognitive components of his attitude.

   5a. When the affective and cognitive components of an attitude are mutually consistent, the attitude is in a stable state.

   5b. When these components are mutually inconsistent, to a degree that exceeds the individual's tolerance limit for such inconsistency, the attitude is in an unstable state.

   5c. When an attitude is unstable, a reorganization is likely to occur in order to resolve the inconsistency.

   5d. If a person changes his cognitive component after listening to a message, there will be a tendency for him to change his affective component as well.

   5e. Conversely, a message or an experiment that changes a person's affect or feelings about an attitude object may also bring about a change in his cognitions.

   5f. If the inconsistency cannot be reconciled, the message and its concerns will be pushed into a zone of indifference or unawareness.

Cognitive Dissonance Theory

6. Cognitive dissonance is a state of psychological stress which occurs where an individual becomes aware of the "nonfitting" relations among his cognitions, feelings, values, and behaviors (Widgery 1972).

   6a. The existence of dissonance creates psychological tension or discomfort and will motivate the individual to reduce the dissonance and achieve consonance.

6b. When dissonance exists, not only will the individual attempt to reduce it, but he will actively attempt to avoid situations and information which will increase the dissonance.

6c. The greater the importance of the dissonant elements, the greater will be the pressure to resolve the dissonance.

6d. An individual may resort to three basic methods in order to reduce dissonance.

(1) A person may change cognitive elements related to his behavior. (He may deceive himself about the facts. Avoidance of the truth.)

(2) A person may change a cognitive element related to his environment. (He may exhibit some behavior that will change a dissonant situation.)

(3) The person may seek out new information that will help him reduce the dissonance.

6e. Individuals who commit belief-discrepant acts will generally experience cognitive dissonance.

(1) The less the pressure (i.e., offered reward, threatened punishment, or greater choice) put upon the person to perform the belief-discrepant act, the greater the dissonance.

The Social Judgment-Involvement Approach

7. A primary factor affecting the influence of a persuasive communication upon attitude and opinion change is the individual's judgment of the degree of discrepancy between the position of the communication and that individual's own attitude or opinion (as measured on an attitude scale).

7a. If the communication advocates a position that is not too discrepant from that held by the communication recipient, *assimilation* will result in which

(1) the individual will perceive the communication as advocating a less extreme position;

(2) the individual will evaluate the communication favorably;

(3) the individual will be strongly influenced.

7b. If the communication advocates a position very discrepant from that held by the communication recipient, contrast will result in which

(1) the individual will perceive the communication as advocating a more extreme position;

(2) the individual will evaluate the communication unfavorably;

    (3) the individual will be either minimally or negatively influenced.

7c. The social judgment involvement theory (with its assimilation-contrast hypothesis) conceives of the individual's stand on a social issue as not a single point but as a range of related *acceptable* positions or as a *latitude of acceptance.*

7d. The *latitude of rejection* is the range of all of those points of view the individual finds unacceptable or objectionable.

7e. *The latitude of neutrality or noncommitance* lies between the latitudes of acceptance and rejection.

7f. Latitudes of acceptance and rejection vary with the degree of ego-involvement.

    (1) High ego-involvement results in a narrow latitude of acceptance and a wide latitude of rejection.

    (2) Low ego-involvement results in a wide latitude of acceptance and a low latitude of rejection.

7g. The amount or degree of *assimilating* and *contrasting* that occurs depends on the individual's judgment of the "placement" of the message.

    (1) If a persuasive communication advocates a point of view falling within an individual's latitude of acceptance, assimilation will tend to occur.

    (2) If a persuasive communication advocates a point of view falling within an individual's latitude of rejection, contrast will tend to occur.

    (3) At the transition point between the latitude of acceptance and rejection, neither assimilation nor contrast will occur.

    (4) A message producing the greatest degree of discrepancy, but remaining within the individual's latitude of acceptance, will have the greatest degree of influence.

    (5) A message passing into the latitude of rejection steadily decreases in influence and may eventually become negative.

    (6) Low ego-involving topics are more likely to be persuasive than high ego-involving topics because the latitude of acceptance is wider.

The Functional Approach

8. The functions which attitudes perform for an individual may be grouped under four headings: (1) instrumental, adjustive, or utilitarian; (2) ego-defensive; (3) value-expressive; and (4) knowledge.

8a. The instrumental function implies that we tend to develop favorable or unfavorable attitudes toward attitude objects in order to maximize rewards and minimize punishments.

8b. An attitude serving the instrumental function can be changed:
    (1) if it no longer leads to satisfaction;
    (2) if the acceptance of another attitude can be shown to be more instrumental;
    (3) if the individual's level of aspiration has changed.

8c. The ego-defensive function implies that we develop certain attitudes in order to protect ourselves from accepting certain unacceptable truths about ourselves and certain disturbing realities in the environment around us.

8d. An attitude serving the ego-defensive function may be changed by:
    (1) the removal of threat;
    (2) setting up a climate for the ventilation and catharsis of feeling;
    (3) helping the individual to acquire insights into his own mechanisms of defense.

8e. An attitude formed to serve the value-expressive function enables a person to give expression to his central values.

8f. An attitude serving the value-expressive function may be changed by:
    (1) causing the individual to feel some degree of dissatisfaction with his self-image;
    (2) fostering dissatisfaction with old attitudes as being inappropriate to his value system.

8g. An attitude formed to serve the knowledge function helps a person to understand and give meanings to situations.

8h. An attitude serving the knowledge function may be changed by:
    (1) providing the person with new information;
    (2) demonstrating the inaccuracy of the person's store of information.

Additional Readings

Insko, Chester. *Theories of Attitude Change.* New York: Appleton-Century-Crofts, 1967. Chapters 3, 6, 8, 9, 10, 12, and 13 touch upon most of the theories discussed in this chapter. However, we suggest these chapters because of their inclusion of several bits of research conducted to test the various theories.

Kiesler, Charles, Barry Collins, and Norman Miller. *Attitude Change: A Critical Analysis of Theoretical Approaches.* New York: Wiley & Sons, 1969. Excellent in-depth discussions plus criticisms of dissonance theory and social judgment theory are presented in chapters 5 and 6.

Wagner, Richard and John Sherwood. *The Study of Attitude Change.* Belmont, California: Wadsworth Publishing Company, 1969. Chapters 2, 4, 6, 7, and 11 detail full explanations of several theories discussed in this chapter.

part three

Elements
of the
Persuasive
Process

4

The Effects of
the Source on
Persuasive Communication

We spend an estimated three-fourths of our waking hours in some form of communication—reading, writing, speaking, and listening. It can be argued that the greatest percentage of this time is actually spent in the role of receiver. This means that a great number of individuals or groups act as the basic source of our information, attitudes, and values. The source may be a friend, relative, political candidate, radio-TV commentator, social organization, author of a book or essay, or national government. Each source is a potential agent for initiating or perpetuating the persuasive process. Each source is different, possessing certain particular characteristics that affect the transmission, reception, and acceptance of his information.

Imagine sitting around a dinner table with friends talking about a politician just heard on television. In attempting to explain your reaction to his speech you might suggest that "he really sounded great," or "I really believe in him," or "I feel he knows what he's talking about." These evaluative judgments were probably based more on your reaction to the source as a fellow human being than to the message he communicated. At other times our reactions to speakers may run from, "what he said makes me trust him," to "he's the teacher so I'll have to accept his word." These reactions reflect both our concern with the relationship between the source and his message and the power of a source in a particular situation to influence our judgments. More importantly, our reactions to the source, no matter what the bases, can affect the outcome of a persuasive situation.

In classical terms, the role of the source in the persuasive process was called *ethos*. Even today, ethos is still used by many as a label to encompass all source variables that affect the ultimate persuasive effect. Rosenthal (1971) suggests that ethos is not a basic element of the persuasive process but an end product of logical (cognitive) and emotional (affective) responses by receivers, that is, a specific type of persuasion.

The terms "ethos" and "ethical appeal" are sometimes confused when describing the source's role in persuasion. Ethical appeal refers to specific types of speech content. For example, a speech which employs a number of self-references or conciliatory elements is described as having ethical appeals. Ethos consists of whatever enhances the speaker's role in the persuasive situation.

A more contemporary term used to describe the receiver's perception of the communicator is *source credibility*. Source credibility is the degree of credulity or acceptability a receiver gives to a source. The degree of believability or acceptability may range from high to low (Wenburg and Wilmont 1973).

In the persuasive situation, the communicator generates visual and aural cues which stimulate a response from us. These responses are the result of our life experiences. We develop certain evaluations, positive or negative, regarding people, their ideas, conditions, and things. Because our evaluative structures are the product of our life experiences, they are subject to change as we accumulate new experiences. The source has the responsibility to activate the attitudes or values in our evaluative repertoire that will allow him to produce a persuasive effect. The total impact of the source is to a great extent determined by his skill in locating and activating the correct response in the receiver.

When a communicator delivers a message with the intent of influencing the behavior of his auditors, we may conceive of the communication as presenting two distinct objects as the principal foci of listeners: the message and the source. We are not suggesting that a speaker concentrates on either the message or his personality, but that a persuasive effect can be activated by one or the other. In other words, the communicator's image or message may emerge as the agent of activation for the listener. Persuasion can be classified as personal or nonpersonal (Rosenthal 1971). If the message activates the dominant response, the response is called *nonpersonal* persuasion. If the communicator activates the dominant response, it is called *personal* persuasion. Personal persuasion involves a complex pattern of reactions by the receiver to the source. Some listener responses to the source's personality are of the observable behavior variety; for example, reactions to physical appearance, attire, voice, diction, and self-reference in his message. Some listener responses are indirect responses to the source's personality created by the message. The message can provide a picture of the source. The organization of ideas, amount of supporting materials, and language, can all be used by receivers as reflections of the source's personality. In fact, the communicator's choice of words, subjects, thoughts, and structure may reveal more about the source than any deliberate personal reference or observable behavior.

The source is only one part of the total communication process, and cannot, in reality, be separated from the total persuasive process. The source interacts with the message, receiver, situation, and channel. We will, however, attempt to isolate and identify the effects of all five in persuasive situations. Because all parts of the total persuasive situation are interrelated, differences which we may observe in actual communication situations may not be accounted for when we examine only one part of the process. Thus, our conclusions about the source, his importance, and his effect can only be tentative. We will divide this chapter into three major areas: (1) source credibility; (2) source-receiver similarity; and (3) power. For the purpose of discussion, we will examine each variable as a separate entity. But remember, just as the source is only one part of the total persuasive process, source characteristics will operate and affect us simultaneously.

Let us begin by examining what is meant by source credibility and the role of source credibility in the persuasive act.

Source Credibility

Components of Source Credibility

Let's say we are listening to Germaine Greer, a women's liberation leader, berating the attitude of males toward females in our society. We accept her admonitions as a basis for eliminating sex status differences in the United States. Why were we influenced by her comments? Why are some speakers, regardless of what they say, listened to and followed? What do we see in certain individuals that immediately commands our respect when they speak? Answers to these questions have been sought by researchers and theorists concerned with persuasion since antiquity.

These are not simple questions to answer. The perceptions of a source by a receiver are not formed by single characteristics, such as age, sex, or socioeconomic position. Credibility is a complex set of perceptions by the receiver formed by past, present, and future expectations of a source. If we are listening to Ms. Greer, her credibility might be the sum or product of our perceptions of her sex, age, socioeconomic position, knowledge of her subject, sincerity, and so on.

Since the time of Aristotle, source credibility has been recognized as a multidimensional construct. In the *Rhetoric*, Aristotle listed the components of ethos as good sense (intelligence), good character (moral), and good will toward the audience. He believed these three qualities of the source induce the audience to believe what the speaker says apart from the proof he might use to support his statements.

Hovland, Janis and Kelly (1953) distinguished between two components of source credibility: *expertness* and *trustworthiness*. The receiver's attitudes of trust and confidence toward the source arise from the receiver's belief that the speaker is knowledgeable, intelligent, and sincere. In a discussion of sex, Dr. David Ruben would be perceived as having more expertise than William Buckley. Ruben would be judged as more credible or having higher credibility than William Buckley. Kelman (1961) felt that expertness and trustworthiness were reflected in a source who knew the correct stand on an issue and communicated his knowledge without bias.

Recently, researchers have made a number of probes to uncover the component structure of source credibility. They have generally used procedures developed by Osgood, Suci and Tannenbaum (1957) to construct semantic differentials. In semantic differentiation, the researcher develops a set of bipolar adjectival scales which the receivers (subjects) used to rate a number of sources. Each source is rated against a series of scales. Subjects' ratings are then used to discover which scales belong to dependent clusters or components of a receiver's perception of the source. Figure 4-1 illustrates the kind of scales used.

Berlo, Lemert and Mertz (1969-70), using these procedures, attempted to find exactly how many dimensions account for receiver evaluations of a source, whether the dimensions were independent of

David Ruben

Trained	___:___:___:___:___:___:___	Untrained
Just	___:___:___:___:___:___:___	Unjust
Objective	___:___:___:___:___:___:___	Subjective

FIGURE 4-1.   Semantic Differential Scales

each other, and the types of responses characterizing each dimension. On the basis of two studies, they uncovered four components: safety, qualification, dynamism, and sociability. The two major factors were *safety* and *qualification*. The safety factor is defined by such scales as safe-dangerous, just-unjust, objective-subjective, and selfish-unselfish. It is similar to the previously mentioned component of trustworthiness. The source is perceived to be safe when he is just, calm, objective, unselfish, and patient. The qualification factor is similar to the expertness dimension. It is defined by such scales as experienced-inexperienced, trained-untrained, authoritative-unauthoritative, and intelligent-unintelligent. A source is rated as qualified if he is perceived as trained, experienced, authoritative, skilled, informed, important, educated, and an expert. The third component is *dynamism*. It is characterized by such scales as frank-reserved, fast-slow, energetic-tired. A dynamic source is one who is perceived as frank, fast, energetic, extroverted, bold, active, aggressive, and decisive. When we speak of the dynamic quality of the source, we usually think in terms of the speaker's style of delivery. The fourth dimension is *sociability*. A speaker who is perceived to possess this dimension is sociable and cheerful. This last component appears to play a minor role in the receiver's perception of source credibility. More recent studies have supported the existence of safety, qualification, and dynamism components as integral parts of the receiver's perception of source credibility (McCroskey 1966; Whitehead 1968).

In addition, Berlo suggested that dynamism was independent of, but related to, safety and qualification. Dynamism was conceived of as an intensifier—the qualification and safety components were heightened or diminished by the source's dynamism. Dynamism, however, may work as an additive factor rather than as an intensifier. It provides a basis for receivers to differentiate between communicators of high and low credibility and increases the credibility of dynamic sources (Schweitzer 1970; Schweitzer and Ginsburg 1966). Remember, however, that dynamism does not appear to be as significant a source credibility component as either safety or qualification.

Can we separate the source from his topic? Let's say we first evaluate Senator Fulbright talking on foreign policy and, second, Senator Fulbright talking on air pollution. Would we use the same bases for evaluating Senator Fulbright speaking on two distinct subjects? The answer is yes. Receivers use trustworthiness and competence to evaluate source-topic relationships as well as sources in topic-free situations (Bowers and Phillips 1967).

We have been examining the receiver's perception of source credibility as if it could easily be represented by three or four components. However, the structure of source credibility may be much more complex.

Two studies found between twenty-seven and sixteen components for a high credibility source and between twenty-eight and sixteen components for a low credibility source (Schweitzer and Ginsburg 1966; Whitehead 1968).

The fact that different component structures have been observed may indicate that a number of variables affect the perceptual basis for evaluating a source. The perceived credibility of a source is not primarily dependent upon objective attributes, but rather upon the way a receiver perceives these attributes (Wotring 1969). Tucker (1971) remarked that the component structure may vary over concepts, subjects (receivers), time, and cultures. It appears that the components of source credibility vary considerably on the basis of sources, populations, organizational sources (National Education Association, American Medical Association, United States Steel), public figures (Nixon, Ted Kennedy, Agnew), and situations (classroom lecture, sermon in a church, speech to a social organization) (McCroskey, Jensen, Todd, and Toomb 1972; McCroskey, Jensen, and Todd 1972; Applbaum and Anatol 1972).

The receiver's criteria relevant to the evaluation of source credibility can be affected by the nature of the audience, the nature of the source, the type of issue under consideration, and the speaking situation. Source credibility would appear to involve general and group-specific components. Two general components re-appear regardless of the audience, source, issue, or situation: trustworthiness and expertness.

The Effects of Source Credibility

A receiver's tendency to accept conclusions advocated by a source will depend in part upon how competent, trustworthy, and dynamic he believes the source to be. Haiman (1949) had three groups listen to the same speech attributed to three speakers of varying competence. He found that the speaker rated as most competent produced the greatest attitude change. Hovland and Weiss (1951) found that trustworthy sources (high credibility) were more successful than untrustworthy sources (low credibility) in producing attitude change.

There is little question that low credibility sources are not as persuasive as high credibility sources. When, prior to its presentation, a persuasive message is attributed to a low credibility source, the receiver is forewarned that the information may be unreliable. This forewarning is likely to cause receivers to ignore the message's persuasive appeals and not to be influenced by the source. We know that the effects of low credibility can be eliminated by not identifying the source until after the message is presented (Greenberg and Miller 1966). This increases the probability that the message's persuasive appeals will be more attentively received and subsequent attribution of the message to a low credibility source will have less of an effect. Conversely, it is better to identify high credibility sources early in the speech to create a favorable attitude toward the message presented (Greenberg and Tannenbaum 1961). Even with an untrustworthy, high credibility source the overall effect is usually in the direction favored by the communicator. The arguments in his message may counteract negative effects resulting from his untrustworthiness (Hovland, Janis and Kelly 1953).

We would expect that the most favorable source would always be the most effective agent of persuasion. However, this is not always the case. Enduring attitude change in the face of counter-persuasion will be more successful by a source of questionable trustworthiness (Bauer 1966). In certain persuasive situations a low prestige source may be more persuasive than a high prestige communicator. A low prestige source can gain in effectiveness when he advocates a position opposed to his best interests (Walster, Aronson and Abrahams 1966; Stone and Eswara 1969).

The differential effectiveness of high and low credibility sources appears to disappear over time. This phenomenon is referred to as the "sleeper effect." It has been suggested that the character of the source is forgotten at a more rapid rate than the content of his communication. Kelman and Hovland (1953) found that receivers immediately after exposure to a low credibility source linked both source and message together. In contrast, the majority of receivers immediately after exposure to a high credibility source were concerned only with the communication content. As time passed for those who heard the low credibility speaker, the thoughts about the source disappeared and the initial inhibition toward the low credibility source's advocated position disappeared.

These studies illustrate the relationship between source and message variables, a relationship which functions to determine the actual outcome of a persuasive act. This relationship is no more apparent than with the interaction of source credibility and fear appeals in a message. Hewgill and Miller (1966) found that a high credibility source using appeals that elicit strong fear for persons highly valued by the listener (son, wife) will produce greater attitude change than using appeals that elicit mild fear.

Since the message interacts with the effect of the source, we might ask if message organization affects source credibility. Sharp and McClung (1966) found that while organized messages did not lower credibility, a disorganized message did. While a disorganized message lowers the credibility of an initially highly credible source, an organized message will increase the credibility of a moderately credible source (Baker

1965). The manner in which message organization affects the source creditibility components is puzzling. McCroskey and Mehrley (1969) found that the organization of a message had no effect on the character and dynamism dimensions of credibility, though it did affect the authority dimension. Jones and Serlousky (1972), on the other hand, found that disorganization affected the competence dimension, but not the authority dimension. Despite these contradictory findings, it would appear that an organized message can increase source credibility, while a disorganized message can lower speaker credibility.

When the source has high credibility, receivers generally accept his comments without critical evaluation. What would happen in situations where receivers normally evaluate the source's comments critically? Receivers who are highly ego-involved on the persuasive topic are recognized as critical listeners. It appears that a highly credible source still produces more attitude change than a low credibility source with highly ego-involved groups (Gantt 1970). However, the highly credible source is not as successful in producing the same amount of attitude change with highly involved groups (Sereno 1968). This may stem in part from the fact that ego-involved receivers tend to decrease their overall evaluation of the source. Since the source is not perceived as credible, his overall effect is diminished.

Communication Channels.   How often have we heard the expressions, "one picture is worth a thousand words," or "seeing is believing." They refer to a belief that viewing something as it occurs is of more value or more believable than hearing about the same event. When a friend tells us about the four-foot fish that got away, we have a tendency to consider his story as just another "fisherman's tale," unless he can show us a picture of the fish. The assumption that visual materials, slides, photographs, movies, tapes, and so on are more credible than orally presented materials is not new. In fact, authors and teachers alike have suggested that visual aids, when properly used, lend credence and clarity to a communicator's words.

The pictures we see, the words we hear, the odors we smell, and the objects we feel are all forms of communication. However, pictures, sounds, odors, and tactile feelings are all communicated to us through different *channels*. While the concept "channels" has a number of meanings, for our purpose in this chapter we will loosely define "channel" as the mode through which a message is transmitted.

The question we must ask is: Do the channels we use to communicate a persuasive message affect the source's credibility? Seiler (1971) suggested that the use of visual aids designed to supplement and clarify a persuasive message by a speaker enhanced his credibility. The effect of visual aids upon source credibility appears greatest for speakers who are initially perceived as being of low credibility. Low credibility speakers through the use of visuals can overcome their perceived lack of trustworthiness and authoritativeness. The visuals become a form of support that strengthens a speaker's acceptability by his audience. The use of visual aids by low credible sources also appears to affect the audience's retention level. In situations where speakers did not use visual aids, audiences listening to the high credibility speaker retained more information than those listening to a low credibility speaker. However, when visual aids were used by the low and high credibility speakers, there was no difference in the amount of information retained by the audiences. Visuals may negate the effect of or enhance the low credibility sources by reinforcing the information presented by the speaker (Seiler 1971).

While source credibility and audience retention are affected by the use of more than one channel during a persuasive situation, the use of visual aids does not appear to affect either the attitude change of the audience or the overall effectiveness of the speaker.

In the classroom, we are exposed to live presentations, but when watching a television program, the speaker may be prerecorded. The actual persuasive attempt was developed hours, days, weeks, or even months before its presentation on the television screen. A question we might ask is: Does varying the mode of presentation affect source credibility? Croft (1969) suggests that source credibility varies depending upon the channel or mode of presentation. One study of live, audio, and videotaped presentations of the same message did not find a difference in the audience's ratings of source credibility (Meyer and Gute 1972). However, film has been found to be considerably more credible and has a greater impact on receiver's beliefs than either tape or written communications (Addis 1970). Bettinghaus (1968, p. 173) suggests that, in situations where the persuasive effect of the message will depend to a considerable extent on the credibility of the source, oral communication will be more effective than written communication. This occurs because the audience is not able to relate to the impersonal nature of the source of a written message.

Channel variation does appear to affect source credibility. The low credible source may enhance his credibility by utilizing visual materials in conjunction with his normal presentation.

Delivery—Vocalic Cues.   We all recognize that in our day to day interactions with others, certain vocal characteristics of the source affect our reactions to the speaker. Many communicators develop characteristic vocalic patterns, and experienced speakers may use several patterns of vocal cues when they judge them appropriate. For example, the identical news item would be presented differently by newsmen Walter Cronkite, Harry Reasoner, and David Brinkley. An experienced politician's vocal cues will change radically depending upon whether he is addressing his constituents on a street corner or presenting a television news conference to the nation.

We form various personality stereotypes of the source based upon the vocal qualities of the communicator (Allport and Cantril 1934). These vocal stereotypes are learned within the framework of the receiver's culture. For example, a man is categorized as effeminate if he possesses a high-pitched voice or a girl may be called sexy if her voice is low-pitched and breathy.

Vocal communication refers to those elements of voice quality, rhythm, pattern of pitch, stress, inflection, and juncture which characterize a speaker's delivery, but which are not inherent in the verbal message (Pearce and Brommel 1972). When both verbal and vocalic elements are present, as we find in normal speech, vocalic communication is considered paralinguistic. When verbal message units are eliminated from voice, the vocal cues are described as nonverbal messages; for example, inflection, pitch, force, and timing which function as cues to the receivers. Vocalic communication contains several types of information. The voice tells the audience how the speaker wishes them to interpret the words in the text by functioning as oral punctuation, marking the terminal points of phrases and indicating the relationships between structural units. In addition, certain patterns of vocal communication contain additional information regarding the interpretation of the verbal message, "I'm just kidding," "Please take my comments seriously," "I'm being honest with you," and so on.

Communicators develop manners of presentation which lead receivers to draw desired or undesired inferences about them which, whether accurate or not, affect the continuation and effectiveness of the persuasive act. If a source is perceived as unscrupulous or incompetent because of his vocal cues, the credibility of the source can be altered by the receivers. To the extent that a communicator is perceived as having high or low credibility and desirable or undesirable personality characteristics on the basis of vocal cues, the entire persuasive attempt may succeed or fail. We might ask ourselves: What vocal characteristics affect the audience's perception of a source's credibility?

One set of vocal cues that affect an audience's ratings of source credibility are *nonfluencies.* Speaker nonfluencies encompass a wide range of verbal-vocal behaviors: (1) vocalized pauses — the utterance of "uh" between two words of a message, "I—uh—believe that . . .";

(2) repetitions—the first syllable of a word, followed by the utterance of the complete word, "I be–uh–believe that . . ."; (3) sentence corrections—"I feel . . . believe that . . ."; (4) stuttering—"I b–b–believe that . . . "; (5) and tongue-slip correction—"I believe that black mos . . . muslim. . . ." It appears that as the quantity of nonfluencies exhibited by the speaker increases, the perceived credibility of the source decreases. This is particularly true when we compare the quantity of repetitions to pauses (Miller and Hewgill 1964). If we examine the credibility dimensions, it appears that expertness and dynamism, but not trustworthiness, are affected by nonfluencies. It is not hard to imagine that we might consider the pause or repetition as a sign that the speaker lacks certain information or is unsure of his knowledge but is absolutely honest and sincere in his comments (Sereno and Hewgill 1968).

Despite a decrease in source credibility, the attitude change of receivers does not appear to be related to nonfluencies. This does not necessarily refute our earlier contention that credibility and attitude change are related. Remember, a speaker's trustworthiness may be more closely related to attitude change than other elements of source credibility. Trustworthiness may be the critical factor in affecting shifts in receiver's attitudes toward the topic. Since nonfluencies do not appear to alter the audience's perceptions of the speaker's trustworthiness, these nonfluencies would not be expected to affect the amounts of attitude change.

Addington (1970) examined the effects of the speaker's sex and four vocal variables—speaking rate, pitch variety, vocal quality, and articulation—on source credibility. While credibility differences between male and female speakers were not due to their vocal cues, competence, trustworthiness, and dynamism were affected by delivery style. Competence, for example, was most sensitive to changes in the sound of the voice and least affected by speaking rate. While increases in pitch variety had little effect on creditability ratings, decreases in pitch variety led to lower credibility. Articulation had the greatest effect on altering source credibility. We usually categorize articulation problems as speech disorders which educationally, socially, and vocationally handicap the speaker. However, contrary to Addington's findings, it has been discovered that a normal-speaking individual is not perceived as superior to a speaker with defective speech (Schliesser 1968).

Another question we might ask is: Does the overall delivery style of the speaker affect source credibility? It has been found that the speaker's voice style conditions the receiver's perception of source credibility. When a speaker uses a conversational style, he is described as more trustworthy, less dynamic, and more favorably evaluated than when he uses dynamic delivery. Expertness does not appear to be affected by delivery style (Pearce and Conklin 1971; Pearce and Brommel 1972). In terms of speaker effectiveness, the speaker is least effective when he is introduced as lowly credible and uses dynamic delivery and most effective when he is introduced as highly credible and uses dynamic delivery (Pearce and Brommel 1972).

Receiver Comprehension and Source Credibility.   There is some question as to the effect of credibility upon a receiver's comprehension of speech content. Tompkins and Samovar (1964) found that the non-artistic proof of a speaker did not affect the immediate recall of information by receivers. Artistic proof refers to those means of persuasion which are intrinsic to the persuasive act and which the source furnishes through the development and performance of the persuasive act; for example, alterations in content and/or delivery. Nonartistic proof is not supplied by the speaker. It exists beforehand and has only to be used by the speaker.

King (1966) indicated that neither artistic nor nonartistic forms of source credibility affected the ability of an audience to remember a speech. One form of artistic proof is the use of testimony and self-reference in the persuasive message. Ostermier (1967) investigated the relationship between a communicator's use of self and prestige references and its effect upon source credibility and attitude change. Self-reference is a reference in which the source reveals and stresses his first-hand experience with a topic. Prestige reference is a reference in which the source reveals and stresses a personal association with others who have had first-hand experience with the topic. We know that receivers exposed to messages presented by unfamiliar sources rate that source as less competent, trustworthy, and dynamic, than messages presented by unfamiliar sources using self-references. This does not work when using prestige references. It is possible that prestige references do not remove the effect of unfamiliarity with the source. Attitude change also increases as increases to self-reference are made, but not to prestige references.

Whitehead (1971) suggests that authority-based assertions play an indirect role in persuasion; that is, they serve as catalysts for the establishment of credibility. However, Warren (1969) found that when neutral speakers utilize highly credible sources of testimony, they do not enhance their own credibility.

The amount of credibility an individual is seen to have is a function of who the receiver is, what the topic is, how the speaker presents his message, and what the situation is. The actual influence of the source will depend on his relationship with the receiver. When we find out how the audience perceives a source, we can predict his potential effect on the persuasive situation. If we do not know the receivers or are not certain how a group of receivers will perceive a source, we must apply our knowledge of the general characteristics of source credibility to improve our chances to produce a persuasive effect. We have examined how certain perceptual differences between the source and receiver may be influential in determining the outcome of persuasion. In the next section we will investigate how the source may be influential in affecting the outcome of a persuasive act when the receiver perceives some degree of similarity between himself and the source.

Source-Similarity and Identification

Identification

We have all at one time or another imagined ourselves as astronauts, heart surgeons, professional athletes, or perhaps the President of the United States. We may have even bought a car, dress, or cereal product because the person in the television commercial was like us or something like what we wanted to be.

One factor affecting the attraction of a source for a receiver is *identification*. What is identification? Let's say a black politician wishes to persuade a group of women liberationists to support his candidacy for local office. He might include in his presentation a comment such as, "We have all been subjected to society's discriminatory practices," or "We are all somewhat disenfranchised by the present governmental system." The source attempts to show that his interest, beliefs, or background is the same as his receivers. Burke (1950, p. 15) suggests that a source persuades you by using your language, gesture, tonality, order, image, attitude, idea, or identifying his ways with yours. In other words, to persuade the source manipulates language in such a way that it gives "signs" of the commonalities between speaker and receiver. By using linguistic strategies the speaker identifies himself with the receiver and, thereby, achieves persuasion.

One specific strategy is to refer to the experience of the listener, to appeal to what the listener has seen, heard, read, felt, believed, or done. The source can associate or identify his purpose with the knowledge, interests, and motives of his audience. Hopefully, the receiver will adopt the speaker's position because it appears consistent with his previous commitments. When the receiver perceives that he shares certain attitudes with the source, it may lead him to share new attitudes. King (1971) suggests that if a source is similar to a receiver he will be more successful in establishing identification on a specific concept or position. Conversely, identification on any given position will be more difficult when dissimilarity between speaker and receiver has been established. Let us now examine the specific role of source-receiver similarity in the persuasive process.

Source-Receiver Similarity

What makes a source appear similar or dissimilar to the receiver? A speaker may assert that he shares interests, feelings, and beliefs with the receiver. He may emphasize similar origin, parentage, schooling, religion, work, or economic class. Sources may call the audience's attention to certain membership-group similarities; for example, age, sex, fraternities, social organizations, and so on. He may indicate a similarity in attitudes toward issues, people, or objects.

There are four basic types of source-receiver similarity: (1) relevant; (2) irrelevant; (3) attitudinal; and (4) membership-group. A similarity is relevant when it relates directly to the issue advocated, the source's credibility, or producing the attempted attitude change. Conversely, an irrelevant similarity is one that does not relate to the issue being discussed, the source's credibility, or producing attitude change. For example, in many communication situations we use irrelevant similarities to break the ice. Let's say a speaker is addressing a college audience on the topic of water pollution. He might begin his speech by mentioning that he is a fan of their football team. The similarity in interests is irrelevant to his communicative purpose. If he begins his presentation by indicating that he belongs to the same ecology organization to which the majority of audience members belong, he has used a relevant similarity to gain audience interest. A speaker who indicates that he holds the same attitudes as his audience is expressing attitudinal similarity. Whereas, a speaker who identifies himself with an organization that the audience is also a member of, for example, the ecology club, is expressing membership-group similarities.

If a source attempts to create the impression of similarity between himself and receiver, do attitudinal and group-membership similarities create the same effects upon the receiver's impression of the source's attraction, respect, and trust? We do know that a receiver's attraction for a source increases as attitudinal similarity between the two increases

(Byrne 1961). This appears to be independent of the source's respect or prestige (Byrne, Griffitt and Golightly 1966). We might explain the increased attraction by assuming that similarities work as positive reinforcements for the receiver toward the source. Receivers will judge similar sources as more attractive than dissimilar sources. Membership-group similarities, on the other hand, appear to be less significant determinants of source attraction. While establishing membership-group similarities between the source and receiver can increase a source's attraction, it would appear that attitudinal similarities are much more effective in the persuasive situation.

While we can link source-receiver similarity to source attraction, there is little evidence that source-receiver similarity affects the receiver's image of the source's honesty, integrity, objectivity, or intelligence. Simons (1970) suggests that there is a weak positive relationship between attitudinal similarity and the receiver's perception of the source's trustworthiness. An even less dependable relationship exists between membership-group similarities and source trustworthiness. The relationship between similarity and source trustworthiness is dependent upon the receiver's perception of the membership group identified by the source. Receivers belonging to the same group as the source may find the source more worthy of respect or trust than dissimilar, nonmember sources. However, because of the receiver's knowledge of his group, he might recognize that sources of dissimilar groups would have greater competence and dependability than his own group members.

We might ask if source attraction is as significant in determining a receiver's attitude toward a position advocated by the source as respect and trust for the source. Source credibility studies would indicate that attraction (dynamism and likeability) plays a considerably smaller role in the evaluation of the source than respect (expertise) or trust (trustworthiness). In turn, attraction to the source plays a smaller role in affecting attitude change. Thus, emphasis on source-receiver commonalities, especially membership-group similarities, may not have great persuasive value.

Earlier in the chapter we suggested four types of perceived similarity or dissimilarity (relevant, irrelevant, attitudinal, and membership-group). What is the relationship between the type of source similarity and attitude change? Brock (1965) showed that customers buying a can of paint would change the brand, regardless of price, when a salesman recommended the product based on personal experience, that is, experiences anticipated by the customer when using the product. Berscheid (1966) found that relevant similarity contributed to attitude change;

irrelevant similarity did not. It would appear that, while relevant attitudinal similarities have positive effects on attitude change, relevant
membership-group similarities have less of an effect on attitude change.

The relationship between membership-group similarity and attitude
change is difficult to interpret. The advantage of emphasizing certain
membership-group similarities may be outweighed by losses in overall
credibility.

King (1971) suggests that the receiver has two tasks: (1) the
evaluation of message source and (2) the evaluation of the advocated
position on the topic. Evaluation of a source involves the determination
of the appropriateness of a particular source for a particular message.
This evaluation is a joint function of message type, degrees of similarity,
and type of similarity. A similar source is appropriate to the degree that
he is subjectively similar, while a dissimilar source is appropriate to
the extent that he is objectively dissimilar in the direction of increased
competence.

We have now examined the role of identification and source-receiver
similarity upon the evaluation of the source and eventual attitude change.
We will now move on to consider the effect of status and power of the
source upon the persuasive process. Once again, we will examine how
differences in the relationship between source and receiver lead to
increased or decreased persuasive effect.

Status and Power

Status

Originally, status was used as a legal term referring to the sum of the
legal capacities of an individual, his power to enforce legal rights and
the obligations of his position upon himself and others. Status in these
terms still exists. For example, a policeman is granted certain duties
(allowed certain behaviors) which enable him to enforce laws established
by federal, state, and local authorities. If you've ever received a traffic
ticket for speeding, you've seen the policeman exercising his "status."

Today, status has a much broader definition. It has come to mean
the place of an individual in society and is usually defined by a collection
of rights and duties. These rights and duties are defined either formally
or informally by society, organizations, small groups, or single individuals.
The president of a social club, for example, is given certain formal duties
and rights by the constitution of his organization. Informally, the mem-

bers of the club may grant certain rights, honors, and prestige to the president: the president's ideas may be accepted without serious questioning; he may be allowed to dominate discussions concerning group business; he might even be given certain authority and powers that extend beyond the confines of the organizational environment, for example, his advice to a group member on where to eat or rent a home might be readily accepted.

The actual status behavior of an individual we call his *role*. In persuasion, we are concerned with the relationship between communicators' roles, the relationship of status-roles between source and receiver. Let's examine the following list that illustrates several status-role relationships:

High Status	*Low Status*
university professor	university student
university student	high School student
university president	university professor

Notice in our list that individuals can occupy more than one status-role. In the classroom, the college professor is perceived as higher status than the college student. However, if the university president were to enter the classroom, the professor would be of lower status than the president. Thus, the status one holds is relative to the status of the other individual with whom he is interacting. In addition, an individual can be perceived as high status in one role and lower status in another role relative to the same receiver. Let's reexamine the relationship between college president and college professor. Both have relatively high status within the general community. On the university campus, the college president would have the higher status. However, at a convention in the professor's area of specialty, the college president may be of lower status than the professor. In this last example the *environment* of the interaction would dictate the status relationship between communicators.

The role-status of an individual can also function as a variant of the topic of conversation. Let's say that we are listening to a speech instructor discuss the effect of source on persuasion. We would probably perceive him as high status. But what if he began discussing the intricacies of the 1-3-1 basketball offense? Would we still give the teacher the same status? Probably not.

The importance of status-role relationships in persuasion is that the higher the status attached to a position, the more likely an individual occupying that position will be influencial in that situation. A teacher in class may dictate the kinds of questions that are to be asked by students. He can do this merely by answering certain types of questions.

Bettinghaus (1968) remarks that the status that an individual is seen to possess is not responsible for the persuasibility of any receiver. But the perceived status differences between sources and receivers may lead one individual to be perceived as more worth listening to, as more believable, or as more influential. In any communication situation we should realize that there are many differences among individuals— intelligence, personality, age, ability, needs, frequency of communication, and so on. For any of us to regard ourselves as equal to others in all situations would place us at a disadvantage. It would lead us to mis-perceive the intent and action of those with whom we interact.

These inequalities lead to status differences among individuals. Our position in a communication setting or in the status hierarchy is a major factor affecting how others perceive us. The more we communicate the more status is attributed to us, and the greater our status the more power we can possess. The greater our power, the more communication we will initiate and the more power attempts we will not only try but also com-plete successfully.

Our position within a status hierarchy is closely related to differ-ences in individual power. Once we have acquired status, we may exert power over others regardless of the means used to acquire that status. Let's say that George Robbins is the president of Telemex Inc., a com-pany engaged in the production of electrical conductors. His son, George Jr., graduates from college with a degree in basketweaving. Immediately, the father names the son as executive consultant in charge of line man-agement. His immediate status in the organization gives him considerable power over managers, who are better trained than himself. His status is derived from the type of position into which he was placed, but even more so from the relationship between the president of the company and himself.

All of us have been in situations where we were unsure of our power status, or, knowing our status, were uncertain of what to do. In general, we do all sorts of things to minimize status differences. Most often we imitate the behavior of those whom we perceive as having higher status. We modify our beliefs to match those selected by others. Our social etiquette is modified by others. We mortgage our incomes for things we don't need in an attempt to acquire status.

Even between two people, who know nothing about each other except their relative status positions, the lower status person will most often concede to decisions of the higher status individual. Recognize that we are influenced by the high status of others, even though that status may be unrelated to the problem we are considering (Moore 1968, 1969).

If we find ourselves powerless, isolated, and dissatisfied with individuals and conditions that comprise the status hierarchy, we may reject higher status power attempts. Today, many people—young and old alike—who feel isolated from elected representatives, neighbors, family, and colleagues, have rejected the "establishment."

In a previous section of this chapter, we investigated the role of vocal cues in the determination of source credibility. We might also ask if vocal cues are important to the persuasive process by indicating to the receiver the status of the source. Within our educational institutions, there is a belief that training an individual to speak like an "educated man" is a useful education goal. It is based on the assumption that speaking in an acceptable manner will assist individuals both educationally and vocationally.

Putnam and O'Hern (1955) established that listeners are able to identify the background or status of a speaker merely by listening to his voice. Accordingly, we might assume that a source would be perceived as having a specific status by varying his vocal patterns. This becomes important in persuasion since the assignment of different "credentials" to a source will produce different amounts of opinion change (Hovland and Weiss 1951). This assignment of credentials to a speaker can occur strictly on the basis of speech cues alone. Receivers, regardless of their own status, assign speakers status and distinguish among speakers according to status. Receivers perceive high status speakers to be most credible and low status speakers as the least credible (Harms 1961).

The receiver is also able to identify the source's social status position (Moe 1972). As Moe points out, this supports Watson's (1925) contention that vocalizations are responses subject to principles of conditioning. Sound recognition is learned behavior and reflects societal environment. As the child grows and matures, educational and vocational selection influence the speech sound production and language usage. The learned vocal habits affect the source's ability to communicate, to be accepted, and to appear credible in a persuasive situation.

The impact of language cues transcends even racial differences between source and receiver. Individuals perceive sources who utilize standard English as more competent and trustworthy than nonstandard English speakers regardless of the speaker's race (Buck 1968). As Bochner, Bochner, and Hilyard (1972) suggest, receivers respond to certain dialect forms as educated, intelligent, reliable and correct, and respond to other dialect forms as uneducated, unreliable, and incorrect.

What is it about a dialect that makes a receiver evaluate it as correct or incorrect? It would appear that receivers, regardless of their own social status (upper-class white or lower-class black), hold as a linguistic norm the white standard American English. This would be the traditional language-learning in the American school system. English and speech teachers have generally advocated certain standard forms of syntax as "right" while other forms, often having the same meaning but not the same grammar, are pronounced as wrong or incorrect.

In respect to the dimensions of credibility the social dialect of the speaker generally influences the receiver's judgments of the speaker's character, but not his authority. Despite the specific dialect, individuals are perceived as being equally competent. This is consistent for high status and low status receivers. Middle-class receivers, it appears, tend to use the speaker's dialect more as a determinant of speaker's ethos than persons of high or low status. Differences of speakers' perceptions occur within both the authority and character dimensions. It appears that the middle-class receiver may judge a person solely on the basis of his dialect.

Power

Power is developed from the social relationship between source and receiver. It is not merely an attribute of the source. A student (receiver) will accept the influence attempts of his instructor (source) because he wishes to accomplish the goal of getting an *A*. The teacher's control of the grading is a basis for the power relationship between student and teacher. Before we investigate the relationship between source influence and power, we must accept certain basic assumptions. First, the source has power over the receiver only within a specific range of activities. Our instructor would have no power in attempting to dictate whom we date or marry. Second, the power relationship between source-receiver is not one-sided. In any relationship between two individuals, each person may have some power over the other. One person may have more power than the other or neither may have superior power over the other.

The source's power includes his individual resources, motivation, and intent for exerting power. The source's resources are those elements he possesses that other people value. He may have needed information, money, or personal characteristics that are important in the persuasive situation; for example, the ability to speak well in front of others. He may provide others with praise, recognition, affection, or punishment. The motivation will be the source's attitudes toward the receivers and toward the task. He may wish to use his power to help others, to help himself, or simply to get self-gratification from using the power in a particular situation. He may desire to control the group interaction or to win approval from the audience for his behavior.

Although the source's ultimate power varies from one persuasive situation to another, the source's personality and abilities are important for developing or using power. Bass and Wurster (1953) found that individuals who were more intelligent, educated, and of higher rank than others were more successful on power attempts. Browne (1949) found that those who are in a position to influence others have higher feelings of authority and feel they have more responsibility than others. Lippitt and others (1952) found that individuals viewed by others as possessing power also perceived themselves as power holders. They were more successful in power attempts, received more deference behavior, showed more indirect influence on others (imitation by others of their behavior), were best liked by others, and made more frequent power attempts.

The amount of communication by an individual in a communication situation can affect his power. Riecken (1958) reported that when the most talkative member of a group gives the solution, it is usually accepted. The member who talks the most is most likely to promote his solution successfully. Gold (1958) found that the perception of friendliness, gentleness, playing with others, smartness, being unaggressive, and doing things for others are attributed to high power persons. It is perhaps significant that coercive power is not an important influence source for high power sources.

We have noted that some individuals are influenced on the bases of personal abilities accepted by other individuals or because they are in a higher ranked position than others in the communication situation. Bass (1960) noted that leaders may be successful because of their charismatic nature, because they are viewed as father figures or because their position gives them control of reward valued by group members. A supervisor who, on the basis of his position within the status structure, can mediate rewards for subordinates is more influential with his subordinates than a less powerful supervisor.

Individuals who believe their power to be superior to others make more frequent power attempts, resist influence attempts of others more often, and are more self-assertive. In contrast, those who believe their power is inferior accept more suggestions and make fewer power attempts. If a receiver perceives his power to be inferior in a specific persuasive situation, he is more prone to be influenced by a high power source.

A distinctive power source is the title of the position one holds; for example, professor, doctor, supervisor. Torrance (1965) found when members of air crews were placed in groups, the pilots were more influential than crewmen. If a person is told he is the leader—whether or not he has any real power—he will participate more actively and direct and organize group efforts more than other members (Berkowitz 1956). Different situations and issues determine how much influence a given individual has. Opinion leaders, for example, specialize in particular content areas. On public questions, older, better-educated individuals have power potential; in matters of fashion, younger women are more likely to be influential.

Power may be a function of the rewards which the source controls. Bennis and others (1958) indicated that if an individual correctly perceives the rewards others desire and can mediate these rewards, he is usually successful in his influence attempts. If the individual incorrectly perceives the desired rewards or fails to mediate them successfully, his power decreases. Rewards can be praise, promotion, money, educational opportunities, recognition, and so on.

Power may also be based on the source's control of punishment. The power potential exists if the receiver clearly understands what the punishment will be. Deutsch and Krauss (1960) contend that unless an individual can communicate that he possesses the ability to punish, he cannot use punishment as a source of power. If the receiver does not know what he can do to avoid punishment, it is not an effective power resource. In the group environment, the influencer's manner of participation in the group can affect his power. Kipnis (1958) found that when a leader offers rewards and participates in the group, he produces more attitude change than when he does not participate or when he uses punishment as a basis of power. Collins and Guetzkow (1964) argue that punishing power is not as efficacious as rewarding power, but in terms of inducing compliance in an actual situation, positive or negative sanctions seem about equally effective.

If the source is to be effective in producing attitude change, the source must be directly concerned about changing the receiver. It has been shown that when a group's task is depicted to members as involving a higher need for unanimity, the group's members exert more influence over one another than when the task is described as allowing more deviation (Gerard 1964).

The source's influence over the person by virtue of his power is that the source has potential for observing whether or not the person has complied. Receivers show more influence in their public resources (which the source can detect) than in their more private opinions. But, remember, public acceptance tends in time to be introjected as private belief. Maintenance of a private ideology that conflicts with public behavior would be a demanding and dangerous expedient and one that could create great discomfort and frustration for the receiver.

Propositions

1. The role of the source in the persuasive process is called either ethos or source credibility.
   1a. If the source, not the message, activates the desired persuasive response, it is called personal persuasion.

2. Source credibility is a set of perceptions by the receiver formed by past, present, and future expectations of a source.
   2a. Source credibility is a multidimensional construct.
   2b. The three major dimensions of source credibility are expertness (qualification), trustworthiness (safety), and dynamism.
   2c. The dimensional structure of source credibility may vary over concepts, receivers, time, cultures, organizational sources, public figures, and situations.

3. Receivers tend to accept conclusions advocated by sources perceived as competent and/or trustworthy.
   3a. A high credibility source will generally be more successful than a low credibility source in producing attitude change.
   3b. A low credibility source can enhance his success by not identifying his credibility until after the presentation of his message.
   3c. A low prestige source can gain effectiveness by advocating a position opposed to his best interests.
   3d. A source of questionable trustworthiness may be more successful in producing enduring attitude change in the face of counter-persuasion.

4. An organized message can increase source credibility, while a disorganized message can lower source credibility.

5. A high credibility source can produce more attitude change than a low credibility source even with highly ego-involved receivers.

6. The use of visual aids can enhance the credibility of low credibility sources.
   6a. The use of visual aids by low credibility sources increases audience retention of information.
   6b. The use of visual aids does not appear to affect receiver attitude change.

7. Live, audio, and video-taped presentations of the same message by a source do not affect his perceived source credibility.

7a. The use of film is more credible than either taped or written communication.

7b. Oral communication may be more persuasive than written communication.

8. The vocalic or delivery cues of the source affect source credibility.

8a. Ratings of source expertness and dynamism are lowered by increases in speaker nonfluencies.

8b. Attitude change does not appear to be related to nonfluencies.

8c. Perception of source competence is most sensitive to changes in the sound of voice and least affected by speaking rate.

8d. Decreases in pitch variety lead to lower credibility.

8e. When a speaker uses a conversational style, he is described as more trustworthy, less dynamic, and more favorably evaluated than when he uses dynamic delivery.

8f. Expertness is not affected by delivery style.

8g. A speaker is least effective when introduced as low credibility and uses dynamic delivery and most effective when he is introduced as high credibility and uses dynamic delivery.

9. Source credibility may affect receiver comprehension of speech content.

9a. The use of self-reference, a form of artistic proof, may increase credibility and attitude change.

10. When a receiver identifies with a source, it may enhance the source's chances of producing attitude change.

11. The receiver's attraction for a source increases as attitudinal similarity between the two increases.

11a. Membership-group similarities are less significant determinants of source attractiveness.

11b. Source-receiver commonalities, that is attitudinal similarities and membership-group similarities, may not have great persuasive value.

12. The status of the speaker can affect his persuasiveness.

12a. The greater his status, the more power the source possesses.

12b. The greater the status-power, the more successful will be the persuasive attempt.

12c. Status can be identified from speech cues.

12d. Receivers perceive high status speakers to be the most credible and low status speakers as the least credible.

12e. Social dialect of the speaker generally influences the receiver's judgments of a speaker's character but not his competence.

13. The source's power will affect his success in a persuasive situation.
    13a. The source's power includes individual resources, motivation, and intent for exerting power.
    13b. Power can be a function of the rewards and punishments the source controls.

Additional Readings

Anderson, K. and T. Clevenger. "A Summary of Experimental Research in Ethos." *Speech Monographs* 30(1963):59-78. A classic article summarizing experimental evidence pertaining to (1) the influence of ethos upon the effect of the communication; (2) techniques for generating or changing ethos, and (3) measurements of one or more aspects of ethos and attempts to assess the relative levels of individuals or groups.

Jacobson, W. D. *Power and Interpersonal Relations.* Belmont, Calif.: Wadsworth Publishing Co., 1972. Chapter 2, "Power in Operation," pp. 19-38. A comprehensive treatment of the relationship between power and source. The emphasis is on the power-source relationships in group environments.

Simons, H. W., N. N. Berkowitz, and R. J. Mayer. "Similarity, Credibility, and Attitude Change: A Review and a Theory." *Psychological Bulletin* 73 (1970): 1-16. An excellent article summarizing the research dealing with the receiver-source-similarity-dissimilarity relationship and proposing a theoretical framework for future investigations.

5

The Effects of
the Message on
Persuasive Communication

In the preceding chapter, we found that a great percentage of our daily activity is spent communicating — reading, writing, speaking, and listening. A source transmits by speaking or writing his persuasive ideas to a receiver. In turn, the receiver listens to or reads these persuasive appeals. The source's ideas are communicated to the receiver through a *message*. A persuasive message may be transmitted in many forms: a speech, conversation, telephone call, textbook, letter, photograph, billboard, and so on.

Messages are composed of symbols, verbal and nonverbal, which can elicit particular meanings and responses from receivers. In persuasion, the source develops a message with a specific response in mind. For successful persuasion, the meaning given the symbols composing the message must be similar for source and receiver; persuasive communication is dependent upon the use of symbolic messages having shared meaning for sources and receivers. Imagine a persuasive situation in which a husband is talking to his wife at home. He slouches into a chair, hands trembling, voice quivering, and shouts the following: "Sue, I'm worried. The Governor has said we'll get a raise, but you know how two-faced he can be. Inflation is so bad we may be forced to cut down on our activities. Will you help me write a letter to our state senator urging him to support our proposed raise?"

A number of messages may have been communicated by the husband to his wife in this persuasive situation. The quivering voice, trembling hands, and slouching into the chair acting as nonverbal symbols may have indicated to the wife that her husband was tense, nervous, and disturbed. The oral-verbal message may have provided additional information indicating his specific distress and the behavioral response he desired. For his persuasive appeal to be successful, it must be assumed that the wife correctly interpreted the nonverbal symbols and, thereby, established the correct context for the subsequent verbal communication. Second, it must be assumed that she understood the oral message. For example, the husband states that inflation may "cut down on our activities" or "you know how two-faced he can be." The wife must share the meanings for these two ideas for the message to make sense and provide justification for the intended response. Unless the meanings of the messages are shared by source and receiver, attempts at persuasion are fruitless.

Let's imagine, once more, sitting around a dinner table with friends talking about a politician we've just heard on television. The politician's speech is his persuasive message. In attempting to explain our reaction to the speech we might suggest, "he shouldn't have put his best arguments last," or "he sounded disorganized." These evaluative judgments reflect a concern over the form or organization of the message. Messages do not exist as single words, but are created from the placement or ordering of groups of words (paragraphs, chapters, arguments, summaries, and so on) to provide the specific meaning of the persuasive communication for the receiver. We might also suggest, "his message attempted to frighten us," or "he only stated his side." These reactions reflect a recognition of the importance of the contents of the message in a persuasive communication. The source must decide what materials will appeal to the receiver and, thus, encourage the receiver to accept the source's position. At other times our reactions to the politician's speech may run from, "I don't like the way he sounds" to, "he's rather pompous, don't you think?" These reactions reflect a concern for the manner in which the message is presented to the receiver. The source decides how best to present his organized content to the receiver. The presentation of a message is sometimes called *delivery*. However, in today's society, the term delivery has a more restricted meaning—the presentation of a formal speech or lecture.

This chapter is divided into three sections: (1) form of the message; (2) content of the message; and (3) presentation of the message. We will consider only message variables relating to persuasion. Although we will examine each message variable in isolation, it must be emphasized that message variables do not exist in isolation; they are only one part of the total message. In turn, the message, while discussed separately from source, channel, receiver, and situation, never occurs without the presence and effect of these other persuasive elements. It is beyond the scope of this text to investigate all message variables and their interrelationships within the persuasive situation. We will examine only those message variables that have been extensively researched and appear to affect attitude or behavior change.

Form of the Message

Why organize a message? Why not just give an individual the right information? He'll change the way he feels, believes, or behaves. The assumption that providing information without consideration of its form will change attitudes is widely held but not always correct. Despite all the money and time spent by advertisers devising persuasive appeals based on this assumption, most of their work is wasted. Adding new information without consideration of its form is an effective agent of change in very specialized situations, that is, when information refers to some person, object, or thing for which we have no existing attitudes. This is indeed a rare situation. New information that contradicts an existing attitude is usually distorted to fit our existing cognitive structures. Jack Haskins (1966) in a review of advertising and psychological literature found "no relationship between what a person learned, knew, or recalled on one hand, and what he did or how he felt on the other . . . Telling him *(the receiver)* the facts" does not necessarily influence his attitudes or behavior.

One variable that does affect the persuasive appeal of information (new or old) is the message's organization. Since communication is a process, and each communication effort is a unique attempt at expressing a message, the organization of a message is a situational phenomenon. A speaker organizes his message according to the situation. In our examination of message organization, we limit discussion to the form of a message as it applies to introductions, conclusions, ordered versus disordered messages, and the question of primacy-recency.

Introductions–Conclusions

It is difficult to conclude whether an introduction is needed or what type of introduction is preferred in a persuasive situation. It would be foolish to assume that introductions are of no value when so many speakers use them and so many teachers of speech communication recommend their use. However, reaching any conclusions about the effectiveness of introductions is difficult. Since what comes before something else in a message has an effect on what follows (see primacy-recency in this chapter) and since the introduction of speakers has an effect on the audience's attitude toward the speaker and his subject matter (see chapter 4), it is obvious that introductory material in a message will have an effect on the other parts of the message, the perception of the source and message by the receiver, the retention of the message by the receiver, and the persuasive impact of the message on the receiver.

Introductions appear to have a persuasive effect upon the receiver. Allyn and Festinger (1961) found that when receivers holding a position strongly were told in advance about the content of a communication arguing against their position, they had less change in attitude than when they were not told about the communication content. The introduction also interacts with the source to affect the receiver's attitudes. Receivers change less when a disliked source in his introduction announces his persuasive intention than when he does not mention his intent (Mills and Aronson 1965). In the same regard, receivers change more when a well-liked source admits his persuasive intent. Despite these findings, we still do not have conclusive evidence of either the effect or need for introductions. The inclusion of an introduction is a situational phenomenon that seems related to the issue, the source credibility, and receiver involvement in the topic.

The use of conclusions in messages is no less a situational phenomenon than introductions. It has been suggested that the effectiveness of conclusions is influenced by the kind of communication, audience, issue, and degree of explicitness with which the conclusions are drawn (Hovland, Janis, and Kelley 1953; Cohen 1964; Karlins and Abelson 1970).

We might ask, is it better for the source to state his conclusions explicitly or let the receiver draw his own conclusions? Hovland and Mandel (1952) presented receivers with two messages that were exactly the same except that one drew the conclusions at the end (explicit) and the other did not (implicit). They found that more receivers changed their opinions in the direction advocated by the source when the conclusions were explicitly stated. Cooper and Dinerman (1951), working with a film presentation, discovered that implicit messages influenced the more intelligent members of the audience but not the less intelligent. It has also been found that stating conclusions in a message is more effective in changing the opinions of the less intelligent (Thistlethwaite, deHaan, and Kamenetsky 1955). The more intelligent may resent having conclusions drawn for them, particularly when they are obvious conclusions. However, where an issue is highly complex, stating the conclusion explicitly may be more effective (Krech, Crutchfield and Ballachey 1962). What if the receivers do not favor the source's position? In this situation, Weiss and Steenbock (1965) found that a persuasive message presenting conclusions is more effective in changing attitudes.

The findings would seem to indicate that when using highly complex messages, addressing less intelligent receivers, or when receivers are initially unfavorable, it may be wise to state the conclusions explicitly. When dealing with an intelligent audience, particularly with simple problems, it would be best to have implicit conclusions. In some situations, the audience may view a statement of conclusions as "propaganda" and become more hostile or suspicious, thus resisting any persuasive attempts.

We have all been confronted with the communicator who asks us directly to take some form of action or adopt a certain belief. We might ask, Where should a direct appeal be placed in persuasive messages? Appeals for receiver change appear more effective if they are placed in the conclusion rather than anywhere else in the message (Leventhal and Singer 1966). While conclusions that ask for a large amount of change produce more change than conclusions asking for less change, the change attained is less than the speaker asks for (Hovland and Pritzker 1957).

Ordered Versus Disordered Messages

Should a speech be presented in some orderly manner or not? Smith (1951) found that minor disorganization has no significant effect on attitude change, but major reorganization (rearranging major units of the speech such as the introduction, transitions, and conclusions) leads to significantly less attitude change than when the material is presented in correct order. Thompson (1960) and Darnell (1963), on the other hand, found differences in retention due to rearrangement (rearranging sentences within various parts of a speech), but no differences in attitude change.

Baker (1965) manipulated "disorganization cues," having the speaker apologize in the speech for his lack of organization, and found no significant differences in attitude change between groups hearing the organized or disorganized messages. However, most research indicates that the presence of disorganization brings about a reduction in attitude change (McCrosky and Mehrley 1969; Jones and Serlousky 1971).

The disorganization of a speech appears to affect attitude change, an audience's retention of a message, and the source's evaluation, but it is not clear if disorganization affects the listener's understanding of the message. Beighley (1952), who randomly rearranged paragraphs in the presentation of two speeches, found no significant differences in comprehension due to the rearrangements. In contrast, Johnson (1970) found that the disorganized speech led to significantly less comprehension than did the organized version.

It should be obvious that not all the answers regarding the effect of order in a message have been found. The conflicting results may be due to factors not yet thoroughly investigated. For the present, it seems that logical order in a speech as perceived by the receiver is more persuasive and may lead to better comprehension, while helping the source appear more credible.

Order of Arguments

Let's imagine we have a persuasive message to which we want a group of receivers to respond. In this message are a number of very important arguments we want the audience to remember. Hopefully, these arguments will provide the impetus for the desired change. Where do we place the arguments? Tannenbaum (1954) exposed groups of receivers to a tape-recorded news program containing twelve news items. He rotated the news items so that each group heard a different order of items. Receivers were then tested to see how many news items they could recall. Recall was better for items at the beginning and end of the newscast, but not items in the middle. In addition, Shaw (1961) found that what is said first or last (versus in between) can influence actual behavior even if some of the communication is forgotten. We might ask ourselves, Which position is more effective in enhancing the impact of vital information? Unfortunately, research results are conflicting and no final conclusion can be made regarding whether the opening or closing parts of a communication should include the more important material (Cromwell 1950; Sponberg 1946). It has been suggested that when an audience is not interested in the communication, the major arguments should be placed first. Where interest is high, it seems advisable to place the arguments last. The placement of important information first for a relatively disinterested audience may arouse or maintain interest. If the important arguments are placed last, the audience may lose all motivation and not pay attention to the persuasive appeal (Karlins and Abelson 1970).

Let's imagine that we intend to deliver a persuasive appeal utilizing both sides of the issue. We might ask, Where do I present the side I favor—first or last? This question has received a great deal of attention in persuasion research and is called the *primacy-recency* problem. The specific question investigated asks, Will the message presented first (primacy) or last (recency) have the greatest effect on attitude and behavior change?

Early research by Lund (1925) indicated that arguments presented first were significantly more effective in producing attitude change than arguments presented second. In 1952, Hovland and Mandel replicated the Lund study. However, their results were entirely opposite. Recency, not primacy, seemed to be more effective in the persuasive process. Hovland, Janis and Kelley (1953) concluded that it was unlikely that either presenting strong arguments first followed by weaker arguments or putting weaker arguments first and important arguments last would invariably turn out to be superior. They felt that other factors might well produce varying outcomes and suggested that some of the important factors were receiver attention, learning, and acceptance of the arguments. Putting major arguments first would be more effective when the receiver is not too interested in the persuasive appeal, but when attention and desire to learn are present, then ending with the strongest arguments would be more effective. Cohen (1964) added that "the advantages of one order over the other depend on the particular conditions under which the communication is presented, including the predispositions of the audience and the type of material being presented."

Let's examine several generalizations drawn from a review of primacy-recency literature (Cohen 1964). When two sides of an issue are to be presented by different communicators, being the first speaker may not be advantageous. The message's effect may be tempered by various conditions (time, place, audience, and so on). However, when one speaker presents two sides of an issue in one presentation, we are usually more influenced by the side he presents first.

The receiver will play an important role in determining the proper placement of arguments. When we make a public response about our position after hearing one side of an argument, the second side we hear is less effective in changing our attitudes. This may be based on our need for social acceptance. Once we publicly take a position it may be difficult for us to change for fear we will be viewed as inconsistent and/or dishonest. If our needs are aroused before a communication and the communication satisfies these needs, the communication is more readily acceptable than if we perceive the need after the communication. If some specific need is aroused within us we are eager to listen and apply any information presented that will satisfy that need. If, on the other hand, the need arousal follows the information, it may be difficult for us to reconstruct the information in our minds and then apply it to the need. If, early in a speech, a communicator presents ideas with which we can readily agree, we may find ourselves accepting those ideas and becoming more responsive to him as a communicator. This responsiveness may make us less critical of later ideas and views with which we cannot readily agree. Whereas, if ideas with which we disagree are presented first, we may become more critical of the communicator, hence becoming even more critical of acceptable ideas presented later in the speech. If we are listening to a communicator whom we respect, we are influenced more when he presents the arguments for his position first, followed by the arguments against his position. We are less likely to be influenced if he presents the arguments against his position first and follows with arguments for his position.

Our ability to handle and retain information plays a role in determining the effectiveness of argument placement. When we receive a series of communications about a variety of subjects the primacy factor seems to operate at first but diminishes as the series of communications progresses. There seems to be a limitation as to how much information our minds are capable of handling at any given time. When we are receiving a great deal of unrelated information at once, we have a tendency to remember what we hear first, but as the mass of information continues to build up, subsequent information tends to inhibit the effectiveness of material received earlier. When one side of an issue is presented and there is a time lag before the other side is presented, there is a maximum forgetting of the first side and minimum forgetting for the second, so that the last side presented has an advantage. When two sides are presented at the same time, both sides have equal forgetting potential. Under this condition, the first issue presented has an advantage.

In summary, Cohen states that "taken as a whole, the findings regarding primacy and recency seem to rule out any universal principle of primacy in persuasion." Rosnow and Robinson (1967) make the following statement regarding the possibility of either a law of primacy or recency:

> Instead of a general "law" of primacy or recency, we have today an assortment of miscellaneous variables, some which tend to produce primacy ("primacy-bound variables"), others of which, to produce recency ("recency-bound variables"). Still others produce either order effect, depending on their utilization or temporal placement in a two-sided communication ("free variables"). Non-salient, controversial topics, interesting subject matter, and highly familiar issues tend toward primacy. Salient topics, uninteresting subject matter, and moderately unfamiliar issues tend to yield recency. If arguments for one side are perceived more strongly than arguments for the other, then the side with the stronger arguments has the advantage—"strength" being the free variable. Another free variable is "reinforcement." When incidents that are perceived as rewarding or satisfying are initiated close in time to a persuasive communication, opinions tend to change in the direction of the arguments closer to the rewarding incident. When an incident is dissatisfying, or punishing, opinions tend to change in the direction of the arguments farther in time from it.

In this section, we discussed the organization of a message including information on introductions, conclusions, ordered versus disordered messages, placement order of arguments, and primacy-recency. In the next section, we will examine the content of the communication, the specific information that the source transmits to the receiver. We will attempt to discover what types of information or persuasive appeals have the greatest influence upon attitude and behavior change.

Content of the Message

When we attempt to persuade another person or group, we are not only concerned with *how* we order the available information, but also *what* information we select or disregard as we formulate our persuasive message. In this section, we will be concerned with the content or substance of the messages, we will examine the use of evidence, one-sided versus two-sided messages, fear appeals, emotional versus factual appeals, and humor.

Evidence

Many textbooks currently available on persuasion and persuasive speaking recommend that a speaker utilize documented supporting materials in order to produce attitude or behavior change. However, research in this area has produced conflicting results regarding the value of including evidence in a persuasive message (McCroskey 1969; Gilkinson, Paulson, and Sikkink 1954; Anderson 1958; Dresser 1962, 1963).

While there is much research that still needs to be done in regard to the effect of evidence in a persuasive message, a few generalizations can be drawn. The effect of evidence in a message seems closely related to the perceived credibility of the source. A less credible source seems to gain credibility by the inclusion of evidence, while a more credible source does not seem to profit much from it. If, however, a highly credible source is speaking after a message that included evidence has already been given on his subject, then he loses credibility if he does not include evidence in the message. The effects of the inclusion of evidence seem related to the topic, with some topics being enhanced by the inclusion of evidence and others not. If we are listening to a speaker who is trying to convince us that we should brush our teeth, the topic may need little or no evidence for support. If the speaker is trying to convince us that integration will lead to the removal of racial prejudice, evidence to support this topic seems essential. The effect of the inclusion of evidence seems to be influenced by the delivery of the source, with poor delivery lowering the impact of the inclusion of the evidence. The effect of the evidence seems to be influenced by the intelligence of the audience members, with the more intelligent receivers being influenced more by the evidence. An audience's familiarity with the evidence presented seems to have an impact on the effect that the evidence has. For example, if we had just completed reading articles supporting the contention that integration reduces racial prejudice, we would be more receptive to a speaker citing such evidence than if we had not been exposed to this material before. Finally, the effect of evidence will be influenced by whether the receivers perceive the evidence as "good" evidence or not. For example, if we are listening to a speaker quoting evidence on a specific topic, that evidence should seem to us to be relevant to the topic and from an acceptable source, such as the AMA on a medical issue. If we do not perceive the evidence to be relevant and acceptable we would be inclined to discount the speaker's message (see McCroskey 1969).

We might ask two additional questions: (1) Does the intelligence of the audience relate to the effect of evidence in a message? and (2)

Does evidence play a role in counter-persuasion? Kline (1969) found that the effect of evidence varied with the receiver's intelligence. That is to say, the inclusion of factual evidence and the specificity of that evidence will make more difference for receivers of high intelligence than for those of low intelligence. In regard to counter-persuasion, McCroskey (1970) found that evidence does appear to serve as an inhibitor to future counter-persuasion.

It seems obvious that the research on the effect of evidence in a message underscores the interaction occurring in the persuasive process. We have seen that evidence interrelates with the source, the receiver, the perceptual processes of both, the presentation of the message, and the other elements of the persuasive process.

One-Sided Versus Two-Sided Messages

In an earlier section of this chapter, the effects of placing strongest arguments at the beginning of a message (primacy) or at the end of a message (recency) were examined. We will now question whether one side of an issue or two sides of an issue should be included in the message. We realize that most issues have at least two sides. Therefore, we must make a decision whether to discuss both sides.

Hovland, Lumsdaine and Sheffield (1949) investigated whether it is more effective to present evidence supporting the main goal of the persuasive appeal or to include opposing arguments too. Their results indicated that, for receivers initially opposed to the position presented by the message, giving both sides of the issue was more effective. For receivers initially favoring the stand taken by the message, the one-sided presentation was more effective. A further study by Lumsdaine and Janis (1953) exposed subjects to counter-arguments after having them initially exposed to one-sided and two-sided messages. Their results indicated that those who had been exposed to the two-sided presentation were more resistant to counter-propaganda than those exposed to the one-sided communication. In a more recent study, McGinnes (1966) provides cross-cultural support for the earlier Hovland, Lumsdaine and Sheffield study. Using Japanese university students, he found that two-sided communication was superior to one-sided appeals when individuals were initially opposed to the position advocated. For those students who initially agreed with the speaker's position, the one-sided communication tended to be more effective.

The educational level of the receiver appears to play a role in whether a speaker should use a one-sided or two-sided message. The two-sided presentation is more effective for better-educated men, while the one-sided presentation is more effective with less educated. When the amount of education and initial position are examined together, the one-sided communication is more effective with the less-educated subjects who initially favored the position advocated in the message, while the two-sided communication was most effective with the better-educated subjects regardless of their initial position (Hovland, Lumsdaine and Sheffield 1949). However, an investigation by Bettinghaus and Basehart (1969) found no support for the generalization that two-sided messages are more effective than one-sided messages for changing attitudes of more highly educated individuals.

Thistlethwaite and Kamenetsky (1955) found that using two-sided messages leads to less change in attitudes when receivers are not previously aware of the opposing arguments, but failure to include both sides will weaken the effect if receivers are previously aware of the opposing arguments.

From research done on inoculation effects and on the issue of one-sided versus two-sided messages, the following generalizations seem appropriate (Karlins and Abelson 1970). One-sided messages seem to be more effective when the audience is aware of the source's persuasive attempts, when the audience is generally friendly to the source, when one position is all that will be presented, when the audience is not aware of counter-arguments, and is not expected to hear counter-arguments, or when only immediate, temporary opinion change is desired. Two-sided messages seem to be more effective when the audience initially disagrees with the communicator, when the audience is aware of counter-arguments before the presentation or will be exposed to them, when the audience members are more intelligent, and where the communicator wants to be fair and objective in his message.

Fear Appeals

In a Los Angeles mayoral race several years ago, one of the candidates, the incumbent, attempted to scare voters into voting against his opponent. He charged that his opponent was a political radical and that his election would ruin the city. In this particular election, the incumbent's use of fear appeals was not successful and he was soundly defeated at the polls. The use of fear appeals in speaking situations is not a new phenomenon. Aristotle, the father of rhetorical theory, discusses the use in Greek persuasive speaking in his classic work, *The Rhetoric*. It would appear that the use of fear appeals can be both successful and unsuccessful

in the persuasive situation. Therefore, to fully understand the value
and use of persuasive appeals to fear, there are several questions we
must answer: Are appeals to fear generally successful in the persuasive
situation? Are there different types of fear appeals? When are fear
appeals successful or unsuccessful? Within the last three decades a great
deal of research has been centered around answering these questions.

Janis and Feshbach (1953) examined three types of fear appeals
and their effect in producing change among groups of high school students regarding dental hygiene. Group one received a strongly threatening lecture which included the possibility of cancer among the many
consequences of poor oral hygiene. The second group received a mildly
threatening lecture that condemned people who neglected their mouths
to nothing worse than a few cavities. The third group received a lecture
with an intermediate degree of fear. They found that the more threatening the lecture, the more worry students expressed immediately after
the lecture. After a period of one week, however, they found that the
group subjected to the least amount of fear was found to have conformed
most to the message. They concluded that under conditions where people
will be exposed to competing communications dealing with the same
issue, the use of a strong threat appeal will tend to be less effective than
a minimal threat appeal in producing attitude change. We might suggest
that high fear appeals produce more threat and receivers are more likely
to employ defense mechanisms. Thus, they become more resistant to
high fear appeals in a message.

However, mild fear appeals are not always the superior form of
fear appeal in producing attitude or behavior change. Leventhal and
Niles (1964), for instance, found that a low fear appeal message was
more effective than moderate or high fear appeals in enforcing an individual's intentions to stop smoking. Leventhal and Watts (1966) exposed
audiences at a state fair to high, medium, and low fear appeals on the
topic of antismoking. In their persuasive message, they recommended that
the audience stop smoking and take an X-ray at a nearby mobile unit
to detect the presence of cancer. They found that audiences exposed
to the high fear appeals stopped smoking more significantly than those
exposed to the other fear appeal conditions. However, the audiences
exposed to the low fear appeals were more likely to have the chest
X-ray. They suggested that extreme fear produced an avoidance reaction within the audience members that forced them to avoid the
possibility of further fear coming from X-ray. Thus, the high fear appeal
group selected an alternate method for reducing the threat—they stopped
smoking.

Dabbs and Leventhal (1966) examined the effect of high and low fear communication upon the attitudes and behavior of college students exposed to written materials. The researchers recommended in the messages that the students should receive a tetanus inoculation. Students exposed to high fear appeals were more likely to want and obtain shots than individuals who received the low fear appeal messages. "The manipulation of fear . . . influenced both intentions to take shots and actual shot-taking behavior . . . A positive relationship between fear arousal and persuasion was observed." Kraus, El-Assal and De Fleur (1966) also found that high fear appeals were very successful in modifying behavior using the mass media as the agent for transmitting the message.

It would appear that the personality of the receiver interacts with the level of fear in the message. Some individuals may not be able to avoid high fear appeals because they are unable to develop adequate defense mechanisms. Niles (1964) found that students who rated themselves "highly vulnerable" to a communication on antismoking showed more attitude change toward stopping smoking when exposed to moderate fear appeals than to high or low fear appeals. On the other hand, "low vulnerable" subjects showed more attitude change when exposed to an increase in fear arousing appeals in the message. Dabbs and Leventhal (1966), in the study reported earlier, found that individuals of "high self-esteem" complied with the recommendations of the researchers. Individuals who were classified as "low self-esteem" complied equally well to both high and low fear appeals.

The effectiveness of fear appeals appears to be related to a number of other factors as well. Berkowitz and Cottingham (1960) found a strong fear appeal more effective than a weak appeal when the communication was of low interest value or low relevance to the audience. The dramatic nature of the high fear appeal may make the message more interesting. Insko, Arkoff and Insko (1965), examining the effects of fear appeal on attitudes toward smoking, concluded that audiences exposed to high fear appeals were quicker to make inferences from the message that diseases caused by smoking could and would affect them and, therefore, the high fear appeal was more effective in producing immediate attitude change. Miller and Hewgill (1964) found that a high credibility source using a high fear message was more effective than when he used a low fear message. His credibility may make the appeal more believable or lend more credence to the information provided, thus making it more difficult for the receiver to discredit the influence attempt. Powell (1965) discovered that a strong fear appeal posing a threat to the receiver's family produced a greater change in attitude than a mild appeal. Our defense mechanisms may not be able to cope as easily with a threat on a loved one as a threat to ourselves. Simonson and Lundy (1966) found that irrelevant fear facilitated the acceptance of a persuasive message. They suggested that this might have occurred because irrelevant fear served as a distractor.

Many factors influence the effectiveness of fear appeals in the persuasive situation. Some studies indicate that mild appeals are more effective, while other studies indicate the reverse. Fear appeals seem to be effective in changing behavior when: (1) immediate action can be taken on recommendations included in the appeal and (2) specific instructions are provided for carrying out the message's recommendations (Leventhal, Jones and Trembly 1966; Leventhal, Singer and Jones 1965). Cronkhite (1969) recommends that the communicator present a specific plan of action and demonstrate that it is effective and feasible whenever a strong fear is used. The source may use the strong fear appeal followed by a specific plan of action with confidence when his receivers have a history of being able to cope with their problems and when the suggested action is aggressive in nature, does not create a further threat, and does not appear too difficult. The fear appeal should be realistic enough that the receiver cannot easily say it does not concern him and should not present an excess of fear that might appear ridiculous rather than frightening.

Emotional Versus Factual Appeals

We often hear individuals say that it is better to appeal to the heart than the head. Many people feel that a speaker is more successful in producing attitude change if he appeals to the emotions of his audience. Whether emotional or factual appeals are more successful in producing attitude and behavior change is difficult to answer. Hartman (1936) examined the effectiveness of appeals in soliciting votes for Socialist candidates in the 1936 elections. He found that written pamphlets using emotional appeals were more successful than factual appeals in getting individuals to vote for the Socialist candidates. The Opinion Research Corporation (1952) prepared booklets attempting to marshal opinion against excess profits taxes. The booklet with emotional arguments was more successful than the booklet using factual arguments.

Weiss (1960) found the opposite effect. He prepared three written messages with the same conclusion—criminals should be severely punished for their crimes—and three different forms of supporting evidence:

one message utilized emotional appeals, a second message used factual appeals, and the third message combined emotional and factual arguments. He found that factual arguments were more effective than emotional arguments in changing opinions. In addition, no differences of opinion existed between students reading factual or emotional-factual messages. However, the persuasive advantage of factual arguments was only temporary. Two weeks after the initial testing, students expressed similar opinions about the treatment of criminals—regardless of the appeal read. Several other studies have also found partial support for the superiority of factual appeals (Bowers 1963; Carmichael and Cronkhite 1965; Weiss and Lieberman 1959). Carmichael and Cronkhite (1965) suggest that the effectiveness of the appeal is sometimes dependent on the mood of the audience. It would appear that no type of appeal is always superior. Much depends on the issue to be discussed and the composition of the audience.

Humor

Many politicians and advertisers use humor to persuade their audience. The humor used by Truman and the Kennedy brothers has been suggested as a factor contributing to their political success. Approximately forty-two percent of television commercials use some humor (Markiewicz 1972). Cannan (1914) stated: "No tyrant, no tyrannous idea ever came crashing to earth but it was first wounded with shafts of satire: no free man, no free idea ever rose to the heights but it endured them." However, Feinberg (1967) states: "The notion that satire has played an important part in reforming society is probably a delusion satirists themselves know better." We might ask ourselves, Does a humorous persuasive message increase the amount of persuasion?

Gruner (1965, 1966) found that humor (at least satire) was not a potent persuasive device in messages. However, the initial opinion of receivers might determine when a humorous message is more persuasive. It is suggested that humor functions as a distractor; receivers initially opposed to a message position would be more persuaded by a humorous rather than a serious message. Those initially neutral or in favor of the position would be equally persuaded by either a humorous or serious message (Haaland and Verbeatesan 1968; Osterhouse and Brock 1970; Zimbardo, et al. 1970). However, it is possible that receivers generally laugh more at those whom they do not sympathize or identify with. When the humor in a message supports the message position, those who are initially opposed to the position might not be amused, and might react against the persuasive attempt. Those initially opposed to a position should be less persuaded by a humorous than a serious message. Satire may operate as a reinforcer of attitudes. "When people already hold opinions which satire expresses, these opinions are reinforced." However, "The satirist who expresses unpopular views has no social effect, no matter how entertaining he may be" (Feinberg 1967). People enjoy humor directed against "enemy" reference groups and least enjoy humor ridiculing their own reference groups (Priest and Abraham 1970). Gruner (1972) found support for the contention that satire can and does operate as a reinforcer of previous attitudes in oral communication situations.

Markiewicz (1972) found that a humorous source was rated more trustworthy than a serious one. If humor enhances the image of a source, the effect of humor would more likely be evident with low credibility or disliked sources. A low credibility source might utilize humor to raise his image before his audience and, therefore, improve his chances of persuading the audience to his particular position.

We have centered our discussion of message content on the use of evidence, one-sided versus two-sided messages, fear appeals, factual versus emotional appeals, and humor. This in no way exhausts the list of message content variables than can and do operate in the persuasive situation. However, these other variables—for example, the use of metaphor—have not been researched thoroughly enough as yet to draw meaningful generalizations to the persuasive situation. We will now proceed from dealing with *what* is said in a message to *how* something is said in a persuasive message. We will examine how the presentation of a message affects the persuasive situation.

Presentation of a Message

In this section of the chapter we will examine how the manner in which a message is presented to an audience or group of individuals will influence the persuasive process. We will examine how active versus passive listener participation, audience distractors, and general delivery affect attitude and behavior change.

Active Versus Passive Participation

Let's imagine a situation in which you desire to persuade an audience that air pollution can be controlled by the development of rapid transit systems. You have a choice—you can talk to the audience about your position or you can ask your listeners to write an essay on the subject. Would you be more successful in giving the talk or allowing the audience to participate actively in the persuasive process? Watts (1967) examined this problem. It was found that, initially, both active and passive participation can lead to opinion change. However, over time, the active participants showed greater persistence of the initially produced opinion change. Furthermore, active participation lead to greater involvement and superior recall of the topic and side supported.

Karlins and Abelson (1970) present a sample of diverse research situations in which active participation is superior to passive participation in producing attitude and behavior change:

> (2) Active participation, in the form of group discussion, is often more effective than passive participation (hearing lectures or reading appeals) in changing attitudes (Hereford, 1963; Lewin, 1953). . . . (4) Active participation in T-groups or sensitivity training leads to marked behavior modification (Rubin, 1967). (5) A person who actively (rather than passively) learns about a situation often changes his attitudes about that situation. Thus, visitors who took guided tours through a state school for mental defectives changed their opinions about the patients and the institution (Kimbrell & Luckey, 1964); and children who studied Spanish had more positive attitudes toward Spanish-speaking peoples than children lacking such education (Riestra & Johnson, 1964).

We might conclude from these findings that the effect of a persuasive appeal is enhanced by requiring active, rather than passive, participation by the receiver.

Distractors

Let's imagine ourselves at a school cafeteria. A friend invites us to have dinner with him and during the meal asks us to support a petition he is circulating around campus. Our friend has used a method of distraction (eating our dinner) in order to enhance his persuasive attempt.

Leon Festinger and Nathan Maccoby (1964) had two groups of fraternity men listen to an antifraternity message while watching a movie. One group viewed the film of a speaker giving the antifraternity lecture; the second group watched an irrelevant silent comedy while listening to the sound track of the first film. They found that the distracted group (those watching the comedy film) were more persuaded by the message—expressing more antifraternity attitudes. Haaland and Venbeatesan (1968), however, found less attitude change when receivers were subjected to visual and behavioral distraction while listening to a persuasive communication. The type of distraction experienced by the receiver may be an important factor in the persuasive process. "Generally, persuasive appeals become more powerful when presented in conjunction with moderately distracting stimuli which positively reinforce the individual" (Karlins and Abelson 1970). Food and sex appear to operate as positive reinforcements for receivers. Using these stimuli as detractors may enhance the effectiveness of persuasive appeals (Janis, Kaye and Kirschner 1965; Zimbardo, Ebbesen and Fraser 1968). Negative reinforcements (foul odors) are generally ineffective in enhancing the persuasive process.

General Delivery

The manner in which a speaker delivers his message to an audience has a tremendous influence over the effectiveness of that persuasive effort. Heinberg (1963) found delivery to be almost twice as important as content in determining general effectiveness of introductions and also three times as influential as content in determining effectiveness in attempts to have an idea accepted. Delivery includes the way a message is spoken and presented to an audience. It also includes the nonverbal aspects such as the way the source looks when he presents a message, facial expressions, gestures, and the like.

It appears that delivery can influence the degree of attitude change that takes place in the listener. Heyworth (1942) found that fluency and effectiveness were highly correlated. Bettinghaus (1961) found that effective delivery contributed to persuasiveness in the presentation of a message. While McCroskey and Arnold (1969) did not find an effect on immediate attitude change attributable to delivery quality for live, video-taped, or audio-taped speakers, they did find a delivery effect on delayed attitude change. In addition they found that when good delivery was coupled with good message quality, it produced immediate positive attitude change; but when good delivery was coupled with poor message quality, it did not. While it has been found that nonfluency has no effect on immediate attitude change, McCroskey and Mehrley (1969) found that "extensive nonfluencies seriously restrict the amount of attitude change any source can produce."

Effective delivery also appears to enhance a speaker's credibility (Bettinghaus 1961). McCroskey and Arnold (1969) found that the quality of delivery had a significant effect on perceived source credibility. Assuming that source credibility plays an important role in producing the impetus for attitude change, it would behoove the source to evaluate the effectiveness of his delivery style.

Propositions

1. Information by itself does not always produce persuasive change.

2. New information may be an agent of change when the receiver has no existing attitudes concerning the attitude object.

3. Message organization will influence attitude change.

4. The organization of a message is a situational phenomenon.

5. Introductions have a persuasive effect on receivers.
   5a. Introductions alerting receivers that the message will argue against their position produce less attitude change.
   5b. Receivers change less when a disliked source announces his persuasive intent.
   5c. Receivers change more when a well-liked source admits his persuasive intent.

6. The conclusion of a message will have a persuasive effect on receivers.
   6a. Conclusions should be stated explicitly when using complex messages, addressing less intelligent receivers, and when receivers are initially favorable toward the message position.
   6b. Conclusions should be stated implicitly when the problem is simple and the receivers are intelligent.
   6c. If the receivers view the conclusions as propaganda, they may resist persuasive appeals.
   6d. Direct appeals for change should be placed in the conclusion of a message.
   6e. Conclusions asking for a great amount of change produce more change than conclusions asking for less change.

7. Message disorganization reduces the amount of attitude change, audience's retention of a message, and the source's evaluation.

8. Receiver recall is better for materials placed at the beginning and end of the message.

9. No universal rule of primacy or recency exists in persuasive situations.
   9a. There is no advantage in being the first communicator when two sides of an issue are presented by two different speakers.
   9b. When a receiver makes a public response about his position after hearing one side of an argument, the second side is less effective in changing attitudes.
   9c. When one speaker presents two sides of an issue in one presentation, we are usually more influenced by the side presented first.
   9d. When a receiver's needs are aroused before a communication satisfies these needs, the communication is more readily acceptable than if the need arousal follows the communication.
   9e. Attitudes change more when desirable ideas precede undesirable ideas.
   9f. The pro-con order is more effective than the con-pro order when an authoritative communicator presents both sides.
   9g. If a time lag exists between the presentation of two sides of an issue, the side presented last has an advantage.
   9h. When no time lag exists between presentation of two sides of an issue, the first side has an advantage.
   9i. When a receiver hears a series of communications about a variety of subjects, primacy operates at first but diminishes as the series of communications progresses.
   9j. Salient topics, uninteresting subjects, and moderately unfamiliar issues tend to yield recency effects.
   9k. Nonsalient, controversial topics, interesting subject matter, and highly familiar issues tend toward primacy effects.
   9l. The placement of reward or punishment in a message will affect primacy-recency effects.

10. The content of a message will affect attitude and behavior change.

11. Evidence may play a role in producing a persuasive change.
    11a. A less credible source gains credibility with inclusion of evidence.
    11b. A highly credible source can lose credibility if he does not include evidence.
    11c. The effect of evidence will be influenced by the message topic.
    11d. The inclusion of evidence is influenced by the delivery of the source.
    11e. Intelligent receivers are influenced more by evidence.

11f. Receivers are influenced by evidence with which they are familiar.

11g. The evidence must be perceived to be relevant and acceptable or the receiver may discount the message.

11h. The medium of transmission used to convey the evidence does not affect the potential influence of that evidence.

12. The presentation of one or more sides of an issue may affect the persuasive process.

12a. Two-sided messages are more effective when receivers initially oppose the message position.

12b. One-sided messages are more effective when receivers initially favor the position taken by the message.

12c. Receivers exposed to two-sided presentations are more resistant to counter-propaganda.

12d. Two-sided presentations are more effective with better educated men, while one-sided presentations are more effective with less educated men.

12e. Failure to include both sides of an issue may weaken the persuasive attempt, if receivers are aware of the opposing arguments.

13. Fear appeals may affect the persuasive process.

13a. The level of fear producing change is influenced by the personality of the receiver and the message topic.

13b. Fear appeals are effective in changing behavior when immediate action can be taken on appeal recommendations and specific instructions are provided for carrying out the recommendations.

14. Neither emotional nor factual appeals are universally effective in persuasive situations.

15. Humor may affect the persuasive process.

15a. Humor as a distractor may produce greater attitude change.

15b. Satire may operate as a reinforcer of attitudes.

16. The presentation of a message affects the persuasive process.

17. Active participation is more effective than passive participation in producing attitude and behavior change.

18. Presentation distractors may enhance the effectiveness of persuasion.

19. The manner of delivery used by a speaker may influence his persuasive attempt.

19a. Extensive nonfluencies may restrict the amount of attitude change any source can produce.
19b. The quality of delivery may affect source credibility.

Additional Readings

Bettinghaus, E. P. *Persuasive Communication.* 2d ed. New York: Holt, Rinehart and Winston, 1973. Chapter 5 provides a very basic explanation of the code system used in persuasive messages.

Karlin, M. and H. I. Abelson. *Persuasion: How Opinions and Attitudes Are Changed.* New York: Springer Pub. Co., Inc., 1970, pp. 5-40. An examination of major issues and studies of persuasive messages.

Miller, G. R. and M. Burgoon. *New Techniques of Persuasion.* New York: Harper & Row, 1973. An examination of recent theory and research not usually found in basic persuasion texts. Topics of particular interest are: (1) uses and limitations of counterattitudinal advocacy and (2) inducing resistance to persuasion.

6

The Effect of
Channels on
Persuasive Communication

In this chapter we will attempt to study some factors pertinent to the channels and media through which persuasive messages are transmitted. In 1967, McLuhan and Fiore published a book entitled *The Medium Is the Massage*. The title reflects McLuhan's position that the medium or channel through which a message is transmitted exerts *more* influence on the receiver than does the actual content of the message. We do not take such an extreme position on the issue of channel and media effects. However, we do believe that they exert some influence (with certain media and channels exerting more influence than others) on behavior, attitudes, and opinions.

We propose to discuss the effects of media and channels under three separate areas of concern. First, we will study the effects of the mass media. In this connection we will try to draw up a *profile* of the audience reached by each medium before going on to detail the effects of the media on the receivers or audience.

Second, we will study the relevance of reference or interest groups to the overall process of persuasion. We contend that the influence of the group may perhaps be the focal point in the total process.

Third, we will discuss the value and comparative effectiveness of face-to-face or dyadic communication. This, too, constitutes another vital channel in the persuasion process.

The order outlined above seems representative of a normal sequence in the diffusion of information. First, messages, opinions, and viewpoints are broadcast by the mass media; those messages are received and interpreted by interest groups or reference groups, following which the information or persuasive induction is either accepted or rejected. Finally, influential members or opinion leaders of the particular interest group transmit the disposition of the group to individuals through face-to-face or dyadic communication. We shall now discuss the first phase — mass media effects.

Mass Media Effects

We consider mass media to be an organized means of reaching large numbers of people quickly, economically, and efficiently. Such media include the *print* media — newspapers, books, and magazines; and the *broadcast* media — radio and television. We shall discuss the print media and their audiences or receivers first.

Print

Lazarsfeld (1940) reported that newspapers were more important than radio in the lives of people who exerted the greatest influence on the affairs of the United States. Although three decades have passed since that survey, during which time we have witnessed the development of television, we contend that newspapers still occupy priority of usage over both radio and television as sources of information and opinions. The *New York Times, Washington Star, Los Angeles Times, The Christian Science Monitor,* and several other newspapers still serve as yardsticks for measuring opinions and responses to government's management of critical situations.

Klapper (1960, p. 110) surmises that the priority given to print usage may be due to the fact that print allows the reader to control the occasion, the pace, and the direction of his exposure to persuasive inductions or propaganda, and permits him easy re-exposure or review whenever the need for clarification arises. How about the value of print media to the communicator or sender? The priority of usage for the communicator is also justified in that print allows him to develop topics, issues, and arguments as fully as is necessary. With print, the persuader is not constrained or frustrated by the rigid time frames prevalent in television or radio programming. Moreover, print is more economical for reaching interest groups (no matter how small or specialized) than is the broadcasting media.

Several researchers contend that the print media, as persuasive tools or channels, demand greater active and creative participation from the receiver. Klapper (1960) summarizes the argument well: "The communication (in print media) is less structured; it does not confront the reader with a visible or audible speaker, as do radio and TV, and therefore permits him greater freedom to assign (meanings) or to imagine nuances, interpretations and the like."

It seems probable, too, that the newspaper reader may not become as personally involved as does the radio listener or TV watcher because he does not feel that he is being personally addressed. If this is the case, one may argue that high ego-involvement, which may normally serve as a *resistor* against incoming persuasive stimuli, will not present a barrier to the printed message. This type of participation and the minimizing of involvement is considered to be "persuasively advantageous" (Doob 1935, 1948; and Berelson 1942).

In view of the public's response to the print-enforced dissemination of information and opinions of the so-called "Watergate Scandal" in Washington, D.C., the argument of print's superiority seems tenable. Others may argue that the "active and creative participation," and "extending of interpretations" on the part of the print user might have been mediated by the concurrent influence of several other media and channels. Perhaps we can go on to construct a *profile of the receivers* or audiences who are most likely to use the newspaper as their main source of information.

Studies have shown that the higher the individual's economic status and the larger the community in which he lives, the more likely it is that the individual considers himself a "regular newspaper reader" and— perhaps more significantly—the greater the chances of his maintaining that he prefers to read "national and foreign news" in a newspaper rather than to hear it over the radio (Samuelson, Carter and Ruggels 1963; Westley and Severin 1964; Doob 1966).

We should not overlook books in this context because they are perceived differently in comparison to the newspaper (here we are dealing with nonfiction books). Books generally reflect trends and tides of merging consensus and opinions. In particular, textbooks tend to mold opinions in large segments of our culture.

One rather important problem for the persuader is that books are read by rather select audiences or receivers. Textbooks "buffet" their classroom captives, but books at large are read by relatively few in our society. Books such as *The Conscience of a Conservative, The Greening of America, The True Believer* are considered by critics to be statements of merging consensus. But how many people have ever read them?

In spite of the narrow audience or limited exposure potential, books do provide a significant "payoff" for the persuader or the propagandist. Many people are inclined to approach a book with awe, wonder, reverence, and surrender. Its content, because of being bound between two covers, is elevated without criticism and proper evaluation. There is a tendency to confer immediate status on book-bound information to the extent that one often hears the statement: "It is true; I read it in a book!"

Whatever the predisposition of the reader or receiver, there is a significant payoff for the source or writer. Books (as is the case with newsprint) permit the communicator to develop a point of view or argument with as much amplification and redundancy as is desired. The reader is able to set his or her own pace, reviewing salient issues and skimming over the inconsequential. In short, the reader also has control over the presentation of material. Doob (1966) suggests that a book, because of the facility accorded to the reader, may lead to the arousal of central rather than segmental responses, and hence their reaction responses are more likely to be strong. Since this type of audience —or receiver—control is at a minimum with the broadcasting media (radio and television), we would expect predispositions to respond or to "move into action" to be not quite as strong. We will discuss the question of media effects later.

Thus far in our brief discussion of the print media, we have alluded to potential comparisons between print and broadcasting media. Let us look at a few fundamental characteristics of the broadcasting media.

Broadcasting Media

The broadcasting media (radio and television) are capable of reaching the entire population "in a single shot." In addition to this vast outreach, television, by way of its visual presentation, provides its audience with a sense of reality. Figuratively speaking, the Viet Nam war was the first war ever fought in the American living room. By bringing the war home, TV angered the pacifists and stirred up protest.

Radio is the more easily used of the two media. However, it is the medium most casually attended and serves (in this country, at least) primarily as a source of entertainment. Let us look at the two media separately.

Radio.   We pointed out earlier that influential citizens tend to depend more on newspapers than on radio. Researchers have also discovered an apparent correlation between economic and educational status and the amount of time devoted to radio listening. The lower the individual's economic or educational status, the more time he or she spends listening to the radio (Lazarsfeld 1940). Here we are speaking of "quantity" of listening and not "quality." Lazarsfeld points out that as cultural level descends "serious" listening also descends; i.e., the individual tends to listen less to political speeches, discussions of public affairs, "educational" programs, and newscasts. His conclusion is that when people have the choice between radio and print for fairly comparable subject matter, the higher their cultural level the more likely they will read rather than listen (Lazarsfeld 1940).

Of what use is radio as a medium or channel for broadcasting persuasive messages? Whatever its limitations, we should remember that radio is usually first out with the news. Television cameras, crews, film editors, and newspaper presses all need considerable lead time in order to transmit information to the public. The public, fully aware of the information lag, turn to their radios whenever crises arise.

Television. In spite of the quickness of radio, television has had a far-reaching impact on our culture. Television, according to Reuven Frank, President of NBC News, "is a medium for transmitting experience." He comments further, "It has never covered a national budget and it never will. The reason we don't put the national budget on is that we know that people will tune out. We don't consciously put things on that no one will watch" (MacNeil 1968). Frank's point of view reflects the nature of a "sense of reality" to which we alluded earlier; it is this "ability to transmit experience" that stampedes many uncritical viewers into believing that TV "tells it like it really is."

We often forget that politicians, propagandists, reporters, commentators, and analysts may unwittingly (and sometimes deliberately) color the description of an event with their own opinion. Moreover, many of the news specials and documentaries seen on TV consist of a "hard news plus analysis and opinion" format, and it is sometimes difficult for the viewer to separate the real facts from the reporter's fiction. Doob (1966) suggests that it is the passivity of the viewing audience itself that has led to the unreliable mixture of fact and opinion. He writes: "Many of the events in the modern world, furthermore, are so complex and swift moving that the viewer practically begs to be told not only what is taking place but also why it is taking place and the 'meaning' behind the externalities."

During the 1970 Congressional campaign, former Vice-president Spiro Agnew questioned the role of TV newscasting as a supplier of meaning. He proposed the introduction of TV panel shows in reverse, with public figures such as governors, senators, and congressmen, questioning news analysts and commentators. He asked, "Don't you think it would be beneficial for the viewing audience to know what they (the media people) believe so that when they characterize certain things, that there be some understanding of what their underlying philosophy is?" The idea does appear preposterous, but the concern may be well-founded and worthy of consideration. The mixture of facts and opinions can be advantageous to persuasion. According to Doob (1966), it may be the news which evokes auxiliary responses but, to perceive the news, the receiver unwittingly perceives the opinion. As soon as the receiver hears the verbal message and sees the visual stimulus, he is told by the communicator what position he should assume.

There is yet one other consideration. We should point out that television, regardless of the lofty ideals bandied about by the Federal Communication Commission, is not primarily committed to entertaining its viewers. Television is in the business of delivering audiences to marketers and advertisers; it primes or softens the viewer so that he will submit to the subliminal entrancing of commercials. MacNeil (1968) sounds an instructive note for the student of persuasion.

> It is this ruthless world that the politician invades at election time, perhaps innocently believing that he is welcome there. It is this world that TV journalists, now and then during the day, are grudgingly permitted to enter with their brief bulletins from outside. It is essential, if either the politican or the journalist is to reach the mind of anyone in this world, that he make himself competitive, that he sufficiently resemble the other goods sold in this market. For the journalist that means mixing show business with his journalism; for the politician it means a willingness to be sold like Geritol.

We see, then, that the audience politicians, persuaders, and propagandists are trying to reach is an audience that TV has built for commercial purposes. Who are the people that comprise this audience? According to surveys, roughly 36 million Americans watch television during the "prime" evening hours. In the fall of 1966, adult males who watched news segments presented by the major networks, CBS, NBC, or ABC, consisted of the following categories: 25.6 percent went to college; 43.7 percent had attended high school but not beyond; and 30.7 percent had a grade school education or less (figures supplied by Brand Rating Index 1967). We see that proportionately more grade-school educated Americans are steady viewers than are high school and college graduates. The average age of the prime-time viewer has also been established—one could say that TV, during the early evening hours, seems to have more appeal for men over fifty and somewhat more appeal for women over fifty than for men of that age group.

We have also learned that people employed as craftsmen and foremen, or who are students, the unemployed or those who are retired, tune in more than people in other professions above or below them. People in smaller towns and rural areas are more avid viewers than the folk in larger towns or cities; and so are people with total household incomes of $8,000 a year or less (MacNeil 1968, p. 4). This household income range is somewhat descriptive of a "low-culture" group. This quality of audience is of some concern to TV managers. The well-known pollster, Louis Harris, informed the television industry that better-educated Americans were abandoning television while it was gaining among the less educated.

What about the joint dependence of television watchers on other media? MacNeil (1968) claims that there are few heavy readers of magazines or newspapers among the regular TV news audiences. His table, represented here as table 6-1, shows the analysis. MacNeil's

Table 6-1

	TV-News Audience	United States Average
Magazine Reading		
Very heavy	17%	16%
Heavy	16	15
Moderate	35	34
Light	13	13
None	19	22
Newspaper Reading		
Very heavy	12	11
Heavy	28	26
Moderate	31	31
Light	10	10
None	19	19

tabulation shows how the TV audience (particularly the news audience) compares with the national average of magazine or newspaper readers. It would appear as if TV newswatchers read more than the general population. However, the sad truth is that only fifty percent of that avid viewing audience watch TV with a reasonably substantial current affairs background. MacNeil's cryptic commentary is: "The rest, roughly 18 million people, must be relying heavily on television. Considering that for reasons of status most of us are likely to overstate the amount we read, *the dependence on television may be even greater than the figures suggest.*" Is this statement of the absence of a sound information background exaggerated? Not at all. Markel (1967) reports that three quarters of a questioned sample of American voters could not identify the "Vietcong," and when CBS conducted a current events test conforming to tenth-grade standards, almost three quarters of the sample flunked. Several TV watchers were unable to name the senators representing their state, let alone their congressmen. And we have heard of a few who could not name the vice-president of the United States!

Our discussion, thus far, leaves one basic question yet unanswered: Do the mass media exert any significant influence on the people who are exposed to them? A review of works by several authorities has presented us with a mixed bag of opinions ranging from findings of minimal effect to findings of maximum effect. We shall attempt to put the findings into perspective.

The Effectiveness of the Mass Media

A great deal of research has been conducted by people in marketing, political science, and advertising to test the effectiveness of the mass media. Some of those studies have employed message retention and learning as the crucial behavior or dependent variable; others have sought to measure attitude change, behavior modification, buying behavior, and so on. Several of the researchers (Belson 1956; Berelson, Lazarsfeld, and McPhee 1954; Campbell, Gurin, and Miller 1954; Hovland 1959; Kraus 1962; Mendelsohn 1964) report very little evidence of attitude or behavioral change. Other researchers caution that such results are a bit misleading. McGuire (1969), for instance, cautions that "there are indeed 'attitudinal' effects, though these are of a more subtle nature than at first supposed."

Schramm and Roberts (1971) also sound a note of caution. They write:

It is difficult to argue with such generalizations. Few, if any, examples of radical changes in basic beliefs, values, or behavior deriving directly from mass communications have been demonstrated. Moreover, it is clear that mass communications are seldom, if ever, the sole agent behind any change. Rather, they function as just one element in a highly complex social system; their impact is moderated and mediated by numerous other factors in the system. In short, whatever the consequences of mass communications, it would be a mistake to conceive of them as anything other than a contributing influence.

On the other hand, generalizations such as the preceding one risk the danger of leading us to underestimate those contributions to social behavior which the mass media do make. For example, the status quo which the media serve to maintain can be characterized as normative means for dealing with the environment. This, in turn, implies that changes in the environment require changes in the status quo — in effect, the establishment of a new status quo. If we are willing to concede that for most of us the mass media function as the primary link with a large proportion of the "environment," and that changes in this environment are occurring at a rapidly increasing rate, then it is difficult to believe that mass communications do not exert a strong influence on social behavior. In other words, to the extent that other factors in the social system impelling toward change seem to manifest themselves more and more frequently, mass communications have more and more opportunity to contribute to social effects.

Schramm and Roberts cite the civil rights movement as a case in point. They suggest that it is reasonable to argue that the civil rights struggle would not have experienced such a rapid (?) development in the absence of mass communications. And in this respect the consequence of mass communications should not be underestimated.

Still others hedge a bit on the argument of "mass media minimal effect" by pointing out that the mass media serves a "primary" effect of maintaining the status quo; that is, the mass media may not drastically change attitudes and behaviors, rather the mass media reinforces, consolidates and strengthens existing behaviors, opinions, and attitudes. DeFleur (1970) offers a more cogent, supportive suggestion in his book *Theories of Mass Communication.* Explaining his "cultural norms theory," he argues that since the mass media are often the major source of information about many parts of the world, and since the mass media coverage seems to endow whatever is broadcast or printed with a kind of validity and status, it would stand to reason that mass communications have the power to shape our impressions and conceptions of norms and events.

Skornia (1965) seems to endorse the previous contention for he argues that radio and television not only can and do teach, but cannot help teaching. He says it is only a question of *what* they teach, whether intentionally or unintentionally. Skornia is particularly critical of television and its harmful effects on children. He claims that while it is unfair to say that television is *the* cause of delinquency and mental unfitness, it is quite unacceptable to say that television is not *one* cause.

After unscrambling the conflicting literature and research findings, we should be able to make some definitive statements concerning the ability of the mass media to exert an influence on their audiences. We propose to discuss the nature of the effects of the mass media under two general headings: (1) emotional arousal, and (2) attitude, opinion, and behavior change.

Emotional Arousal.   Research carried out at the Psychological Institute of the University of Rome showed that the rhythm of film images influences the viewer's respiration and other metabolic behavior. The viewer of television programs became much more emotionally involved than did the reader of print. More crucial to our study in this book, Keilhacker (1958) points out that long before a child goes to school, he is learning what values are important, what is truth, what is honesty, how people succeed, how adults behave. He states that at this age, children are not as much spectators of film as they are co-actors (see Skornia 1968, for a statement of Keilhacker's work). Stress or emotional arousal is heightened as children are forced to shuttle back and forth between TV fantasy and the values taught on the "boob tube," and the values that we attempt to instill in them in real life.

Let's forget the effect on children for a moment. What about the effect of television on those who are grown up enough to read this book? How many items that you cannot afford to purchase were shown to you this week on television? Did the advertisers or persuaders try to make the purchase seem easy? Perhaps you are one of those who are prepared to await the end of "ghastly" college days until the time when you'll be able to afford what the advertiser offers! But, what about the effect of such appeals on persons who have no days or years of affluence to look forward to? We wonder whether the effects of "message and situations" interactions could ever be measured in laboratories. Does the broadcast media influence social revolt? Looting? Skornia (1968) asks a series of rhetorical questions that are impossible to ignore:

> What is the breaking point of people subjected in commercials to parades of physical ills; bombardment by slogans; rumors and tales of violence; sales messages in musical, visual, and spoken form; and the volume of claims, counterclaims, accusations, and counteraccusations which make up much of television and radio

offerings? How many irritating commercials can people stand? How many suggestions of infirmities does it take to create hypochondriacs?

Experts in counseling, psychiatry, and psychoanalysis caution against the hazards of introducing frustration, either by overstimulation or by causing the viewer to want something he cannot afford, or will not ever be able to have because of physical, racial, or other reasons.

We may look at emotional arousal from another and perhaps more deliberate standpoint. What is the effect of portrayal of violence or aggression on the screen? Does it set a "reverse" psychological effect in motion? Or does it lead to the "copy-cat" syndrome? This is what Berkowitz (1962) has to say on this matter:

> On the basis of these findings we can hypothesize that people with strong aggressive predispositions will display a relatively strong liking for aggression in television, movies, and comics. There is no evidence, however, that their hostile predispositions are weakened by viewing fantasy aggression. If anything, experimental results suggest that scenes of violence depicted on the screen will have a much greater tendency to incite children to later aggressive acts than to "drain" them of their aggressive "energy."

Bettinghaus (1968) also concurs with the idea of mass media effectiveness in bringing about affect changes. He suggests that when an individual sits in front of his television set and watches a highly emotion-laden message, he does so in the absence of the constraints or taboos that hound him in public situations. Consequently, he may weep, stamp his feet in rage, or even "make an ass of himself."

The evidence concerning the impact of the mass media on emotional arousal is rather limited at the moment. We believe that the paltry literature has been due to the inability of communication researchers to study the effects of the media in "real" life environments. However, the trickle of information (such as it is) convinces us that there is more to the effects of the mass media on the human senses than is apparent. We will now discuss the effect of the mass media on attitudes, opinions, and behaviors. Here, too, a similar hodge-podge of garbled findings confronts us.

Attitudes, Opinions, Behaviors.   The consensus among media researchers is that the mass media has little or no effect on changing attitudes, opinions, and behaviors. Kraus (1962) informs us that during presidential election campaigns the mass media communication was not as effective as face-to-face informal communication among peers. He suggests, moreover, that there is a tendency for those who are exposed to mass media campaigns to change their votes less than those not exposed to them. Bettinghaus (1968) reports that most listeners or readers do not switch their attitudes when they are exposed to a persuasive message. Instead, their original positions tend to be reinforced. Few people are actually converted. Other studies (such as Berelson, Lazarsfeld and McPhee 1954; Lazarsfeld, Berelson and Gaudet 1948; and Star and Hughes 1950) report similar results of attitude and opinion reinforcement rather than attitude and opinion change.

These findings cause us to raise a vital question: If the mass media is so powerless as an instrument for bringing about attitude, opinion, and behavioral change, why do persuaders, propagandists, and advertisers persist in using it? Are they, too, caught up in the myth of media potency? Are they merely squandering billions of dollars in programs that afford no "payoff"? Or, do they count it worthwhile to achieve reinforcement, consolidation, and a strengthening of those who are already committed to the viewpoints advocated? Is this reinforcement or strengthening effect *the* major effect of the mass media? We think so. But we see another angle to the problem. Conceivably, much of the research conducted in this area has dealt with political issues with which subjects are so highly ego-involved that practically no conversion is possible. Moreover, people do not willingly listen to, watch, or read information or messages that run counter to their own beliefs or opinions. People *selectively expose* themselves to and *selectively retain* that which lines up with their "thinking." So, it's much more a question of leading the horse to the water than it is of getting him to drink.

What happens when the persuader uses the mass media to present persuasive messages dealing with less involving issues such as changing from Crest toothpaste to Colgate? Does the same effectiveness prevail? We doubt that. We believe that audiences are more passive when the issues evoke low ego-involvement. And it is this passivity that the media men try to capitalize on. MacNeil (1968) says it well: "The object is to disconnect the audience from uncomfortable realities, to lull it on a sea of gentle inconsequence — and then sell it deodorant." The TV watcher or the newspaper reader does not approach the media to be persuaded; he approaches them in order to escape and in order to kill time. Consequently, direct attempts at persuasion may not be suited to the media—especially radio and television. Finding the American consumer in his passive slumber, the media men of Madison Avenue steal up on him, put a jingle in his ear, and when he awakes he heads directly for the cooler at the nearby supermarket. He's got a lot to live, and Pepsi's got a lot to give.

So, the mass media (as far as crucial gut issues are concerned) comes up short. It does not seem to be *directly* responsible for opinion, attitude, and behavior change. What, then, *does* influence change? Some commentators suggest that the media has an influence that is somewhat dependent on a "two-step" flow of communication. That is, the media posits the idea, and interest groups or reference groups through "opinion leaders" do the actual job of persuading. We will look at these opinion leaders later; first, we must study the dynamics of the group interaction with its members.

The Effects of Group Interaction as a Channel in the Persuasion Process

Persuasion research has recently begun to recognize the group as a persuasive device. Social psychologists have pioneered much of the work in this area, and later, mass communication researchers have been led to view the dynamics of the group as a vital mediator in the influence of the mass media. Earlier in this chapter we alluded to the finding that the mass media seemed weak in its ability to enforce opinion change; this finding, however, may be qualified or perhaps better explained as we study the dynamics of the influence of groups.

The Influence of Groups

It is generally agreed that our attitudes do not develop and thrive in a vacuum. The groups in which we function as members assist in the development of these attitudes. The importance of the group has been heralded by Schramm (1961): "We live in groups. We get our first education in the primary group of our family. We learn most of our values and standards from groups. We learn roles in groups because those roles give us the most orderly and satisfying routine of life. *We make most of our communication responses in the group.*" To a great extent, then, our attitudes depend upon the attitudes and norms of the groups which serve us as yardsticks or frames of reference. Thus, it seems a bit futile to study the effects of channels and media by isolating the individual and treating him as if he were the sole arbiter of his behaviors and opinions.

Once we accept the idea that our group affiliations play an important role in attitude formation, we may be able to appreciate the significance of such factors as primary group relationships, conformity pressures from the group, a willingness or eagerness to share similar experiences and similar exposure to information, and the tendency to seek out people who are similar to us in many respects. We are not suggesting that one has to be a *bona fide*, objective member of any group in order for that group to exert an influence on him. One can certainly *identify* with a group without being a member of that group. This is why we are using the broader definitive concept of the *reference* group. Halloran (1967) is rather instructive on this point:

> The important thing about this development is that it reminds us that individuals may orient themselves to groups other than their own and not merely to their membership groups. Amongst other things, this helps us to explain why attitudes and behavior may deviate from what one would predict on the basis of group membership. Symbolic processes allow the individual to escape from a narrow environment and in analysing social behavior the reference group approach enables us to go beyond the impact of immediate stimulus situations and look at attitudes and behaviour in relation to values and norms that are not necessarily related to immediate group situations. Man relates to groups not only in terms of past and present associations, but also in terms of aspirations, expectations, future goals and objectives, status and prestige.

Shibutani (1955) is also expressive on the issue of the salience of reference groups. He notes that "deliberately, intuitively, or unconsciously, we all perform for some audience." He suggests that complex societies present many *unseen* audiences and that in order to understand behavior (in relation to the mass media) we need to identify these audiences.

What concerns us very much in this discussion are the relationships that develop among members in the group. Two key factors should be considered: (1) cohesiveness and (2) conformity in the group. By *cohesiveness*, we are referring to "the resultant of all the forces acting on members to stay in the group" (Festinger 1950). By *conformity*, we refer to the degree to which a person's behavior corresponds to the norms of his reference group.

Although many studies on cohesiveness and conformity have been conducted in the small group communication area, we believe that such studies are particularly relevant to the study of persuasion. Let us look at these two factors separately even though in our discussion they tend to overlap occasionally.

Cohesiveness. As a rule, highly cohesive groups—that is, groups that are characterized by friendliness, cooperation, interpersonal attraction— usually exert strong influences on their members to behave in accordance with group norms, consensus, and expectations. Also members of such groups are inclined to behave in accordance with the wishes of the group. Two studies support these generalizations. Festinger, Schacter and Back (1950) found that members of cohesive groups in university housing units held uniform opinions and usually acted in conformity with group standards. They found that as pressures toward uniformity increased, the more the cohesiveness of the group increased. The second study (Back 1951) found that members of highly cohesive dyads changed their opinions more toward their partner's position than did members of the less cohesive dyads. Other studies (such as Festinger, Gerard, Hymovitch, Kelley and Raven 1952; Lott and Lott 1961; and Schacter, Ellertson, McBride and Gregory 1951) all point up similar results.

Bettinghaus (1968) argues that members of groups that are more cohesive are more likely to be influenced by persuasion for the very reason (stated earlier) that there are more pressures to be "uniform" in a highly cohesive group than in a less cohesive group. Bettinghaus reasons that when the group becomes the recipient of persuasive communication, there are more pressures to do something about the message. Since the outside pressures are for acceptance of the message, they apparently tend to produce more influence. Bettinghaus' argument makes the process seem too easy to accomplish. We agree that the "pressures toward uniformity" will dispose the group to act faster on the message; however, the "outside pressures" are of little or no consequence in the final analysis. The bulk of the influence to respond (favorably or unfavorably) to the persuasive message should emerge from those key members within the group who are accorded opinion leadership and status by the other members. In any case, a clear point concerning the ability to influence the group still arises from the notion of "high cohesiveness." Cohesiveness leads to increased social influence, which in most instances produces greater conformity to the norms and expectations of the group.

Conformity. The group serves both a normative and comparative function for its members. The *normative* function involves the assimilation of the attitudes and values of the particular group, and with this normative function the group is seen as a source of the individual's values and perspectives. The *comparative* function involves self-appraisal through comparison with a standard; in terms of this comparative function the individual compares himself with the group when making a self-judgment. (See Deutsch and Gerard 1955; and Kelley 1952.)

Conformity increases with identification with the group (cohesiveness), and, as pointed out by Constanzo, Reitan, and Shaw (1968), is further influenced by both the perceived competence of the majority and the subject's perception of his own competence. When a person has high confidence in his ability to make judgments, he conforms less than when he perceives his competence to be low. The implication of this issue of competence and conformity should be obvious.

Conformity is generally rewarded by the group; deviance, on the other hand, is punished, or at least not rewarded. Consequently, most of us tend to conform to the norms of our various reference groups. When persuasive messages run counter to group norms and expectations, we tend to resist those messages.

Given this brief background, we will now point up the relevance of the reference group to the overall concern of channel effects. Several studies (such as Festinger, Schacter and Back 1950) reveal that meaningful communications are generally transmitted along "social" lines defined by friendship, by shared interest, and particularly by shared opinions (Klapper 1960). In this fashion, says Klapper, the audience originally reached by the mass media is increased.

Katz and Lazarsfeld (1955) report on various studies showing that people tend to belong to groups whose opinions are congenial to their own. Those studies also show that opinions become intensified through intragroup discussion, and that the individual's desire to maintain a good standing (or acceptance?) in the group usually acts as a deterrent against opinion change. Thus, in some instances the group influence aids the mass media in facilitating opinion change; in other situations, the group influence frustrates the impact of the media.

In this section, we have alluded to a sort of "silent" influence of the reference group. We have suggested that the mere presence or awareness of the existence of others around us is a sufficient influence on the response that we make to persuasive communication. We need to look to another aspect of the group's influence. In the next section, we will discuss the question of deliberate influence attempts as we talk about the effects of face-to-face or dyadic communication.

The Effects of Face-to-Face Communication as a Channel in the Persuasion Process

A great deal of our communicative interaction is conducted through person-to-person contacts, and for several years media researchers have been analyzing the character of this person-to-person or face-to-face transport of information. Particularly, they have been concerned with identifying those groups from which these "message relay runners" are likely to go forth. Much of these studies fall under the heading of *opinion leadership* or *the two-step flow of information*. The concept was first investigated and defined by Lazarsfeld, Berelson and Gaudet (1948), and later elaborated upon by Katz and Lazarsfeld (1955). They discovered upon analysis that personal contacts tend to be more effective than the mass media in influencing voting decisions. This accounts, of course, for the aspect of face-to-face communication. But they discovered another interesting phenomenon—that is, certain "special" individuals were generally instrumental in initiating these face-to-face contacts. These special individuals were called "opinion leaders." Lazarsfeld, Berelson, and Gaudet suggested the possibility that ideas often *flow* from the mass media *to* the opinion leaders and then *to* the less active sections of the population. It is the latter two-thirds of this process that is viewed as a two-step flow. Our first chore is to find out who these opinion leaders are.

Opinion Leaders

Weiss (1969) suggests that the opinion leader is more conversant with current issues and that he or she is more highly exposed to the mass media. Katz and Lazarsfeld (1955) found that women opinion leaders read more magazines and books than did the nonleaders. Other studies further narrow the issue by suggesting that those who are perceived as opinion leaders tend to be more exposed to relevant media content, to technical or formal professional communications or to commercial sources of information (Emory and Oeser 1958; Katz 1961; Lionberger 1960; Menzel and Katz 1955; Rogers 1962). Studies of the manner in which farmers and doctors adapt to new techniques show that people who are earlier than most in adopting new items are more likely than the others to be in contact with technically competent or knowledgeable professionals (Coleman, Katz and Menzel 1957; Menzel and Katz 1955; Rogers 1962).

Opinion leaders are generally found on all social levels, and are generally of the same social status as the people who acknowledge being influenced by them. However, there is one fundamental area of difference. In the area of public affairs there is a stronger tendency than in other areas for the low and middle status levels to be influenced by the high-status group. In the area of agriculture and the adoption of new agricultural techniques, Rogers (1962) found that here, also, opinion leaders tended to be of a higher socioeconomic status than were nonleaders. The same trend was also found in studies measuring the status of opinion leaders among doctors.

Klapper (1960) sums up the dynamics of the opinion leader's interaction with the people he influences.

> The leader's guidance seems to be sought or accepted in specific areas partly — or perhaps largely — because it provides his followers with the sort of satisfactions they seek in those areas. The marketing leader, for example, is relied upon because the brands she suggests fulfill the particular needs of her followers. In regard to her field of expertness she appears, like other leaders, to be consciously or unconsciously so intimately familiar with group norms that she can guide group members toward their attainment.
>
> In reference to group norms, then, opinion leaders seem likely to be conformist. They appear to be, in this respect, very like *group* leaders (as opposed to persons who are merely *opinion* leaders), who have been similarly observed to embody group norms, and thus to be in a certain sense, the most conformist members of their groups—upholding whatever norms and values are central to the groups.

It is clear, then, that opinion leaders do exert some influence on the people in the environment, and that these opinion leaders generally relay information derived from the mass media. It is also clear that opinion leaders in face-to-face contact with their peers exert more influence than the mass media on opinion change. In this final segment we will discuss some factors which may contribute to the superiority of face-to-face communication.

Mass Media Versus Face-to-Face Communication

The notion that the mass media as a communication channel allows only a one-way communication system, whereas face-to-face communication affords the possibility of a two-way loop, is fundamental to our analysis.

In the first place, face-to-face communication generally draws the receiver into more participation with the communicator. Also, because of the communicator's visible presence, the receiver under the impress of social constraint may be stampeded into acquiescence or agreement more than he would when dealing with the mass media.

Second, face-to-face communication provides a feedback, clarification, and adjustment facility which is not afforded by the mass media. Several studies have shown that, by noticing the effect of various arguments on his visible audience, the source is able to use his time more effectively in the face-to-face situation to modify his arguments to fit the disposition of his audience (Jecker, Macoby and Breitrose 1965; Jecker, et al. 1964; Rosenthal 1967).

Third, as McGuire (1969) suggests, it is possible that attention factors are also involved in the superiority of face-to-face communication which provides much less opportunity for selective avoidance than does mass media communication. Here is his expansion of that suggestion:

> Social constraints usually prevent the receiver from leaving the room when another person begins to express to him opinions with which he disagrees. There is much less constraint against turning to a new page or a new channel when one finds the mass media communicator disagreeing with one's own preconceptions. Of course, as we saw above, there does not seem to be a tremendous amount of selective avoidance in any case. The attention advantage of face-to-face communication obtains even on a more passive, less psychodynamically interesting basis: the wanderings of attention deriving from the simple weaknesses of the flesh, such as boredom, fatigue, and intellectually limited attention, are more likely to interfere with the reception of mass media communications. In face-to-face communication situations, the demands of courtesy and the explicit efforts of the communicator are likely to limit such inattention so that the receiver will absorb more of the message.

Fourth, there is the question of accuracy of transmission—a problem which Lerbinger (1972) has considered. He makes a distinction between *technical* accuracy and *semantic* accuracy. According to his analysis, the printed media is "unquestionably superior" in the technical sense of accuracy. By this he means that messages can be worded, figures and tables can be displayed, pictures can be included according to the dictates and resources of the message-sender or source. However, all of these features do not guarantee that the message will accomplish its mission. Much more is needed in order to achieve semantic accuracy. How does one put across an intended meaning? Surely, meanings do not exist in words; they exist in you, in me. Words don't mean; people mean. To achieve a "sharing of meaning," active two-way communication is necessary. Consequently, face-to-face communication is superior for influencing semantic accuracy.

In this chapter we have studied the effects of the mass communication media, group influence, and face-to-face communication (through personal influence by opinion leaders) on opinion and behavior change. We have shown that each of these channels does exert some influence even though face-to-face communication appears to be superior. However, it would be unrealistic to discard the usage of the mass communication media for the simple reason that the mass media shifts group influence and opinion leadership into high gear. We suggest, then, the practical use of a media-mix. The mixing of media should be influenced by the size and composition of the potential audience, and also by the ability of each medium and channel to move the audience along a given persuasion path. One may utilize the mass media simply to broadcast a new idea and to bring it to the individual's level of consciousness; the follow-up may involve the persuader's approaching the customary opinion leaders in an attempt to get them to campaign in behalf of the idea.

Communication media and channels tend to exert influence on behavior, attitudes, and opinions. The vital media are: print, radio, and television. The vital channels are: face-to-face communication and group influences.

Propositions

1. The print media appears to be used more regularly by some individuals than by others.
   1a. The higher an individual's economic status and the larger the community in which he resides, the greater the likelihood of his being a regular newspaper reader.

2. Print media tends to create a unique psychological climate that affects receiver response.
   2a. Print media demands greater active and creative participation from receivers than does the broadcasting media.
   2b. (Because of the impersonal nature), the print media tends to minimize the arousal of the receiver's ego-involvement, and consequently increases persuasiveness.
   2c. Print media influences stronger predispositions to "move into action" than does the broadcasting media.
   2d. The print media facilitates greater development of viewpoints and arguments than does the broadcast media.

3. Radio and television seem to have limited appeal, and tend to draw a limited audience.

   3a. The lower the individual's economic status, the more time he spends listening to radio.

   3b. As cultural level descends, the tendency to avoid "serious" listening increases.

   3c. The higher the individual's cultural level, the greater the tendency to read rather than to listen.

   3d. Grade-school educated individuals are steadier viewers of television than are college graduates.

   3e. Television viewing by children is heaviest among the duller and emotionally insecure.

   3f. Viewers of television tend to become more emotionally involved in the topic than do newspaper or magazine readers.

   3g. Individuals with strong, aggressive predispositions tend to display a relatively strong liking for aggression on television.

   3h. Scenes of violence depicted on the screen will have a greater tendency to incite children to later aggressive acts than to drain them of their aggressive energy.

4. Generally, mass media communication is not as effective in changing opinions and attitudes as is face-to-face communication in dyads or in small groups.

   4a. The groups in which we function as members influence the attitudes or opinions we develop.

   4b. Our attitude formation depends upon the attitudes and norms of the group which serves as a yardstick or frame of reference.

5. The cohesiveness of a group and one's conformity to a group are two major factors that influence attitude and opinion formation.

   5a. A highly cohesive group exerts a stronger influence on its members to behave in accordance with group norms, consensus, and expectations than does a less cohesive group.

   5b. Members of a highly cohesive group are more likely to behave in accordance with that group's expectations than are members of a less cohesive group.

   5c. Pressures toward uniformity increase as the cohesiveness of the group increases.

   5d. Members of highly cohesive dyads (groups of two) change their opinions more toward their partner's position than do members of less cohesive dyads.

5e. Conformity is influenced by an individual's perception of the competence of the majority, and the perception of his own competence or incompetence.

5f. When a person has high confidence in his ability to make judgments, he conforms less than when he perceives his competence is low.

6. The major influence in groups is exerted by opinion leaders.

6a. Opinion leaders tend to be more conversant with current issues, and are highly exposed to the mass media.

6b. Opinion leaders (except in the area of public affairs) are generally found at all social levels.

7. Face-to-face communication is more effective in influencing opinion change than is mass media communication.

7a. Face-to-face communication generally draws the receiver into greater participation with the communicator.

7b. Face-to-face communication provides more feedback, clarification, and opportunities for adjustment than does the mass media.

7c. Face-to-face communication provides much less opportunity for selective avoidance than does mass media communication.

Additional Readings

Andersen, K. *Persuasion: Theory and Practice*. Boston: Allyn and Bacon, 1971. Chapter 14, "The Relationship of Channel and Setting" and Chapter 15, "The Systematized Campaign Using Multimedia," pp. 267-329. An up-to-date summary of the usefulness of various channels and media is provided. The reader will also find a discussion on the effectiveness of several media in political campaigns.

Bettinghaus, E. *Persuasive Communication*. New York: Holt, Rinehart and Winston, 1973. Chapter 4, "The Influence of Social Groups," pp. 77-96; Chapter 8, "Communication Channels." These chapters provide very good summaries of research.

Halloran, J. *The Effects of Mass Communication with Special Reference to Television*. Leicester, England: Leicester University Press, 1965. The entire book (83 pages) deals with a summary of research findings pertaining to the effects of television as a communication medium. We suggest reading pages 11-42; 63-76.

7

The Effect of Receivers on Persuasive Communication

The study of the relationship between receiver variables—personality variables inherent in listeners, readers, and viewers—and persuasion is crucial to our becoming more effective persuaders. The speaker or writer who makes no assessment of the mental, cognitive, or emotional states of his audience has a rather slim chance of reaching that audience, regardless of his appeal or the structure and organization of his message. It is naive to assume that a single message would have the same impact on every individual who comes in contact with that message. We must remember that receivers vary in terms of personality characteristics, and that the same message is generally interpreted differently by different listeners.

The joke about the paranoid who, after a passerby says "good morning," thinks to himself, "Wonder what in hell that s.o.b. meant by that?" suggests the existence of a wide latitude for interpretation. The receiver's attitudes, state of mind, and personal background often determine what he hears, how much, or whether he hears anything at all. We hope that this chapter will increase our awareness of the existence and the potency of individual characteristics.

What traits dispose certain people to "turn off" and "turn on" during message impact? What makes them open-minded to some opinions, and closed-minded to others? We remind you that we don't have precise answers, but we can discuss receiver variables that are quite critical toward progress in formulating answers. Ten receiver variables or personality characteristics—self-esteem, anxiety and insecurity, Machiavellianism, authoritarianism, dogmatism, ego-defensiveness, cognitive style, intelligence, age, and sex—will be examined in this chapter.

Variables Affecting Receiver Behavior

Self-esteem

The interaction or relationship between self-esteem and persuasability has received the most attention in persuasion research. Its popularity may be due to the fact that self-esteem can be easily manipulated in experimental situations. In spite of the widespread concern with the effects of self-esteem, the results derived from research are conflicting. Many studies report negative relationships between self-esteem and persuasability—that is, the higher the individual's self-esteem the lower his readiness to be persuaded (such results have been reported by Berkowitz and Lundy 1957; Cohen 1959; Hochbaum 1954; Janis 1954; Janis and Field 1954; Janis and Rife 1959; Kelman 1950; Mausner 1954; Mausner and Bloch 1957; Samelson 1957). Other studies, however, have reported positive relationships—that is, the higher the level of self-esteem, the greater the susceptibility to persuasion (such studies are Cox and Bauer 1964; Gelfand 1962; Gollob and Dittes 1965; Leventhal and Perloe 1962; Nisbett and Gordon 1967; Silverman 1964; Silverman, Ford and Morganti 1966).

McGuire (1969) suggests an explanation which may resolve the conflict. He contends that we should be mindful of the situations in which self-esteem had been studied by the various researchers. "For example, according to the situational-weighting principle, the relationship between self-esteem and influenceability will more likely be negative when the influence situation is quite simple. . . . it will tend to be . . . positive with more complex social inductions that allow more individual-difference variance in message reception" (McGuire 1969, p. 250). This "situation-weighting" explanation should clarify questions concerning the apparent conflict. Gollob and Dittes (1965), for example, discovered a negative relationship between self-esteem and persuasability when clear messages were used in the experiment, and a negative relationship when ambiguous messages were used. Nisbett and Gordon (1967) observed a positive relationship between self-esteem and persuasibility when individuals dealt with a more complex, argumentative message.

What, then, may we say about self-esteem in terms of its importance to the persuader? Perhaps this: Individuals characterized by high self-esteem, or high self-concept, or high self-image tend to be persuaded more when rational and properly constructed arguments are used in messages. Conversely, such individuals of high self-esteem may tend to resist messages that attempt to force issues without arguments that justify those issues. Individuals of low self-esteem tend to resist persuasive messages of a complex nature, and receive messages that are clear-cut and explicitly stated.

Several other researchers have tried to explain the relationship in terms of specific situations. Holtzman (1970) suggests that some individuals are receptive to persuasion because of their craving for acceptance by significant people in their environment. These individuals tend to go along with a point of view simply because going along affords a chance to "hit it off" with the persuader. This persuasibility trait may be more pronounced in emotionally disturbed persons.

Individuals of high self-esteem are generally sure about their opinions, and are consequently less anxious. On the other hand, individuals of low self-esteem, as Cohen (1964) suggests, are hounded by certain expressive defenses that make them sensitive or extremely concerned about their social environment. Two types of expressive defenses utilized by low self-esteem individuals are projection and regression.

Projection is the defensive mechanism used to escape the anxiety created by a threat to one's self-concept. Projection may be manifested in the spectator who dashes into the midst of a Gay Liberation parade and proceeds to assault the marchers with a baseball bat; or it may be manifested in the women who metes out violence to other women who picket in support of Women's Liberation. It has been argued that members of the "Silent Majority" react so violently to long hair and other examples of "free" life style because they themselves feel contempt for society's artificial restraints, but feel that such contempt is unpatriotic or immoral.

Regression is the defensive device certain individuals use to escape coming to grips with decisions or judgments. The individual tries to regress to an earlier "safe" period in his life. He becomes a child again. Several psychologists have suggested that a form of regression caused many Jews to *allow* themselves to be herded into gas chambers. They were so paralyzed with fear, their alternatives were so limited, that they blinded themselves to reality and behaved like children, willing to be led by their captors, and did as they were told. This same kind of mental paralysis is sometimes seen in customers on a car lot, and voters at election time.

Projection and rejection are important to persuasion because they cause certain individuals to be vulnerable to suggestion and external influence. Under the influence of these two defensive mechanisms individuals become extremely susceptible to fear and threat appeals. Demagogues are particularly adept at playing on these projection and rejection tendencies. We may have observed the practice at work among speakers who stir up antiblack sentiments among certain segments of the population by exaggerating the prospect of property devaluation, a black takeover of community control, and wanton rape.

Persons of high self-estem are able to deny or ignore challenges from their environment in ways that help them maintain a semblance of stability. For example, one may consider the case of the person who is repelled by the militancy of the Arab guerilla movement, but could identify with their vigor, determination, and nationalistic fervor; or, the case of the person who, though repelled by the thought that Civil Rights legislation prevents him from keeping his neighborhood lily-white, is able to identify with a black man's insistence on decent housing in a decent neighborhood.

In summary, self-esteem may be defined as the value individuals place on themselves. Individuals of low self-esteem are more persuasible or influenceable because they feel unsure and anxious about their own opinions. They are more likely to accept threatening messages than persons of high self-esteem.

Anxiety and Insecurity

In the last section, we referred to anxiety in relation to defensive projection. We consider anxiety to be a distinct receiver variable which may facilitate persuasion in some situations and hinder it in others. We also consider insecurity to be an equally forceful variable. However, since both anxiety and insecurity seem to trade with each other in terms of cause and effect, we shall discuss them within the same section.

According to psychologists, there are two basic kinds of anxiety: (1) neurotic, characterological, or trait anxiety, and (2) situational or state anxiety. Neurotic anxiety—the type of anxiety that "never goes away"—is common among low socioeconomic groups. In a constant state of anxiety, individuals tend to be apprehensive about everything, and behave defensively toward others. Nunally and Bobren (1959) observed that such neurotically anxious individuals are unresponsive to messages, even highly persuasive messages; and Janis and Feshbach found that strong fear appeals had very little impact on the neurotically anxious. Situational anxiety is the normal response felt in threatening situations. Generally, this anxiety makes us susceptible to suggestions. Thus, situational anxiety may work as a facilitator if the suggestion is relevant and hopeful.

Insecurity, as Triandis (1972) describes it, refers to a personality characteristic that causes a person to be intolerant of ambiguity. Insecure individuals tend to endorse extreme positions or cling to fanatical orientations. They choose a side seemingly on a mental toss of a coin. Triandis explains the phenomenon:

> This occurs because to be able to "live with" the gap among his cognitions is too threatening to the insecure person, that is, such a person is unable to tolerate this gap. By adopting one or the other of these two positions, the insecure person reduces his dissonance, since there is only one clear, "correct" position to which he must adhere. This position suggests that the left-wing fanatic and the prejudiced have a common psychological basis for their attitudes—insecurity. (p. 127)

In 1962, Triandis conducted research into the characteristics of insecurity of two cultures, Greeks and Americans. He found that, in both cultural groups, the more insecure individuals were more prejudiced. He noted, too, that in both cultures the highly prejudiced subjects reported that they were punished inconsistently and without explanation by their parents. Triandis contends that such upbringing is likely to be confusing to the child and contributes to insecurity throughout growth.

Childhood experience is not the only influence on insecurity. There are other causes of insecurity which a persuader may be able to assess through audience analysis. Loss of status also leads to insecurity. The person who comes from a middle-class family, but who is himself unable to hold a middle-class job, loses status. Bettelheim and Janowitz (1957), and recently other researchers, have found that this type of person is likely to be more prejudiced than a person whose social class is the same as the social class of his parents. Kaufman (1957) studied individuals who expressed much concern about their status (status concern) and found a significant positive correlation between status concern and anti-Semitism.

The effective persuader must first identify the cause of the insecurity, and then proceed to relate to the individual in a way that increases his self-acceptance and self-worth.

Machiavellianism

Machiavellianism refers to an amoral, manipulative attitude toward other individuals, combined with a cynical view of men's motives and of their character (Guterman 1970). Most high Machiavellians (Machs) manifest emotional detachment in dealing with others, and are often lacking in commitment to conventional moral norms (Christie 1968).

High Machs tend to appear cool and calm when confronted by influence attempts. They change their opinions or comply with requests *only* if they are furnished with sufficient justification or rewards. Low Machs tend to be pushovers or soft touches. They accede to demands for opinion change merely because someone appeals for change.

The relationship between Machiavellianism and susceptibility to persuasive influence has been studied under several conditions. In three different group discussion studies (Geis, Krupat, and Berger 1965; Rim 1966; Harris 1966) low Machs consistently reported opinion change after a face-to-face discussion of particular issues; high Machs showed no change at all. Harris (1966), in a follow-up study, investigated the effects of written persuasive communication consisting of either scientific information or polled opinions on high and low Machiavellians. Harris found that both highs and lows shifted their opinions in the direction of the factual, scientific information; however, *only lows* changed in the direction advocated by the "mere" opinion data. Christie and Geis (1970) summarize the patterns persisting in a wide range of research on Machiavellianism and persuasion.

1. High Machs and low Machs are equally persuaded by factual information or rational arguments.
2. Low Machs but not high Machs are also moved by sheer social pressure.
3. Although low Machs seem to be more susceptible in live face-to-face interaction, they are also moved by written communications representing beliefs or wishes of others.

Earlier in this section, we mentioned that high Machs change their opinion only if they are furnished with sufficient justification or reward. This tendency goes against the arguments we developed in support of the effectiveness of forced-compliance or role-playing situations as vehicles for bringing attitude change. You will recall the dissonance theory prediction that attitudes and opinions sometimes change in order to be consistent with a certain behavior performed with little or no coercion or reward. This is known as the principle of insufficient justification (discussed in chapter two). Low Machs tend to change their opinions to bring them into line with "unjustified" behavior; whereas high Machs appear to be less influenced by what they have said publicly or by the behaviors that they have role played.

Epstein (1969) had college men give voluntary arguments contrary to their own private convictions. All subjects read one of two booklets, one with a positive "sponsor" and one with a negative "sponsor," giving arguments against fluoridation. Half the subjects were placed in a role-playing situation in which they improvised talks against fluoridation for possible use on radio programs. Epstein found that low Machs shifted on a post-test measure toward antifluoridation attitudes after role playing more than after silent reading only. High Machs showed the opposite pattern by becoming more antifluoridation when presented with factual arguments than in the role-playing condition. Burgoon, Miller, and Tubbs (1972) and Widgery and Tubbs (1972) report findings consistent with Epstein's research.

In summary, high Machs tend to resist "raw" social pressure. They are persuaded to change opinions or beliefs only when there is high rational justification, and change their opinions or beliefs less when there are high costs or risks. Low Machs seem unmindful of costs or risks for compliance, especially in situations involving sheer social pressure in face-to-face encounters, and acquiesce with the wishes of others readily.

Christie and Geis (1970) suggest a few pointers for working with high Machs:

> High Machs have appeared immune to persuasion by the subtleties involved in dissonance manipulations . . . but it cannot be concluded that they are less persuasible than lows. . . . they were more likely than low Machs to follow the suggestions of an attractive, high-prestige partner. And in Epstein's study they showed more change after silently reading factual arguments than after role-playing. . . . the more reason, incentive, or reward high Machs are given for changing, the more they change. With smaller incentives or greater costs they change less or in the opposite direction. (pp. 253-54)

For a description of the Machiavellianism scale, see Christie and Geis 1970, pp. 10-34.

Authoritarianism

Adorno and his associates, in their book *The Authoritarian Personality* (1950), described a personality trait that they called *authoritarianism*. In order to measure this trait, the authors developed a scale, called the F scale, which is easy to administer and is assumed to measure the magnitude of authoritarianism of a given individual.

A cluster of nine authoritarian character traits was advanced as typical of the authoritarian personality. These were:

1. *Conventionalism*—a rigid adherence to conventional middle-class values;
2. *Authoritarian submission*—a submission to authority figures and an uncritical attitude toward idealized moral authorities of the in-group;
3. *Hostility toward those who violate social norms*—a form of authoritarian aggression. A tendency to be over-ready to perceive, condemn, reject, and punish people who violate conventional norms;
4. *Dislike of subjectivity*—an aversion to the subjective, the imaginative, the aesthetic, the tender-minded;
5. *Superstition and stereotyping*—beliefs in mystical determinance of the individual's fate; the disposition to think in rigid categories;
6. *Preoccupation with strength, power and toughness*—concern with the dominant-submissive, strong-weak, leader-follower dimension, identification with power figures, exaggerated assertion of strength and toughness;
7. *Destructive cynicism toward human nature*—a rather generalized hostility—the vilification of the human;
8. *Projectivity*—a tendency to project unacceptable impulses—a disposition to believe that wild and dangerous and wicked things go on in the world;
9. *An exaggerated concern with sex and sexual goings on.*

Triandis (1972) provides excellent amplification of the nine authoritarian traits:

> Authoritarians tend to employ a particular cognitive style. Specifically, they avoid introspection, reflection, speculation, and imaginative fantasy; they believe in mystical determinants of individual fate. They also have characteristic attitudes concerning a variety of attitude objects. Thus, they accept ingroup authority figures without questioning them; they desire powerful leaders; they

approve of severe punishment of deviants, particularly sexual deviants; they perceive others as deviant and mankind as anarchic; they have a preoccupation with power, viewing human relations in terms of dominance and submission; they admire military men, athletes, and financiers. By contrast, those low in authoritarianism view authority figures as being sometimes correct and sometimes incorrect; they prefer equalitarian leaders; they emphasize warmth and love in interpersonal relationships; they are tolerant of deviance; they admire scientists, artists, and social reformers.

The central theoretical thesis of the authors of the authoritarian personality is that prejudiced and hostile attitudes are expressions of inner needs or impulses created as a result of certain child-rearing experiences; the inner needs are manifested not only in prejudiced attitudes but also in a variety of perceptual, conceptual, and behavioral styles. (pp. 120-21)

The key factor in the relationship between authoritarianism and persuasion is the authoritarian's *very* high regard for authority figures, and his tendency to slight or ignore less significant individuals. Remember, too, that he is extremely status conscious, and has a preference for middle-class values. The authoritarian individual is not influenced by rationality or logic of messages, but rather by the power, prestige and status of the source. For example, if Governor Wallace of Alabama represents a positive authority figure to an authoritarian, that individual is likely to go along with Wallace's suggestions, whether they concern pancake batter or people's rights.

The results of two studies demonstrate the "authority-centeredness" of this type of person. Rohrer and Sherif (1951) found that individuals who had been identified as authoritarian (by the F scale) were influenced by the remarks of authority figures, regardless of whether the remarks were "pro-black" or "anti-black." Nonauthoritarians were influenced more by the content of the messages. Harvey and Beverly (1961) found that authoritarians changed their opinions when advised to do so by a high-status source, whereas nonauthoritarians resisted such an influence attempt. Harvey and Beverly stumbled upon an interesting feature—they observed that nonauthoritarians could recall points and arguments accurately, whereas authoritarians tended to forget message content.

In summary, we may reason that the authoritarian type of person would be swayed largely by appeals from authorities and powerful individuals. Persons who are not authoritarian would be swayed largely by arguments based on relevant information.

Dogmatism (Open- or Closed-Mindedness)

Rokeach (1960) pioneered research into the receiver variable known as open-mindedness (low dogmatism) and closed-mindedness (high dogmatism). Dogmatism refers to the way people respond to opinions, ideas, beliefs, and classes of people. The main concern in the study of the dogmatic individual is not *what* attitudes he holds, but *how* he holds them. Rokeach's study was derived from previous studies on authoritarianism. He discovered that even extremely "liberal" individuals were rigidly committed to certain ideas. In short, there seemed to be closed-mindedness in left-wingers as well as right-wingers.

To understand open-mindedness versus closed-mindedness, we must first analyze what Rokeach calls "belief systems." Each person has a system of involvement such as education, religion, politics, and so on. For a given individual, Catholicism may be an orientation in his belief arena; and Protestantism, an orientation in his disbelief arena. The low dogmatic or open-minded person, though committed to orientations in a belief system, is fully aware of the overlap or common grounds that exist between his belief and disbelief systems. He is aware, for instance, that Protestantism preaches a need for goodwill toward all men, just as Catholicism does.

The magnitude of dogmatism depends on one's degree of involvement (often considered a separate receiver variable; see Sereno 1969), or how much one's ego is invested in a given issue. It is not uncommon to find that a person can be reasonable and open-minded about the Women's Liberation movement as a sociopolitical principle, but can be unreasonable and closed-minded about his wife's becoming an active member of the women's rights crusade.

Rokeach defined dogmatism as a rigid set of beliefs and disbeliefs organized around a commitment to absolute authority which provides a framework for varying patterns of intolerance. Let us look at the operation of low dogmatism and high dogmatism as manifested in behavior.

The more dogmatic the individual, the more he will reject any common ground between his belief system (for example, Catholicism) and his disbelief system (for example, Protestantism). The highly dogmatic individual fails to see any sort of overlap between the two systems — he looks at the world in terms of black and white, ignoring all the varying shades of gray. He tends to label "irrelevant" any argument that points up the similarity of Catholicism's and Protestantism's concern in the war against poverty. The greater the dogmatism, the more he views any part of Protestantism as a threat, and he will reject it totally without compromise.

Also, the greater the dogmatism, the more dramatic his opinion change or belief (for example, about celibacy) *if it is advocated* by a high authority figure (for example, the Vatican Council). Nevertheless, his basic dogmatism persists, and his change of belief is very specific to one particular issue and not a wide range of issues.

Highly dogmatic persons tend to *narrow*. They avoid ideas or people that threaten their belief systems. They are careful to read only certain types of publications, or meet with select groups of people of similar ilk, become involved in reactionary fringes, and join in crusades to ban certain books and ideological teachings.

The high dogmatist manifests a tendency to overly admire or "truckle" to positive authority figures and to hate and defame negative authority figures. Applbaum, et al. (1973) contend that those who attempt political assassination are often dogmatic people who see their counter beliefs epitomized in one man.

The foregoing observations are important to the study of persuasion. However, we need to realize that the world is not made up of "high dogs" and "low dogs." We are all dogmatic to a certain degree, and sometimes our ego-involvement in and commitment to an issue determines just how dogmatic we are. We contend, however, that extreme chronic dogmatism creates a problem for the persuader. We must be prepared to cope with it.

Remember: The open-minded or lowly dogmatic person tends to compare various belief systems, evaluate them, and accept or reject issues according to their merit. The closed-minded or highly dogmatic person clings to his belief, and refuses to look at any other evidence. The open-minded individual evaluates the logic and reasoning of arguments or messages. The closed-minded individual depends largely on the word of positive authorities. The effective communicator should know his audience and tailor his messages and references to suit the disposition of the receiver.

Ego-defensiveness

Some attitudes provide us with rationalization for our shortcomings, and make it possible for us to face the world and ourselves. (See our discussion on the functional approach in chapter three.) The student who hungrily seeks recognition for his work in class, but does not receive it, often cannot bring himself to the realization that his classwork may not be outstanding. He may then resort to the belief that "the teacher is nothing but a damned turkey who couldn't tell the difference between good and bad work!" He takes this attitude because it is ego-defensive for him.

Frequently, extreme ego-defensive attitudes are changed only under skillful psychoanalytical techniques. The fellow with the constant "chip on the shoulder" would generally have to seek some form of psychiatric assistance. However, the ego-defensive syndrome can sometimes be dealt with at an elementary persuasion level. The Katz, Sarnoff and McClintock (1956) research is worthy of extensive coverage, and we reproduce here Karlins and Abelson's (1970, pp. 93, 94) paraphrase of it.

An experiment by Katz, Sarnoff and McClintock (1956) studied attitudes toward Negroes. A major hypothesis was that people's anti-Negro attitudes which have a personal (ego-defensive) basis can be influenced by showing that the attitudes exist to protect the personality rather than because the facts about Negroes logically support such attitudes. Another side of the hypothesis is that people whose anti-Negro prejudice does *not* have a personal (ego-defensive) basis can be influenced more readily by presenting them with factual information about Negroes.

Accordingly, the experimenters prepared two kinds of influence materials. One was for the ego-defensive group. It explained how scapegoating works, and how anti-minority attitudes are often the result of personality conflicts that have nothing to do with the attitudes themselves. This explanation was followed by a case history of a college girl which showed the connection between her prejudices and her personality. The other kind of influence material was for the nonego-defensive group: a resumé of the achievements of Negroes in America and how they have made good whenever opportunities were available to them.

Nearly 250 college students participated in the study. At a first session, they filled out questionnaires designed to reveal their attitudes toward Negroes and took some psychological tests which helped categorize the motivations underlying their attitudes as personal (ego-defensive) or factual.

For the second session, held a week later, the students were assigned to three groups, without regard to the answers they had given the previous week. One group read the material which explained the relationship between attitudes and personality. A second group read the informational material. The third group was a control group and read nothing. After exposure to their respective reading matter, the first two groups filled out the attitude questionnaires again. The control group did likewise. Six weeks later, all three groups once more answered an attitude-toward-Negroes questionnaire. They found that the ego-defensive people in general did respond better to the material that attempted to help them understand themselves than to the purely informational material. But as the experimenters had predicted, the individuals who were *extremely* ego-defensive did *not* respond well to this kind of influence attempt. The reason advanced was that for these people, the attitudes they held were so crucial to the maintenance of their personalities that some kind of psychiatric treatment would be a necessary forerunner of successful persuasion.

Cognitive Styles or Integrative Complexity

Cognitive styles are receiver variables that enable an individual to sort out the bits and pieces of information that make up the world of ideas and subjects. Some psychologists (for example, Harvey, Hunt and Schroeder 1961; Schroeder, Driver and Streufert 1967; Karlins 1967; Karlins and Lamm 1967) refer to cognitive style as variations in *integrative complexity*. A person who is low in integrative complexity is called "concrete."

Much of the research in cognitive styles or integrative complexity has been conducted under the rubric of conceptual systems theory, and from its findings we may be able to predict how people think and how they may be persuaded.

A concrete person is rigid and closed-minded in his thinking, and is not a complex thinker. Harvey (1967) summarized the characteristic traits of concreteness:

> The concrete thinkers tend to (a) make few differentiations among categories that are concerned with issues that are central or ego-involving to them; (b) tend to judge in an extreme, black and white manner; (c) depend on the status and authority aspects of the sources of messages; (d) form quick judgments in ambiguous situations; (e) have a greater need for cognitive consistency; (f) have difficulties in changing sets and in behaving flexibly; (g) have trouble solving problems that require different ways of looking at situations; (h) are more insensitive to subtle cues; (i) have a smaller capacity to act "as if" and to take the role of others; (j) are more sure of their opinions; and (k) tend to follow the rules.

The abstract person is flexible and original in his thinking. The abstract person, or one high in integrative complexity, is "creative" (Karlins 1967; Karlins and Lamm 1967). Seudfeld and Vernon (1966) found that abstract individuals will be less easily swayed by propaganda appeal and have a greater head for information in their environment than will concrete individuals.

Intelligence

Research, to date, has presented a mixed bag of findings on the relationship between intelligence and persuasion. We will highlight what seems to be typical of the results.

The more intelligent and extroverted individuals are more persuasive and *less* persuasible in arguing their point of view with a disagreeing person (Carment, Miles and Cervin 1965). The most intelligent students were the least influenced by crudely propagandistic statements (Wegrocki 1934).

Hovland, Janis and Kelley (1953) used troop indoctrination films, *Why We Fight,* as message stimuli and found that the films were more effective on soldiers of high intelligence. However, there were reversals in this trend especially on opinion questions, but not so much for factual questions.

On the basis of their investigation, Hovland, et al. (1953) conjectured that intelligence consists of separate components: (1) learning ability — the brighter people learn and remember more; (2) critical ability — the brighter people can sort out the reasonable arguments from the specious ones; (3) inference-drawing ability — the brighter people can see the implications behind the facts. They then proceeded to draw the following conclusions which seem adequate as guiding principles for persuasion:

(1) Persons with high intelligence will tend—mainly because of their ability to draw valid inferences—to be *more* influenced than those with low intellectual ability when exposed to persuasive communications which rely primarily on impressive logical arguments.

(2) Persons with high intelligence will tend — mainly because of their superior critical ability — to be *less* influenced than those with low intelligence when exposed to persuasive communications which rely primarily on unsupported generalities or false, illogical, irrelevant argumentation.

Age

We may conclude, on the basis of evidence, that maximum persuasibility is generally found at eight or nine years of age (Barber and Calverley

1964; Messerschmidt 1933a, 1933b; Reymert and Kohn 1940). After age nine persuasibility takes a steady sharp decline and levels off at adolescence (Hull 1933; Stukat 1958; Weitzenhoffer 1953), declining with age more for boys than for girls (Hovland and Janis 1959).

Psychologists suggest that as people become older, they tend to develop more conservative attitudes (Freedman 1961) because of a lessening adaptability to environmental changes and novel sociopolitical situations, whereas young people tend to welcome change and sometimes demand it.

Sex

There seems to be clear-cut evidence that women are more persuasible than men (Carrigan and Julien 1966; Janis and Field 1958; King 1954; Reitan and Shaw 1954; Scheidel 1965; and Whittaker 1965). However, men should look into the possible causes for this relationship before embarking on male ego trips. There are several explanations from which to choose. We shall present most of them in the following outline.

1. American cultural influences require females to conform more than males (Hovland and Janis 1959). Karlins and Abelson (1970) suggest that as the American female progresses in her battle for equal rights with males, we should expect differences in persuasibility to diminish and eventually disappear.
2. Persuasibility of women may be due to better message reception by females than by males (McGuire 1969a). Some psychologists contend that women possess greater verbal skill and may better assimilate ideas from verbal messages.
3. Perhaps men experience a greater feeling of imposition and more reduction of their freedom of choice than do women. Thus, men tend to oppose influence (Triandis 1971).
4. When we speak of "women being more persuasible than men" we are referring to the "average" woman. This does not mean that *all* women are more easily swayed than men. There is overlap between the sexes as far as susceptibility to persuasion is concerned—with some females being less persuasible than males and vice versa (Karlins and Abelson 1970).
5. Finally, it should be noted that data supporting sex differences in persuasibility come from laboratory studies which deal with issues of minor relevance to the participants. A woman swayed in a psychological experiment is not necessarily as easily swayed

in the real world, where more ego-involving, important issues are involved. To put it another way: Could the same male who persuaded a female in the lab also convince her outside the lab? We suspect not as easily nor as often! (Karlins and Abelson 1970)

Propositions

Receivers vary in terms of personality characteristics. These personality characteristics influence receiver perception and reception of persuasive communication. Some of the personality characteristics (variables) which seem to affect receiver perception/reception of messages are:

1. Self-esteem
2. Anxiety and insecurity
3. Machiavellianism
4. Authoritarianism
5. Dogmatism
6. Ego-defensiveness
7. Cognitive styles
8. Intelligence
9. Age
10. Sex

1. Self-esteem
   1a. Individuals characterized as high in self-esteem are persuaded more by rational and properly constructed arguments, and less by messages that attempt to force issues without sufficient justifying arguments.
   1b. Individuals characterized as low in self-esteem tend to resist complex messages, and accept messages that are clear-cut and explicitly stated.
   1c. Individuals characterized as low in self-esteem are generally more responsive to authority-bound messages and information linked to the support of a majority.

2. Anxiety and Insecurity
   2a. Highly anxious individuals tend to respond favorably when assured that a message or proposition has widespread acceptance, and unfavorably when no assurances are given.
   2b. Highly anxious individuals resist messages that arouse high levels of fear.

    2c. Situationally anxious individuals are generally susceptible to convincing arguments.

    2d. Insecure individuals tend to be more intolerant of ambiguity than individuals who manifest no traces or fewer traces of insecurity.

    2e. Insecure individuals tend to endorse extreme positions and cling to fanatical orientations.

    2f. The more insecure the individual the greater the tendency to be prejudiced.

3. Machiavellianism

    3a. High Machiavellians manifest greater emotional detachment in dealing with others than do low Machiavellians.

    3b. High Machiavellians manifest a lower commitment to conventional norms than do low Machiavellians.

    3c. High Machiavellians tend to manifest opinion change *only* when furnished with high reward or justification.

    3d. Low Machiavellians tend to manifest opinion change following a face-to-face discussion of the issues; high Machiavellians generally will not manifest opinion-change under such conditions.

    3e. Both high and low Machiavellians tend to shift their opinions in the direction advocated by factual, scientific information; however, only low Machiavellians tend to shift opinions in the direction advocated by mere opinion data.

    3f. High Machiavellians are more likely to follow the suggestions of an attractive, high-prestige partner than are low Machiavellians.

4. Authoritarianism

    4a. High authoritarians tend to manifest a high regard for authority figures, and tend to disregard less significant individuals.

    4b. High authoritarians are influenced less by the rationality or the logic of messages, and more by the power, prestige, and status of the source of messages.

    4c. Low authoritarians manifest a greater ability to recall the points and arguments of a presented persuasive message than do high authoritarians.

5. Dogmatism

    5a. The more dogmatic the individual, the greater the tendency to reject a notion of common ground or overlap between his belief system and disbelief system.

    5b. The less dogmatic the individual, the greater the tendency to accept a notion of common ground or overlap between his belief system and disbelief system.

5c. The more dogmatic the individual, the greater the tendency to view the advocacy of the disbelief system as a threat.

5d. The more dogmatic the individual, the greater the opinion change in response to the suggestion of a positive authority source.

6. Ego-Defensiveness

6a. Extreme forms of ego-defensiveness will be modified or reduced *only* under treatments entailing skillful psychoanalytic techniques; milder forms may sometimes be modified under conditions of normal persuasion.

6b. Moderately ego-defensive individuals respond better to material that facilitates self-understanding than to purely informational or issue-centered material.

6c. Extremely ego-defensive individuals *do not* respond (in the direction of the message) to self-enlightening messages.

7. Cognitive styles

7a. Abstract individuals generally manifest a high degree of integrative complexity.

7b. Concrete individuals generally manifest a low degree of integrative complexity.

7c. Concrete individuals are rigid and closed-minded in thinking, and are not able to cope with complex material.

7d. Abstract individuals are flexible and original in thinking, and cope successfully with complex material.

7e. Abstract individuals are less swayed by propaganda appeals than are concrete individuals.

8. Intelligence.

8a. The higher the intelligence of the individual, the greater the tendency to be influenced by messages relying largely on logical arguments.

8b. The lower the intelligence of the individual, the greater the tendency to be influenced by messages relying on emotional appeals.

9. Age

9a. Maximum persuasibility is generally found in subjects between the ages of eight and nine.

9b. The older a person becomes, the greater the tendency to acquire more conservative attitudes.

10. Sex
   10a. Females tend to be more persuasible than males.
   10b. The greater persuasibility of females may be attributable to their tendency to conform more than males (cultural expectations?).
   10c. The higher persuasibility of females may be due to the female's greater facility to assimilate messages.

Additional Readings

Applbaum, R., et al. *Fundamental Concepts of Human Communication.* New York: Harper and Row, 1973. Chapter 9, "Receiver Variables," pp. 134-47. An overview of a few of the important personality characteristics that affect listener or audience responses.

Bettinghaus, E. *Persuasive Communication.* New York: Holt, Rinehart and Winston, 1973. Chapter 3, "Personality and Persuasibility," pp. 57-75. An excellent chapter presenting a brief discussion on the structure of beliefs, problems involved in studying personality, and a few variables that influence or hinder message acceptance.

Karlins, M., and Abelson, H. *Persuasion: How Opinions and Attitudes Are Changed.* New York: Springer Publishing Company, Inc., 1970. Chapter 5, "The Audience as Individuals," pp. 83-106. A quick, excellent compendium of findings presented with helpful explanations.

part four

Strategies of Persuasion

8

Product Advertising

The communication and persuasion function of advertising is to aid consumers in the search for goods and services and to satisfy their needs and wants. Advertising is a rather expensive means of persuasive communication. It involves the use of such media and channels as magazines, newspapers, radio, television, posters, and pamphlets in order to transmit messages.

Tillman and Kirkpatrick (1972, p. 174) define advertising as "the mass communication of a promise." Their use of the term "promise" hints at a major responsibility on the part of the advertiser. This mass communication of a promise, in order to be helpful to the consumer, should be informative, educational, and persuasive. It should inform the consumers or receivers of (1) the existence of want-satisfying products and services; (2) where to obtain them; and (3) the qualities possessed, expressed in terms that will enable consumers to choose intelligently. The communication should be educational from the standpoint of increasing consumer knowledge and enhancing judgment in the process of reaching a buying decision. It should be persuasive enough to motivate people to try something new.

According to Sandage and Fryburger (1971) the advertiser should know both the consumer and the product. They state that "the linking of the two (i.e. consumer and product), and success as an interpreter calls for some knowledge of how advertising functions as communication, as well as how it affects and is affected by consumer behavior" (p. 239).

In this chapter we will try to acquire some knowledge of how advertising works, and how it affects and is affected by receivers or consumers. We will discuss the two common views of advertising, and will indicate our preference. We will talk about (1) the various audience responses that either hinder or facilitate advertising as persuasive communication, and (2) the factors which seem to influence audience or receiver response. Message factors are also discussed under *content factors* and *structure factors*. Both content and structure will be viewed as attention-getting devices. The question of believability will also be explored in terms of limits and leeways governing the construction of advertisements. Finally, we will talk about the channels utilized in advertising; we will discuss the general effects of channels and also some artistic concerns about presentation.

Two Views of Advertising Communication

The two ways of viewing advertising communication evolve out of two different ways of viewing the audience in persuasive situations. There is the traditional view (Cox [1964] calls it the "egotistical" view), and the "realistic" or more sophisticated view.

The traditional or egotistical view leads the communicator or advertiser to think of the audience or consumers as "a relatively inert and undifferentiated mass that he can persuade and influence at will" (Cox, 1964). This view has been called egotistical because it imputes great powers to the communicator and reduces the audience to a swayable, impressionable mass. Cox summarily describes the view this way: "Proponents of this view would probably hold that if you 'hit them hard enough' (or 'loud enough, long enough, and often enough'), sooner or later they will buy your product."

The traditional or egotistical view considers the advertisement as the stimulus (S) that triggers the desired response (R). According to Sandage and Fryburger (1971), the process thus becomes a "one-way flow," S–R. The advertiser acts, and the audience reacts. Bauer (1964) sees the traditional or egotistical view as "a model of exploitation of man by man" quite common in tactics of "brainwashing," "subliminal advertising," and "hidden persuasion." Bauer notes:

> The model of a one-way exploitative process of communication . . . is probably further reinforced by the experimental design in which the subject is seen as *re*acting to conditions established by the experimenter. We forget the cartoon in which one rat says to another: "Boy, have I got this guy trained! Every time I push this bar he gives me a pellet of food." We all, it seems, believe that *we* train the *rats*. (Bauer 1964; p. 322)

As we can see, this traditional or egotistical view exaggerates the power of advertisers and minimizes or underrates the power and initiative of audiences.

The realistic view is more valid. It considers advertising to be a two-way flow. In this two-way flow, the audience is regarded as a collection of individuals who respond to communication and messages in several different ways, depending on their individual predispositions. What is important is not what the message brings to the audience, but rather what the audience brings to the message. While the communicator, the message, and the channel or medium play major roles in the communication process, it is the audience that decides whether (and how much) it will be influenced. The audience's attitudes, beliefs, values, goals, status, and so on determine whether the advertiser's message will be heard, believed, and acted upon. (We will discuss a few of these audience predispositions in the next section.)

For the moment, let us briefly consider the impact carried by the audience in the two-way flow of the advertising process. For an audience to be influenced (in keeping with the intentions of an advertiser), several conditions must be met:

> The audience must, somehow, be *exposed* to the communication.
>
> Members of the audience must interpret or *perceive* correctly what action or attitude is desired of them by the communicator.
>
> The audience must remember or *retain* the gist of the message that the communicator is trying to get across.
>
> Members of the audience must *decide* whether or not they will be influenced by the communication. (Cox 1964)

Cox considers these four conditions—exposure, perception, retention or integration, and decision—as the gateways to effective persuasion in the advertising process. Let us consider each of these four gateways or categories of audience response to advertising communication.

Categories of Audience Response to Advertising Communication

How does advertising (as a strategy of persuasion) really work? To answer this question we need to focus on a sequence of psychological events occurring in the receiver of the message. In order to be influenced, a person must see the advertisement, comprehend it, remember it, accept it, and tentatively decide to buy the product. However, we should realize that it is prior experience (learning) that determines what will be seen, heard, thought of, and done in response to the advertisement. Four basic categories may be used to characterize the various responses to advertising communication:

Exposure: The audience is within range and is capable of seeing and/or hearing the message.

Perception: The audience sees and/or hears the message and relates to prior learning the word/picture/sound symbols making up the message.

Integration: The audience accepts or rejects the message; believes or disbelieves; remembers or forgets; modifies or retains relevant attitudes and perceptions.

Action: Members of the audience buy, try, serve, repeat purchase, advocate, or openly endorse product advertised. (See Sandage and Fryburger 1971, p. 243.)

Exposure

We can say that a person is exposed to advertising when he or she is able to receive or perceive it. However, we must realize that the person generally exercises a choice in the matter. Exposure to the media and its advertising messages tends to be *selective* and *voluntary.* According to Sandage and Fryburger (1971), it is selective in that the person chooses only a fraction of all media available, and different people choose different things.

Most people expose themselves to advertising messages that interest them, or which support and reinforce existing attitudes. They avoid ads that are uninteresting, irritating, or incompatible with their opinions or attitudes. Erlich, Guttman, Schonbach, and Mills (1957), for instance, found that new car owners were much more likely to read ads for the car they had just bought than were owners of the same make but an earlier model. The explanation or conjecture is that the new car owners were seeking reassurance by selectively exposing themselves to reinforcing or supportive messages. Cannell and MacDonald (1957) found that a mere thirty-two percent of a sample of male smokers consistently read articles on health (i.e. articles dealing with the relationship between smoking and lung cancer), while sixty percent of nonsmokers read the articles.

Such findings raise a crucial question! How will an advertising message reach its intended audience in light of the tendency toward selective exposure? Sandage and Fryburger (1971, p. 245) offer the following helpful strategy:

> *Whereas exposure to media tends to be voluntary,* exposure to much advertising is involuntary, i.e., the person does not seek the advertisements. The ads "come along with" the program or editorial content and one becomes involuntarily exposed to the ads as a result of his voluntary exposure to the medium. Exceptions, of course, are exposures to classified ads, to the "yellow pages," to mail order catalogs, and to regular sources of shopping information, such as grocery store and department store ads.
>
> From the advertiser's viewpoint the factors affecting exposure are most significant in media decisions. He should place his messages in media that are congenial to his market's predispositions. However, he also might enhance exposure to his messages if he adopts an appealing style and consistently schedules them in appropriate media. Then the audience will be inclined to keep the line of communication open when the commercial comes on or the ad page comes in view.

The matter of "an appealing style" is most important as a strategy to counter selective exposure. We will consider the style and appeals later in this chapter. For the moment, let us look at another category of audience responses—perception.

Perception

Perception involves more than being aware of, or hearing, or seeing an advertisement through the senses. Perception also involves the attachment of meaning to messages, and relating messages to prior experience. We send and receive communication through signs and symbols whose very existence depends on meaning. Walter Lippmann (1922) noted: "For the most part we do not first see, and then define. We define first and then see."

Perception is selective. We see what we want to see, and hear what we want to hear. Murphy (1947, pp. 377-78) explains the conditions that lead to selective perception:

> Needs determine how the incoming energies are to be put into structure form. Perception then is not something that is registered objectively, then "distorted". . . . Needs keep ahead of percepts. The needs are always controlling; perception instead of being the lawgiver, takes orders from the need. . . . It is the need pattern that plays the chief role in determining *where we shall look*, to what outer stimuli we shall attend, and what other factors shall be allowed to enter the control box (selector system).

In short, our needs at a given moment will influence our manner of perceiving a message. A study conducted by Stayton and Weiner (1947) showed that individuals who have a greater desire to own a Volkswagen tend to see the car as physically smaller than those who express a lesser desire. Several other studies demonstrate that new parents are more quick to notice camera ads. Women with graying hair are more likely to notice hair coloring ads. New homeowners are more likely to see and read advertisements concerning lawn care.

Even when people are accidentally or involuntarily exposed to an advertisement, they sometimes misinterpret or distort (i.e. selectively perceive) the intended meaning or thrust of the message. Kendall and Wolf (1949) report a study in which cartoons intended to ridicule prejudice were misinterpreted by sixty-four percent of the people who saw them. Prejudiced subjects were most inclined to misrepresent what they saw; they either saw no satire in the cartoons or interpreted them as supporting their own attitudes.

Hovland, Harvey and Sherif (1957) presented messages supporting prohibition to three categories of people—"drys," "wets," and "moderately wets." They observed that the greater the discrepancy between a person's attitude and the viewpoint of the message, the greater the tendency to regard the message as propagandistic and unfair, and even to evaluate the message as further removed from the receiver's own position than it actually was. On the other hand, when there was little discrepancy between the receiver's own position and the message viewpoint, the receiver judged the message to be fair, factual, and closer to his own position than it actually was.

We know also that habits can cause distortion. We often see and hear what we are accustomed to see or hear. Allport and Postman (1945) cited evidence demonstrating that a picture in which a Red Cross truck was shown loaded with explosives was ordinarily perceived by subjects as a Red Cross truck carrying medical supplies. Why? Supposedly, because that's the way it's expected to be!

So, perception is yet another factor that impedes or facilitates audience response of advertising messages. We have shown that, under certain circumstances, people distort or misinterpret messages to make them more compatible with their own attitudes, habits, or opinions.

Integration

One of the many problems confronting advertising is that a person may or may not believe the message or remember it. Furthermore, the person may not be motivated to change his attitude after having seen or heard the message. Message acceptance is influenced largely by the degree of harmony existing between the receiver's attitudes and beliefs and the content of the message. Believing, remembering, and attitude change (or resisting change) are considered part of all the selective processes which we habitually use to protect ourselves from the entry of unwanted persuasion. This part of the response sequence—message-evaluation, remembering, and fitting the message to existing beliefs, attitudes, opinions, values, and past actions— is referred to as *integration*. Maloney (1964, p. 526) describes the integration responses as follows:

> Stimuli are integrated with memories from prior learning or experience and the effects of such integration are stored in the memory structure. They remain there until they are themselves buried (that is, forgotten) or altered by later inputs, or until they are reactivated to form a decision, a response, or a pattern of response.

Let us explore the principle of integration further. Our attitudes, beliefs, values, goals, and expectations make up what is known as our cognitive structure in which, according to the assumptions of consistency theories, we strive to maintain stability. When an advertisement is inconsistent with our cognitive structure, the message will either (1) be rejected outright, (2) be distorted to make it fit the cognitive structure, or (3) bring about a change in the cognitive structure. Which one of these three situations will most likely happen? According to Cartwright (1964), the outcome "depends upon the relative strength of the forces maintaining the cognitive structure and of those carried by the new message."

Festinger's (1957) theory of cognitive dissonance may be helpful in further explaining what is likely to happen when a message conflicts with components of our cognitive structure. The conflict, according to Festinger, produces cognitive dissonance. The existence of cognitive dissonance, being psychologically uncomfortable, will motivate a person to try to reduce the dissonance and achieve consonance. Also, when dissonance is present, in addition to trying to reduce it, a person will avoid situations and information which would likely increase the dissonance.

Cognitive dissonance may be aroused when a message describing and offering a new product is received. Sandage and Fryburger (1971, p. 248) describe the following case:

> For many years housewives thought that the most effective laundry soaps or detergents were those that produced the most suds—the more suds the better the cleaning action. When the Monsanto Chemical Company introduced "All," a new low-sudsing detergent, their advertising helped housewives reduce the dissonance resulting from the conflicting concept by offering a rational explanation of low-sudsing effectiveness, showing convincing demonstrations, getting washing machine manufacturers to endorse the product, and giving away samples for home trial.

To the extent that cognitive dissonance forces an individual to attempt to bring new ideas into a tolerable alignment with his or her cognitions, the advertiser should design and structure messages which make the individual's task of reconciliation easy.

Action

The goal of the advertiser is to spur his audience into action. This goal is accomplished when the audience or receiver shifts from one brand to another, or tries a new product, or buys more frequently, or buys in greater quantity, or even takes the initiative in telling others about the advertisement.

However, we should note that action is also selective. Even when a person has been exposed to a message, perceives its intent correctly, and remembers its content, he must decide whether or not to be influenced in the manner intended by the communicator. Because of individual predispositions, different people make different decisions as to whether or not (and to what extent) they will be influenced. For some people, attitudes supporting a present buying behavior may be too strongly held to permit a change. Or the advertising message may lack the psychological "punch" to exert any significant impact on an individual's cognitive structure. If these conclusions are valid, what are the implications for advertising? Cox (1965) offers two noteworthy suggestions:

> A great deal of advertising must function either to *reinforce* existing attitudes and behavior (e.g., maintenance of brand loyalty), or to *stimulate* or activate people who are already predisposed to act in the desired manner (e.g., people who enjoy reading murder mysteries are most likely to be on the lookout for, and to be influenced by, advertising of murder mysteries).
>
> A related implication is that advertising is not, in itself, a cause of audience effects, but rather works with and through various mediating factors such as audience predispositions and personal influence (e.g., word-of-mouth advertising).

Cox is not contending that predispositions are so rigid that attitudes and behavior patterns never change. They *do change*. However, his argument is that changing a person's attitude or behavior (as opposed to reinforcing present attitudes or activating those already predisposed) is beyond the scope of most advertising, *except* where:

1. The attitude or behavior involved is of little importance to the individual. People to whom it makes little difference which brand of toothpaste they use are more likely to be influenced to switch brands by toothpaste advertising. Even here, however, some activation of predispositions is involved; people with false teeth are less likely to use any toothpaste. (Cox 1965)

2. The mediating factors (predispositions and personal influence) are inoperative. People may be influenced directly by the advertising for a new product because they have not been able to form attitudes which would predispose them against the product. (Klapper 1957-58)

3. The mediating factors, which normally favor reinforcement, themselves favor change. If for some reason our friends begin buying color television sets, we are more likely to be influenced by advertising for color TV sets. (Klapper 1957-58)

If such assumptions are viable, the foremost function of advertising is to identify and select people who are predisposed to buy a product and present them with such appeals as would elicit the desired response. Audience selection and the quality of appeal are of utmost importance. We should remember that: (1) some people or groups are more predisposed than others to be influenced by advertising for a particular product or brand; (2) within that group which is more predisposed toward a particular product, some individuals or subgroups will be more predisposed to be influenced by certain kinds of appeals, while others will be predisposed by different kinds of appeals.

In this section we have suggested that *exposure, perception, retention,* and *action* are four conditions of an audience's selective responses that may either hinder or facilitate the persuasion of advertising communication. Research has demonstrated that the processes of exposure, perception, retention, and decision do not occur randomly among the population. People manifest varying degrees of predispositions to expose themselves to certain kinds of messages and media and not to others. Different people attach different meanings to the same messages and remember or forget different points of the same message. Different people decide differently whether or not they will be influenced by a message.

As impressive as these selective responses of the audience may be, we should not underestimate the influence of advertising. Advertising does work effectively (as is evidenced by the billions of dollars invested in it yearly!). However, a successful outcome will be realized only when we adapt advertising appeals and messages to existing audience predispositions. Even so, the more realistic expectation is that advertising serves more to modify existing attitudes slightly rather than to change them drastically.

Now that we have discussed the four basic categories of audience responses to advertising communication, let us discuss the several factors that affect audience responses.

Factors Affecting Audience Responses

The factors affecting audience responses seem to emerge from two different psychological environments: (1) the receiver's internal state, i.e. his "psychological make-up," and (2) the external environment surrounding and impressing the receiver. Some of the constituents of the internal state may be level of attention; attitudes, beliefs, opinions, and values; and personality traits. The constituents of the external state may be group influences and prevailing physical and economic realities. We shall study each of these factors or constituents in turn.

Attention

Attention refers to the buyer's sensitivity to incoming information (Howard and Sheth 1969). We may argue that, to the extent that we are studying the effect of a given message on a prospective buyer's responses, what may be more important are the perceptual processes by which he *selectively takes in* information rather than his active seeking of information.

According to Howard and Sheth (1969), *attention* includes a number of aspects:

1. The ambiguity-arousal relation is important; that is, a potential receiver will attend to information only when the message or communication is at a moderate level of ambiguity. If the message is too ambiguous, the receiver will ignore it; too little ambiguity will also lead to ignoring the message.
2. The feedback from attitude (favorable or unfavorable) is also important. The receiver will attend to a message if it issues from a reputable source or if it promotes a desirable product, and will ignore it if circumstances are otherwise.

Attention determines the buyer's or receiver's selective exposure. Sources, channels, and message factors must be utilized to raise levels of attention.

Attitudes, Beliefs, Opinions, Values

Attitude refers to the state of negative or positive affect associated with the product being advertised. Attitude serves a number of functions in determining the effectiveness of communication.

1. The intensity, confidence, or strength of the receiver's attitude will determine (to a certain degree) whether the message will ever become a stimulus to precipitate buying.
2. Attitude is created and changed by a message or communication as a process of learning. According to learning principles, change in attitude may be high in the early stages when its strength is low (much has to be learned), but as more and more is learned (attitude is well established), the message or communication may be less effective in bringing change (Howard and Sheth, 1969).
3. Attitude governs both selective attention and retention of information.

Attitudes and opinion (the verbal expression of an attitude) are usually grounded in beliefs. Beliefs, in turn, are convictions derived from perceived truths. Obviously, what is perceived as true and what is indeed true may be quite different in aspect. To the extent that a belief may be the product of a person's own way of seeing things, one can see how the cards may be stacked against an advertising message.

Values also feature very dominantly in determining response. Values derive from beliefs concerning the desirability or undesirability, rightness or wrongness, justifiability or unjustifiability of situations and choices. Values reflect what should ideally exist (as far as the individual is concerned). Communicators or advertisers would do well to consider the formidable barriers sometimes posed by the receiver's value system.

Personality Traits

Personality may be defined as "an enduring disposition or quality of a person that accounts for his relative consistency in emotional, temperamental, and social behavior" (Howard and Sheth, 1969, p. 75).

The research investigating the relationship between personality and consumer actions has presented us with conflicting findings. Some commentators minimize the role that the study of personality plays in providing recommendations for successful advertising; others celebrate the role of such studies. We take the position that "personality studies" are indeed worthwhile, and that the conflict among findings may be attributable to the imprecision of measurements utilized in the studies conducted. Let us look into a few of these findings.

Evans (1959) used the Edwards Personal Preference Schedule to test for personality differences between Ford and Chevrolet owners. The question was: Is there a relationship between the needs of a buyer and the brand that he buys? Evans's conclusion was that the test was of little value in predicting whether an individual will own a Chevrolet or Ford.

Along the same line of investigation, Westfall (1962) administered the Thurstone Temperament Schedule to a sample of standard, convertible, and compact car owners. He found that the convertible owner is more active, impulsive, and sociable and somewhat less stable and reflective than the standard or compact owner.

Tucker and Painter (1961) report positive relationships between traits called "ascendancy" and "sociability" and the acceptance of new fashions. They also report that the use of headache remedies was negatively related to ascendancy and emotional stability. Gottlieb (1958) reports that compulsive individuals were more likely to use antacid-analgesic products than noncompulsive individuals.

Koponen (1960) studied the relationship between personality and cigarette smoking. He found that the male smoker scored significantly higher than the general male in expressed needs for sex, aggression, achievement, and dominance, but significantly lower than the average in compliance, order, self-depreciation, and association. Koponen reports that a linear relationship seems to exist between such variables and amount of cigarette smoking.

Cohen (1968) administered a test to measure compliant, aggressive, and detached personality systems (see Horney 1937). Cohen's results suggest differences in interpersonal orientation for product use and choice of brand. For example, "high-compliant" persons were heavier users of men's cologne and manual razors.

Concerning responses to the message itself, researchers have studied the relationship between self-esteem and persuasibility. Persons of low self-esteem are more likely to tune out a stimulus, and are more likely to be affected by it if it gets through, than are persons of high self-esteem. Conversely, persons of high self-esteem are less likely to tune out the message and also less likely to be persuaded by the information (see McGuire 1968).

McGuire also reports that personality traits having to do with mental capacity may also make a difference in terms of responses to advertising messages. Chronological age is one such personality trait. Eight or nine years of age is considered as the peak period of persuasibility; it then declines until adolescence, when it levels off.

The findings which we have cited cannot be considered exhaustive. As studies continue with sharper and more precise tools of measurement, we are hopeful that many more relationships between personality traits and audience responses will be discovered.

Group Influences

Group influences point up the emotional tie between an individual and the group. The influence may emanate from (1) a primary group such as family, close friends and neighbors, or from (2) a secondary group such as social class, ethnic group, opinion leaders, and so on.

The individual's emotional ties may be reflected in his incorporation of group values to express his convictions; or may result from a person's attachment to the strength of the group to compensate for his own weakness. Robertson (1970) offers an explanation of the group influence principle:

> The individual considering the purchase of a new car often seeks
> information to reduce uncertainty. His tendency to do this is more

pronounced to the extent that he lacks past experience. Since an automobile is socially visible, he might be expected to seek information about the correct purchase for his position in life. (see p. 82)

Robertson points out that it is not necessary to talk to another person to be influenced by him. Merely seeing a neighbor wear a certain type of shoes or purchase a certain type of furniture polish may influence a consumer to do likewise.

Remember, also, the point made in an earlier chapter concerning Katz and Lazarsfeld's principle of the two-step flow of communication and its role in personal influence. The principle suggests that the mass media directly influences opinion leaders who, in turn, exert their influence on those around them. We can understand, then, how group influence or a person's dependence on it may exert a tremendous mediating effect on responses to advertising messages.

Physical and Economic Reality

Physical and economic reality are, perhaps, the most obvious predisposing factors influencing receiver response. An individual's income, for instance, may determine the type or quality of product that may be purchased, and may even determine his level of interest in a particular class of ads. Age and sex are also predisposing factors.

According to Cox (1965), for some products it is relatively easy to predict, on the basis of physical and economic predispositions, which large group within the population will be most likely to buy. Within this large group it is also possible to identify several subgroups, each of which—though interested in a particular product—could best be reached by different communications or different appeals.

These predispositions—attention, attitudes, opinions, beliefs, values, personality traits, group influence, and physical and economic reality—constitute some of the factors that influence responsiveness to advertising messages. Effective advertising results from message designing that takes such factors into consideration as it fashions appeals to match and mollify different types of audiences.

In the next section we will examine the various devices or strategies utilized in advertising messages that serve to heighten effectiveness.

Message Factors: Designs for Influencing Interest and Action

Our discussion, in this section, deals with matters pertaining to strategies and tactics utilized to heighten audience interest in and responsive-

ness to advertising communication. We will talk about two major factors
—*message content* and *message structure*. Under terms of message
content, we will examine the nature of various types of appeals commonly found in advertisements. Under terms of message structure, we
will look at such features as conclusion-drawing, the nature of arguments, and the use of repetition. Let's examine the various types of
appeals on which most advertising messages are predicated.

Message Content: Appeals

The major function of the advertising effort is to establish a linkage
between the product and the needs of the prospective buyer. According
to Howard and Sheth (1969, p. 371), the essence of message content
is the evaluative favorable beliefs about the brand (or product) that the
buyer should learn. They suggest, too, that the message must be used
in some instances to help the prospective buyer to learn descriptive
beliefs about the product. These two functions—the learning of evaluative beliefs and the learning of descriptive beliefs—are helpful in form-
ing attitude and intention toward the product. The learning of descriptive
beliefs is enforced by stating all of the salient attributes of a product;
however, the learning of evaluative beliefs is enforced by a process that
is much more involved. In order to influence the learning of evaluative
beliefs, one must exercise caution and skill in constructing convincing
arguments and irresistible appeals. What appeals may we use? Advertising experts resort frequently to appeals to needs, appeals to fear, and
rational and emotional appeals. Let's examine each of these basic forms
of appeal.

Appeals to Needs. Is there a list of basic needs to which most people
respond? Marketers and advertisers seem to think so. There are dozens
of "inventories of human desires." The problem is that such inventories
are characterized by much disagreement among authors. Also some inventories propose three basic needs; others propose over a hundred
basic needs. Disagreement notwithstanding, we will utilize here the
simplest and perhaps most widely used inventory of needs proposed
by Maslow (1943):

1. *Physiological needs:* food and water.
2. *Safety needs:* security and protection.
3. *Love needs:* affection and belonging (family and friends).
4. *Esteem needs:* self-respect, prestige, success, and achievement.
5. *Self-actualization needs:* desire for self-fulfillment.

Maslow proposes that lower level needs must be satisfied before
higher level needs become relevant. In other words, it is only after a

person has taken care of his need for survival and safety that he becomes concerned with his love needs, esteem needs, and so on. Robertson (1970) offers an interesting commentary on the question of the relationship between need structure and contemporary advertising:

> Assuming that advertising reflects a society's need structure, a casual examination of current messages should provide adequate evidence that in American society today, most individuals operate at the love or esteem need levels. One does not see a message claiming that "Crispy crackers are more nutritious than other brands"; more typically one sees a message such as "Your guests will enjoy your parties more when you serve Crispy crackers." (pp. 33-34)

Let us examine the nature of the needs (according to Maslow's formulation), in order to observe how they may be utilized as targets of advertising message appeals.

Physiological Needs.   Hunger and thirst constitute a basic motivating force. However, while food and drink provide sustenance satisfying such needs, the prospect of eating and drinking are, themselves, satisfying experiences. Consequently many advertisements resort to visual, aural (sound), and verbal "exciters" in order to provoke sensations of taste, touch, sight, and even hearing. Television and radio commercials bombard us with the fizzing of soda pop, the crunch of fried chicken. Visual symbols conjure up the image of juicy steaks made more succulent and tender after the sprinkling of a certain brand of tenderizer or steak sauce. Successful advertising messages are those which utilize sensory stimulating devices.

Safety Needs.   Safety needs may include our perennial concern for security and health. Basically, the most common threats to our safety are unemployment, loss of income, loss of health, and disability. Let's look at appeals to security and health.
  Security. Churches, the pharmaceutical industry, the medical and dental professions, and life-insurance companies are but a few of the many agencies that must appeal to the security need in order to stay in business. However, one ought to exercise much care and tactfulness when making such an appeal lest he offend the prospect.
  Life insurance companies, for example, have found that an appeal that seeks to influence a prospect to provide security for the family after

the breadwinner's death can be less effective than a more immediate appeal to the breadwinner's self-esteem as a good provider (Sandage and Fryburger 1971, p. 270). There are some circumstances that people tend to avoid thinking about — death is one such circumstance. Consequently other subterfuges must be used in these appeals to soften the impact.

Health. Most of us are motivated by a desire to maintain health. Consequently, many production and promotion agencies capitalize on this safety need — health. Even a rather cursory study of advertisements put out by medicine manufacturers, health spas, dietary food manufacturers, and so on, reveals appeals to the health-maintenance motive.

Closely related to the health-maintenance motive is the comfort-seeking motive. Many products are advertised around the comfort appeal. Such products may include clothing, furniture, shaving equipment, cars, tobacco, and heating.

Love Needs. There seem to be *two* kinds of love needs: (1) the need for an affectional or love relationship with others, and (2) the need to belong to a group of "significant others."

Affection. Affection may include the sex drive. If so, then a reasonably good appeal to the sex drive may be achieved by the suggestion that a person's attractiveness to a member of the opposite sex would be heightened if he or she were to use or purchase a certain advertised product. Such appeals are quite common in ads for perfumes, cosmetics, sport cars, grooming aids, clothing, and jewelry.

There is also the case of parental affection for children, which is manifested in providing reassuring environments, protection, and care. Appeals to parental affection can be appropriately used by insurance agencies, baby food manufacturers, encyclopedia sellers, and manufacturers of safety devices.

Belongingness. A feeling of belongingness may be fostered by our conformity to the social standards of a particular referent group. We are generally always on the lookout for ways of expressing ourselves in such a way that clearly labels us as a member of a particular group. Ownership may be one way of expression. In fact, the advertising themes for Rolls Royce, Corvette, and Mercedes Benz appeal to pride of ownership which is but a facet of the belongingness-fulfillment appeal.

Esteem Needs. We all feel a need to think well of ourselves, and to have others think well of us. We enhance our self-esteen whenever we are assisted in measuring up to the standards we set for ourselves.

To win the esteem of our fellowmen, we must find ways to tell others about the kind of persons we are. Of course, it would be embarrassing and downright "hokey" to go about beating our own drum. So, we resort to indirect ways of doing so. We wear Brooks Brothers suits, drive Porsches, smoke only Marlboros, drink Pepsi (it's for those who think young!), serve Miller beer (the champagne of bottled beer). Why? Because for some of us, these are instruments of self-expression. Advertisers, upon learning of this, bombard us with jingles and slogans around the clock. Through advertising communication it is possible to create what is called "product personality" or "brand image" that will help a person to express himself and gain social approval or esteem.

Self-actualization Needs.   Self-actualization needs are represented by the need for self-fulfillment or the need to become all that we are capable of becoming. Products and services that appeal to the need for self-actualization include educational programs, home study courses, and even some automobiles.

Aside from these appeals to the five basic needs — physiological, safety, love, esteem, and self-actualization — there are other kinds of appeals. Let's look at the effects of appeals to fear.

Fear Arousing Appeals.   Advertising communication may be used to arouse fear and anxiety. However, the crucial question is: Does the arousal of fear or anxiety facilitate the response desired by the communicator? Unfortunately very little research has been conducted in the field of advertising concerning this problem. At best, we must look elsewhere for some probable answers.

Howard and Sheth (1969) view the strategy of fear arousal as belonging to an approach utilized in arousing *irrelevant motives.* The arousal of irrelevant motives is typified by such tactics as appeals to conflict, frustration, power, prestige, affiliation, and fear. The motive aroused in such instances is not product-specific. The rationale is that agitating the person toward a certain intensity serves as a conduit to his becoming interested in the product. What's the effect of this type of appeal?

Howard and Sheth (1969) suggest that if the strength of total motivation (concerning an appeal to an irrelevant motive) is only moderate, the dominant response will be made even more probable. In other words, the buyer will pay attention to the message, will comprehend the arguments in the message, and will change his attitude (and perhaps behavior?) in the direction of the position advocated in the message.

Remember: the strength of arousal should be moderate. If the arousal is strong (i.e. above a certain "optimum-moderate" level), perceptual defense will occur, and consequently both brand comprehension and attitude will not change.

Janis and Feshbach (1953) were among the first to subject fear appeals in propaganda to experimental study. In that study, an illustrated lecture on dental hygiene was prepared in three different forms, representing three intensities of fear appeal: the strong appeal emphasized and graphically illustrated the threat of pain, disease, and body damage; the moderate appeal described the same dangers in a milder and more factual manner; the minimal appeal rarely referred to the unpleasant consequences of improper dental hygiene. The fear-arousing appeals were effective in that they did arouse the motivation of the groups exposed to them. The strong appeal group demonstrated the greatest worry and the minimal group showed the least worry. We should note, however, that more individuals in the strong appeal group expressed greater complaints. This would suggest a sort of ambivalent feeling toward the communication in the strong appeal group. Perhaps the most interesting and important observation in the Janis and Feshbach (1953) study was that *conformity to the directives of the message was highest in the minimal appeal group,* and least in the strong appeal group.

Janis and Feshbach represent only one study; other studies report conflicting findings. Whereas Janis and Feshbach report a negative relationship between intensity of fear appeals, a considerable number of studies have found a positive relationship between intensity of fear appeals and attitude or behavior change (Berkowitz and Cottingham 1960; Leaventhal 1965; Leventhal and Niles 1964, 1965; Leventhal, Singer, and Jones 1965; Leventhal and Watts 1966; Singer 1965; Niles 1964).

In summary, we may say that results on threat appeal seem to suggest that minimal threat in advertising probably has the best long-run effectiveness. We also surmise that several situational and personality factors must be studied in conjunction with intensity of arousal before clear, generalizable results can be achieved.

Emotional Versus Rational Appeals. Another crucial area of investigation is that which deals with the effectiveness of emotional versus rational appeals. Does one type of appeal have clear advantage over the other? There seems to be no clear-cut answer. Some studies have suggested that emotional appeals are more effective than rational appeals (Eldersveld 1956). However, several studies find no difference (Weiss 1960). One of the major problems encountered in the study of the effects of emotional versus rational appeals is that of properly defining what is understood by "emotional" or "rational" (Bauer and Cox 1963; Cox 1962). Howard and Sheth (1969, p. 379) suggest the following approach as a guide to further study:

> We believe that an emotional appeal should be defined as one in which the communication produces only the energizing or tuning-up effect by appealing to the irrelevant Motives. A rational appeal, on the other hand, is one that attempts to show perceived instrumentality of a brand for the buyer's goal satisfaction or changes intensity of relevant and product-specific Motives. A single communication may be classified as a rational or emotional appeal depending on how it affects (as described above) a majority of buyers. In other words, if an appeal only energizes motivation, it is an emotional appeal, but if it also directs behavior, it is a rational appeal.

On a more practical rather than a theoretical level, Seibert (1973) discusses how rational and emotional appeals may convene in advertisements. He suggests that selling ideas may be rational or emotional depending upon which is likely to be more effective in a given advertising situation. Some situations are conducive to a combination of both types of appeals. Here is Seibert's description:

> The safety appeals of the automobile producers stress, in a rational way, those product features that include seat belts, collapsible steering columns, safety glass, padded dashboards, head rests, and safety tires. The safety of a seat belt protecting a tiny tot from harm adds an emotional appeal to the rational selling idea. . . .
> When television tubes were made more rectangular and less circular, there was a rational selling appeal in the demonstration that an enlarged picture resulted. The rectangular tube, furthermore, was not so deep and made possible the production of a narrower television set that fit closer to the wall. Here was another rational appeal. Emotional or subjective appeals are in evidence in the sales ideas for cosmetics, toiletries, perfumes, soaps, and a number of luxury items. The appeal of a fine motorcar may be the satisfaction of ownership and prestige rather than mechanical performance or trade-in value. (p. 225)

Seibert goes on to suggest that advertising messages for industrial goods are more likely to adopt rational appeals. The rational appeal is better suited, in this instance, because the individual's motivation to purchase a machine tool is the performance anticipated —reduction of labor costs, increased productivity, enlarged profits, and so on. Seibert contends that the rational content of an industrial appeal may be lost when the appeal is extended to include attractive color combinations and styles.

The features discussed in this section — appeals to needs, appeals to fear, and rational and emotional appeals — comprise what we have chosen to call "message content" in advertising communication. Let us go on to examine some of the features of "message structure" in advertising communication.

Message Structure

By message structure, we are referring to the way in which a message is presented. Studies have investigated the relative effectiveness of (1) a message that explicitly draws conclusions for the audience as opposed to a message that relies on the audience's drawing their own conclusions, and (2) presenting two sides of an argument as opposed to only presenting one side. Let us see what research evidence has to say in these matters.

Conclusion Drawing

Is it better, as far as advertising is concerned, to present the facts and let the receiver draw his own conclusions? Or, should we draw the conclusions (from the facts) for him? The bulk of empirical research to date suggests that explicit conclusion drawing is more effective in attitude or opinion change (Hovland and Mandell 1952; Hovland, Lumsdaine, and Sheffield 1949; Hadley 1953; Maier and Maier 1957). However, other factors such as education and intelligence must be considered since they appear to affect the relation (Hovland, Janis, and Kelley 1953).

What does an explicit conclusion do for the receiver? How do we assist when we draw the conclusions for him? According to Howard and Sheth (1969), conclusion drawing may help comprehension by providing appropriate integration or absorption of the stimulus. Explicit conclusion drawing serves to reduce ambiguity. However, there could be a danger here, in that ambiguity may be reduced to such a low level that no arousal is created and consequently, the person loses interest in the message. *What is needed is providing a conclusion that will reduce ambiguity to some level but not the minimal level* (Howard and Sheth 1969, pp. 382-83).

It seems, also, that if there are too many factors or features to be remembered in the message, or if the message is complex, it is advantageous to draw the conclusion for the receiver. Also, when the product is new (first of a kind), explicit conclusion drawing may be beneficial.

There is, however, a line of thinking that recommends that we refrain from drawing conclusions for the receiver. Here is the reasoning behind the argument:

> It may be argued that buyers have different evaluative meanings associated with a brand. In other words, a brand may satisfy different configurations of motives, which emerge as different segments in the market. For example, to a segment of the buyers, a foreign automobile may represent status, whereas to another it may represent economy and to still another it may seem to be unpatriotic or un-American. In other words, the buyers buy or reject a brand for a variety of motives. It is impossible to satisfy all segments by the same conclusions in a single advertisement; therefore, if conclusion drawing is left to the buyers, the same advertisement may successfully create favorable attitude and overt action among all the segments. The most recent example of the variety of appeals that a product holds for different segments is the Mustang car (Reynolds 1956). The car was designed for, and communicated to, the youth group, but it was found that many older people were also buying the car. Ford changed its advertising and stopped drawing any conclusions about the kind of buyer that a Mustang owner will be. (Howard and Sheth 1969, p. 383)

Summarily, we may say that it is advisable to draw conclusions for the receiver, but there are at least two instances when we should refrain from doing so. These instances are (1) when the product is familiar to the receiver, and (2) when the product is capable of serving a variety of uses and satisfying users differently.

One-Sided Versus Two-Sided Messages

Is it better to present the pros and cons of a particular product or pros alone? Again, the more definitive answer would depend on whether or not we take such variables as education into consideration. Short of that, our answers must be tentative because research has not really studied certain intervening variables.

We suggest that the existing attitude of the receiver greatly influences the response or acceptance given to a one-sided or a two-sided message. Marketing researchers contend that if the potential receiver of the message is already in favor of the brand or product, a one-sided message is more effective. However, if the receiver is clearly partial to another brand, a two-sided message is more effective. Moreover, marketing researchers have advised that in order to obtain a market share from existing brands for a newly introduced brand, a two-sided message is more effective. They point out that Volkswagen and Avis Rent-A-Car have effectively made use of two-sided messages.

Researchers have also found that two-sided arguments are better for clinching or guaranteeing the endurance of attitude change. Attitude change influenced by two-sided messages is more enduring than that influenced by one-sided messages. This phenomenon of resistance to change has been studied extensively by McGuire and others under the terms of inoculation theory. McGuire (1964) suggests that exposure to counter arguments in a mild form creates a wall of resistance that later arguments cannot penetrate. Howard and Sheth (1969, p. 385) demonstrate the relevance of McGuire's hypothesis to the advertising industry:

> This finding is of some interest to the marketing practitioner, especially when introducing a new product, because counterarguments from competitors are invariably present. This is particularly true of very competitive industries such as drugs and cosmetics where a brand is very often directly attacked in a comparative manner. Listing the limitations of one's own brand, however, may alienate the buyer. Probably the best way would be to show the limitations in a comparative manner in which the advantages are, in the end, stressed.

The message in advertising communication is, perhaps, the major factor that brings about changes in attitude; and with the change in attitudes, other factors in the person's predisposition to respond may also be changed. It behooves us, then, to exercise considerable care and skill in organizing advertising messages. Content and structure must be designed to evoke favorable responses, first, to the message and then, to the product. Beyond the consideration of message content and structure, there is also a consideration of the channels to be used in disseminating or portraying the message. In the next section we will discuss various channel effects.

Channel Factors in Advertising

The channel utilized for communicating or transmitting an advertising message bears several characteristics which tend to affect the manner in which people will respond. Channels may be classified according to two major categories: personal and impersonal. It is generally conceded that personal channels of communication are the more effective since they facilitate a two-way flow of communication. However, in most instances it would be impractical to rely solely on personal channels since the advertiser may be concerned with disseminating a message as widely and as quickly as possible. Consequently, he must rely more heavily on impersonal channels. We shall study the effects of these impersonal channels on the response sequence of the receiver.

General Effects of Channels in Advertising

A major task confronting the advertiser is that of selecting the proper (and most effective) channel. However, there are bound to be limitations regardless of the channel(s) we choose. Crane (1965) touches upon some of these limitations. All the commonly used channels transmit words. All except radio can be used to transmit pictures. Television is more powerful than radio in that it transmits sound, as well as pictures and movements. The printed media (newspapers, magazines, leaflets) may have an advantage over radio because it can provide visual stimuli. Also, most people do read faster than an announcer speaks; consequently print may be more efficient in telling much in a limited amount of time. Print also provides the opportunity for rereading. It is necessary to understand the differences in capabilities of various channels because *the receiver's perception of the message is a function of both the information he has stored and the degree of meaningful representation that the new communication possesses* (Howard and Sheth 1969, p. 356).

For the moment, let us review (in summary form) a few statements of the general effects of channels in advertising. Robertson's (1970) review is rather useful; we quote from it extensively:

1. *The various communication channels are not equally effective at all stages of the purchase decision process.* For example, impersonal channels (radio, TV, posters, billboard, magazine ads) serve as original and additional sources of information about products; however, personal channels (word of mouth, person to person) often serve as "attitude determinants" and as the last source of information prior to purchase. The crucial point to remember is that *purchase* occurs over time, and that the function and usefulness of channels will vary according to the consumer's position on the purchase decision continuum.

2. *Communication channels possess distinct structural and operational features, consequently they tend to perform different functions for the person and to provide different kinds of information.* Although advertising is highly accessible to the consumer and provides a certain

quantity of factual information, it is definitely one-sided information. Thus, the person who desires objective information must often turn to fellow consumers for evaluative information.

3. *A consumer's exposure to more than one channel may increase the likelihood of purchase because of the cumulative effect achieved.* Cox (1961) refers to this as "complementary reinforcement." Channels should, therefore, be viewed as complementary rather than competing.

4. *Channel effectiveness varies by the amount of attitudinal or behavioral change necessitated for purchase of the product.* Impersonal channels, for example, are more likely to function as agents of attitude reinforcement than of attitude change (Klapper 1960). Advertising's potential is greatest under conditions requiring least attitude change. (See Robertson 1970, pp. 51-52.)

A number of researchers concur that interpersonal communication (word-of-mouth) may be the most effective channel of advertising communication (Katona and Mueller 1954; Klapper 1960; and Bell 1963). However, it must be realized that this form of advertising alone will not suffice. One must rely on the cumulative effects of complementary reinforcement. We suggest a reliance upon the most efficient means of communication—such means may entail the use of radio, TV, and the like; but we also suggest the need for a greater awareness of the presence of opinion leaders in the marketplace. By being aware of them, and by pitching our messages (in part) to them, we may enhance the pay-off of our efforts at advertising.

In this chapter, we have stressed a concern for a process in advertising communication. We have discussed the audience in terms of the response potential, and the factors affecting that response. We have talked about the message that confronts the audience—we have looked at such message features as content and structure. Finally, we reviewed a few fundamental observations concerning channel effectiveness. Hopefully, this chapter has helped to focus more intently on a few of the rigors that plague and overwhelm the persuader—in this case, an advertiser.

Additional Readings

Bogart, L. *Strategy in Advertising.* New York: Harcourt, Brace & World, 1967. Chapter 4, "Persuasion and the Marketing Plan"; Chapter 8, "The Uses of Repetition"; and Chapter 10, "The Concept of 'Audience'."

Sandage, C. and V. Fryburger. *Advertising Theory and Practice.* Homewood, Ill.: Richard D. Irwin, Inc., 1971. Chapter 12, "Factors Affecting Responses"; Chapter 13, "Advertising Appeals"; and Chapter 14, "Selecting the Appeal." These chapters provide useful "how-to-do" information.

Wheatley, J. *Measuring Advertising Effectiveness.* Homewood, Ill.: Richard D. Irwin, Inc., 1969. This book of readings contains a series of "quantitative" studies. We recommend it for its description of the kinds of research being conducted in advertising. Part IV, pp. 96-141, and Part VII, pp. 187-233 provide useful information.

9

Persuasion and
the Courtroom

It is unlikely that we can go through an entire lifetime without having
some contact with the courts; we may serve on a jury or be active as
either defendant or plaintiff in civil or criminal proceedings. And, yet,
we know so little of the workings of courtroom proceedings. We have
paid little attention to the process of persuasion as a device for effective
courtroom behavior. A knowledge of the persuasive process as it operates in the courtroom provides us with the tools to cope effectively
with our own courtroom experiences.

The public's view of the courtroom, the actions of the jury, judge,
and lawyer, is generally a picture of the exception, rather than the rule.
Let us examine the typical perception people have of the courts. From
our experience with television, the courtroom is a situation involving
professional gamesmanship between prosecutor, defense, and presiding
judge. Attorneys for the prosecution and defense gather together socially
before the trial to share ideas and experiences; judges meet with attorneys
in their chambers to talk over recent legal developments casually; and
courtroom participants indulge in legal formalities as strict in adherence
as any religious ceremony.

The lawyer is perceived as a major symbol of the law. He is the ultimate persuasive force who commands the knowledge and ability to utilize all the persuasive strategies needed to free the innocent and expose the guilty. The prosecutor, at least in criminal trials, is generally viewed as the "establishment man." He is concerned more with the percentage of successful prosecutions, persuading the jury that the defendant should be penalized, than discriminating between the guilty or innocent. The defense attorney has become the defender of the innocent against the machinery and legal systems of the establishment. The jury is composed of twelve representative men and women, a true cross-section of Americana, an omniscient group that recognizes fact from fiction, the guilty from the innocent. The judge is the guardian of legal procedures. He is unbiased, clear, and at all times concerned with achieving the correct decision within his courtroom.

In an age of enlightenment concerning the role of the lawyer, judge, and jury in the courtroom, television and films continue to bolster this mythical view of the legal process. An intelligent individual will note the discrepancies between legends and realities. This knowledge leads to frustration, distrust, and skepticism with the courtroom process. Therefore, we will seek to clarify the roles played by the lawyer, jury, and judge with particular emphasis upon the persuasive processes operating in the courts.

The courtroom process, as we shall see throughout this chapter, possesses all the elements of our persuasive model in chapter 1. The attorneys, for the plaintiff or defendant in civil cases, the prosecutor or defense attorney in criminal trials, act as the major sources in the persuasive transaction. Secondary sources are the witnesses presented before the court and the presiding judge. We suggest that the witness is a secondary source because his message is controlled by the lawyers and judge in the case.

The messages that are used to provide the facts of the case and the standards for evaluating courtroom materials are developed and presented by the lawyers, witnesses, and judge. The receiver is either the jury and/or judge. A number of civil cases are presented solely to a presiding judge for evaluation. The principal channel of communication, at least on the lower court level, is oral. The use of graphs or other visual materials is also not uncommon. However, appeal courts deal only with written transcripts of lower court decisions. We will concern ourselves solely with the process of persuasion as it manifests itself in lower court proceedings. Figure 9-1 provides a model of the courtroom process.

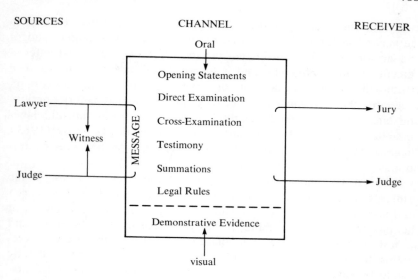

FIGURE 9-1.   The Courtroom Persuasive Process

The purpose of a civil or criminal trial is to provide an equitable method for making decisions regarding the responsibilities, guilt, or innocence of parties involved in the courtroom battle. The courts are to ascertain the facts in the disputes; that is, they are to determine the actual objective acts of the involved parties, to find out what they did or did not do, as these facts bear on the compliance or violation of some law. Jerome Frank (1963) provides a formula to describe the courtroom decision-making process:

$$R \times F = D$$
R = legal rules of society
F = facts of the case
D = court's decision of that case

But, what are the facts of the case? At best, they are only what the trial judge or jury thinks happened. The court usually learns about the real, objective, past facts through the oral testimony of witnesses, the demonstrative evidence provided by attorneys, and the attorneys' interpretation of what constitute the facts of the case. After hearing testimony or seeing the demonstrative evidence, the jury and/or judge must personally evaluate the credibility of witnesses, their testimony, and the evidence. The "facts" consist of the judge's and/or jury's reaction to the various materials presented by the attorneys. Unfortunately, judges and juries possess the same human weaknesses from which we all suffer—perceptual limitations, bias, and influence by persuasive strategies. The "truth-will-out" axiom does not correspond to reality in the courtroom. It ignores the elements of subjectivity and chance. It ignores perjury and bias and it ignores the truthful witness who seems untruthful because he is frightened by the courtroom environment. As Frank (1963) suggests, the description of the actual decisional process needs alteration: $R \times SF = D$. The SF stands for subjective fact.

The development and presentation of the facts of a case reside primarily with the lawyer. It is his task to produce the facts (evidence) for the benefit of his receivers (jury or judge). In the next section of this chapter, we will examine the lawyer's role in the courtroom and several methods and restrictions placed upon him by the courts in presenting the facts of the case. However, we should recognize already that to be successful the lawyer must persuade the jury or judge that the facts of the case support his side.

The Lawyer

The lawyer aims at victory, at winning the fight, but not always at aiding the court to discover the facts. He does not want the judge or jury to reach a sound educated conclusion, if that decision is likely to be against his client's best interests (Frank 1963). Even Cicero boasted of his prowess as a lawyer in winning lawsuits for clients which they should have lost and would have lost but for his clever persuasive strategies in the courtroom.

In the United States, the lawyer's behavior is supposedly governed by a Canon of Ethics. Canon 22, for example, addresses itself to the falsification and improper use of evidence in the courts.

> *Canon 22*
>   It is not candid or fair for the lawyer knowingly to misquote the contents of a paper, the testimony of a witness, the language or the argument of opposing counsel, or the language of a decision or a textbook; or with knowledge of its invalidity, to cite as authority a decision that has been overruled, or a statute that has been repealed; or in argument to assert as a fact that which was not proved, or in those jurisdictions where a side has the opening and closing arguments to mislead his opponent by concealing or withholding

positions in his opening argument upon which his side intends to reply.

It is unprofessional and dishonorable to deal other than candidly with the facts in taking the statements of witnesses. . . . and in the presentation of causes.

A lawyer should not offer evidence which he knows the Court should reject in order to get the same before the jury by argument for its admissibility, nor should he address to the judge arguments upon any point not properly calling for determination by him. Neither should he introduce into argument, addressed to the court, remarks or statements intended to influence the jury or bystanders. (Countryman and Finman 1966)

The lawyer begins, in his attempt to produce the facts before the jury and/or judge, by examining his own and prosecution witnesses. Extracting facts from witnesses is not a simple process. As time passes, a witness is likely to forget or distort events (Hintzman 1965). Time and intervening events may contribute to distortion or change not only in recall of events themselves, but also in their importance in relation to other events. As Frank (1963) suggests, no witness can be expected to be more than fifty percent correct even if he is perfectly honest. One of the chief aims of the cross-examiner is to demonstrate the fallibility of witnesses' memories. What you and I see when two people walk down a street is not the identical two people or streets, but people and streets fashioned from our respective experiences with them. If people of different educational and intellectual levels make the same observation, their testimony regarding that event will be very different.

It has been found that "at the time of exposure, and for a few tenths of a second thereafter, observers have two or three times as much information available as they can later report. The availability of this information declines rapidly . . ." (Sperling 1960). This "forgotten" material is suppressed, repressed, or subliminal and may be brought back to consciousness by new stimuli such as direct cross-examination or testimony of other witnesses (Schiff 1961). The time interval between the crime and trial may be months or even years. The witnesses remembrances of the incident are subject to many stresses, the most important being the "curve of forgetting," a leveling-out process in which most of what happens is forgotten within a matter of hours or days.

Many witnesses rehearse their testimony between the time they observe an event and their presentation in court. The repetition of testimony may serve to facilitate retention of detail or to distort or enhance the details. Some witnesses are neither honest nor unprejudiced. They may be biased and their testimony is affected by their prejudices for or against one of the parties in the suit.

An experienced lawyer will use any number of strategies to minimize the effect on the jury or judge of testimony disadvantageous to his client, even when the lawyer has no doubt of the accuracy and honesty of that testimony. We must remember that counsel and court, through examination and instruction, induce the witness to abandon his habitual thought and expressions.

Let's say we have an honest witness being examined by the prosecution on direct examination. He answers questions promptly, candidly, and makes a good impression on the judge or jury. When cross-examined by the defense, his attitude and mode of expression change. He suspects that traps are being set for him; he hesitates and ponders the answer to a simple question; he creates the impression that he is evading or withholding evidence. The witness's demeanor becomes a basis for the jury to evaluate his testimony. The witness's face, posture, and changing expressions signal additional meanings of the facts to the jury. Longnecker (1913) advises that a lawyer try to prod an irritable but honest "adverse" witness into displaying his undesirable characteristics in their most unpleasant form, in order to discredit him with the judge or jury. The lawyer can sometimes destroy the effect of an adverse witness by making him appear more hostile than he really is. The lawyer attempts to develop within the mind of the jury or judge a perception of the witness that makes it difficult to evaluate between his truth or falsity, sincerity or insincerity, making the evaluation of a witness's credibility difficult, if not impossible.

Wigmore (1937) suggests a different line of attack for the lawyer in dealing with witnesses. The lawyer should put the questions in an intimidating manner in order to coerce or disconcert the witness into believing that his answers do not represent his actual knowledge of an event. Lewis Carroll's King of Hearts captured the lawyer's intimidating posture when he said to a witness: "Give your evidence, and don't be nervous, or I'll have you executed on the spot."

An attorney may present the witness with conflicting testimony made by himself or other witnesses. The contradictory statements may cause him to deny the existence of the conflict or dissonant statements. This denial reflects an ego-defensive attitude which causes him to block out recognition that contradictory statements are realities. Such behavior may discredit the witness in the eyes of judge and jury. If this approach is utilized, the lawyer is attempting directly to persuade the witness of his imperfectibility as an observer and persuade the jury to discount his testimony. The lawyer might also utilize questions which cause embarrassment, shame, or anger within the witness. If he can produce such affective states, the witness's demeanor or utterances may change and the subsequent statements would not be given their true value by judge or jury.

Since a witness's memory may be faulty and the destruction of his testimony may assist in persuading a jury against his particular position, the law allows for a "refreshment of recollection" conducted in the courtroom before judge and jury. It is also common for a form of memory refreshment to take place before the trial when the attorney prepares the case and interviews the witnesses. However, coaching sessions may persuade a witness of the facts in a case. The witness may fill in details of an accident he has never seen. While this may be a deliberate lie, it may also be a result of suggestions by the attorney whose position and credibility lend credence to his position. Thus, the blank spots which may be producing some incongruity are filled in and psychological balance returns to the witness.

Persuading a witness of the facts or getting him to draw certain conclusions is generally more subtle than we realize after years of watching Perry Mason. While a counsel may not lead his own witness, opposing counsel may suggest testimony under cross-examination by means of leading questions. Leading questions are allowed on cross-examination to test a witness's memory, veracity, and accuracy. It is not known how much the answers suggested by the cross-examiner distort a witness's observations. However, we do know that some people are more susceptible to suggestion than others. A person who is oriented to personalities, that is, an individual who tends to get cues for his beliefs and actions from people with authority or status or others from whom he can gain psychological support, is more susceptible to cues from individuals in the courtroom. For example, the authoritarian as low self-esteem witness may look to the judge, attorney, or another witness for the proper response. Witnesses are also influenced by what others have said in their presence or by how attorneys represent other witnesses' testimony.

A victim of a crime may be susceptible to suggestions by the police or district attorney because he is eager to find a likely object for his hostility. A witness for the prosecution in a criminal case usually wants to be helpful. Sometimes there is a threat, or at least he feels a threat, if he does not cooperate with the prosecutor. Accomplices and co-conspirators are particularly susceptible to pressures by the prosecution.

When a witness identifies with one side of the case, it is similar to becoming a member of that group. In effect the "group" is composed of the party and witnesses on the side of the case for which he identifies.

We know there is a tendency to assume the beliefs of members of the group with which we identify. So, too, a witness may support the beliefs of his side by interpreting his observations according to the group's beliefs.

The lawyer is concerned not only with influencing the behavior of witnesses, but also evaluating evidence in terms of how it will affect the judge or jury. He must prejudge how his opponents will interpret testimony gained from witnesses. He must be aware of how his construction of reality will appear to judge and jury. The final test for the lawyer is: Will a witness or piece of evidence successfully persuade the judge or jury to be favorable to his case?

The lawyer has the task of bringing about change. He must bring the judge and jury to a supportive attitude. We have noted that one effective way of bringing about change is to involve the receivers in the planning and installing of change. While the judge and jury cannot be involved in this process, they can be involved emotionally by stimulating a need, a motive to change their present attitudes.

When conflicting evidence is presented to a jury or judge, they must resolve the dissonance caused by the apparent contradiction. A counsel may get the jury to forget the evidence by ignoring it or belittling it so that it appears irrelevant, unworthy of consideration. If we feel a piece of evidence has little or no value, then we are relieved of whatever conflict it has caused.

The counsel may attempt resolution by differentiation. For example, a man is accused of driving his car down the middle of a highway or reckless driving. However, the attorney makes it clear that the plaintiff was not just reckless in running to the middle of the highway but trying to save the life of a dog. The facts are differentiated according to the specific situation. The process of differentiation may not merely resolve a conflict, it may at times change the jurors' attitudes. In our previous example, the jury may change from a negative to a positive attitude regarding the plaintiff, because he is perceived as a warm, compassionate lover of animals.

One effective way to change attitudes is to add social support to reinforce acceptance of a desired change. The degree of social support that a concept yields is related to the source of that concept. The lawyer may be so acceptable to the jury that his words alone provide the juryman the support necessary to reduce his conflict and change his attitude. He may present evidence in such a way that questionable testimony is supported by corroborating witnesses, documents, photographs, and so on.

The lawyer is most successful if he introduces the contradictions, inaccuracies, falsifications of the opposing witnesses, or the weakness of his opponent's interpretations after he establishes a supportive relationship between himself and the jury. A lawyer is like a salesman who must establish his own credibility prior to criticizing his competitor's product.

The key element in the courtroom persuasive process is the receiver (judge or jury). The lawyer's persuasive strategies can be successful only so long as the judge or jury will listen and understand their implications. We will now turn our attention to the role of the jury in the courts.

The Jury

Balzac once defined the jury as "twelve men to decide who has the better lawyer." There is little doubt that the jury is one of the most incredible and exasperating elements in the judicial process. A jury is a group of citizens of predetermined number called together for the purpose of answering a question: Is the defendant innocent or guilty? While more and more cases are decided by judges sitting without a jury, the jury is still widely used as the decision-making element in the courts.

Theoretically, every voting age adult is eligible for jury duty unless he has served more than a year in prison on a criminal charge and has not been pardoned for the offense. In reality, it is not only easy to avoid jury duty, but entire groups within our society are exempt either by law or by custom. Occupational groups having almost automatic exemption are lawyers, physicians, pharmacists, clergymen, teachers, and others in similar capacities. Notice that we have eliminated the best educated and possibly the most intelligent groups in society. But do lawyers want men and women whose training will best enable them to understand the facts of the case? No! (Frank 1963) Other busy or employed individuals can normally avoid jury service by submitting affidavits of indispensability from employers or family.

If none of the reasons cited is acceptable to the court, an individual can still avoid jury duty by confessing to any number of disqualifying factors during jury selection; for example, confession of prejudice for or against one of the litigants, acquaintance with either party to the suit, or opposition to certain pertinent philosophies of life involved in the case. Jurors can also be removed for a myriad of other reasons by appropriate challenges by the defense or prosecuting attorneys. These challenges have frequently delayed impaneling a trial jury for days or even weeks (Abraham 1962).

Erlich (1964) notes that "choosing a jury is a dangerous business. At best, the trial lawyer approaches a buried, five thousand pound bomb. . . . if he has remembered what he was taught in demolition school—the bomb will be reduced to a harmless cannister. If not, there will be an explosion that will reduce his client, and himself, to a large, smoking hole in the ground." Erlich, one of the most successful lawyers in American judicial history, also gives some insight into how many lawyers proceed in their selection of suitable jurors.

> Some lawyers never select any one with an obvious, serious, somber, or sour disposition. Instead they prefer smiles. This is an obvious conclusion and it's frequently correct. . . . Other attorneys are wary of persons whose forebearers were English, German, or Scandinavian. These persons tend to believe in absolute law enforcement and severe punishment for anyone who runs afoul of the law . . . The outdoor or athletic type can take either side and if you can convince him, he will espouse your cause till hell freezes over. . . . Jews are acceptable only if the crime is a minor one. The Jew is severe if the crime is one of violence. A brief examination of the cultural background of the Jew will explain his reasons for being severely opposed to violence. However, if the Jew is a man who is making his living as a bouncer in an East Oakland bar, you may do well to consider him as a favorable juror in an assault and battery case. . . . One hard-and-fast rule that has served me well is this: Never accept a wealthy person if the client is poor, nor a poor person, if the client is wealthy. . . . A businessman is not the best juror if the client is a labor official, nor is the person who is in debt a good juror if the client is a banker or an official of a loan company. . . . A Southerner is often a good juror if the client is a Negro, because the Southerner will often best understand the Negro's problems. . . . Actors and salesmen are almost always desirable; they have seen all sides of life and know the meaning of misfortune and suffering. By the same token writers and artists would also qualify as good jurors. And, of course, so would older men; the older man is more charitable, more understanding and forgiving than the young man. . . . (pp. 109-18)

The typical jury selected will contain twelve men and/or women, augmented by one or more alternates who sit through the course of the trial. Each juror is presumed to listen impartially; may not discuss the trial with anyone; and, at least in theory, is not permitted to read, view, or hear any media dealing with the trial.

There are three basic theories that attempt to explain the methods under which a jury functions:

1. *Naive theory*—the jury merely finds the facts; that is, it does not concern itself with legal rules, but faithfully accepts and applies the rules as stated by the trial judge.
2. The jury not only finds the facts, but applies legal rules it learns from the judge to those facts.
3. *Realistic theory*—the jury is neither able to, nor attempts to, apply the instructions of the court. For example, pretty Grace Brown kills her husband who has committed adultery. The jury believes one should not go to jail for killing an adulterous husband and brings in an innocent verdict. The judge's statement of legal rules (proof of homicide demands a guilty verdict) would be of no value with this type of jury operating. (Frank 1963)

The testimony presented to a juror in a live courtroom is embedded in a rich stimulus field. At a given moment, he may be attending to the verbal and nonverbal behaviors of the witness, the facial expressions of the lawyers, judge, or defendant, a conversation between one of the attorneys and his client, the murmured remarks of spectators, the attractive legs of a female juror seated next to him, or any number of other stimuli.

Jury members reveal four different trends or determinations in their evaluation of the facts (Weld and Roff 1938). First, there is, in a few jurors, a predetermination, an attitude of doubt, which is assumed at the beginning of the trial and maintained as long as possible; this juror will not reach a judgment until he hears all the evidence. Second, there is the juror who is easily swayed by new evidence. Third, some jurors have a tendency to be cautious, deliberative, to balance old and new evidence, and even to anticipate the possibility of future evidence. Fourth, we have the juror who has determined his judgment prior to the closing arguments or presentation of all evidence.

During the trial, jurors are not permitted to take notes. After the jury listens to the testimony and closing arguments by both attorneys, the jury is presented with its charge by the judge. The judge attempts to provide instructions that are fair to both sides in the dispute. Under certain limited circumstances, a judge may express value judgments on the evidence in charging the jury, but this is valid only in isolated cases. He is not to persuade the jurors to make a specific decision. Should he show bias or influence the jurors, it may create a mistrial. The judge's charge is almost always complicated, it sums up the case, pin-points the chief issues involved, and concludes with an admonition that the jury must bring in a verdict of "guilty" or "not guilty"—addressing itself to each charge and/or counts at issue, and, if a choice is permissible under law in homicide cases, determine the degree of punishment.

The jurors must take the judge's charge and retire for deliberation until they reach a verdict. The judge's charge can create a problem because it is worded in the language of the law. As Frank (1963) states: "Juries have the disadvantage of being treated like children when testimony is going on, but then being doused with a kettle full of law, during the charge, that would make a third year law student blanch. . . . If jurors do not understand those words and phrases, and consequently do not apply those rules, then reliance on the rules is unreliable."

It has been estimated that jurors listening to lengthy judge's instructions remember or understand no more than five percent of the material presented. Forston found, however, that individual jurors retain and comprehend about two-thirds of the instructions. Jurors are more efficient as listeners in civil than criminal situations. Face-to-face deliberating juries have the highest level of listening efficiencies: civil (80.6 percent) and criminal (82.9 percent). This study suggests that juries do retain and comprehend a judge's instructions at a higher level than anticipated (Forston 1970).

The whole nature of the deliberation and weighing of evidence by the jury is contrary to the way one makes many decisions in ordinary life. The jury applies legal rules to evaluate the evidence. However, the standards are given *after* all the evidence has been presented. Ordinarily, we apply standards to experiences as they occur. The juror is forced to recollect and reassemble the separate "facts" and fit them into the rules. If the trial is of any length, this requires extraordinary memory on the juror's part. Facts surveyed in mass are apt to confuse and dis-tort the juror's perception of the case. Juries are expected to weigh the relevant evidence, ignore immaterial information, and illegitimate sources of information. However, in one examination of jurors, it was found that four-fifths of the deliberating juries could not correctly answer one or more questions regarding the nature of evidence presented (Forston 1970). Deficient memory of the testimony that has taken place in the courtroom can lead to error later on, in the jury room. It is almost impossible for the wandering mind of the juror to overcome conclusively the dramatics that so often characterize presentation of counsel. To arrive at the truth one observer of juries remarked, "The curtain of flimflam and obfuscation, may well boil down to a jury verdict on the basis of which side, in its judgment, seemed to tell fewer lies."

Sometimes a jury will lack some knowledge or perception of some fact necessary to reach a particular conclusion. This can create a sense of incongruity with respect to known data. In order to dispel this incongruity, the jury may fill the gap by creating further data. Rumor or gossip may be used to fill this gap. The rumor may justify some fear or stress that the jurors have. It also may justify either hostile or affirmative feelings a juror has against one of the parties, witnesses, or attorneys.

In addition, the juror is not able to withdraw to a private room or office for solitary reflection on the evidence. At the close of the trial, jurors are pressed for time in reaching a group decision. If, after a reasonable period of time, the jury is unable to arrive at a verdict of guilt or acquittal, the judge will dismiss the jury, and remit the case to be tried before an entirely different judge and jury.

Throughout our discussion of the jury, we have mentioned problems dealing with the language of the law, the lawyer's presentations, and the complex of environmental stimuli affecting the juror. We will now examine the message and its role in courtroom decision making.

The Message

We have seen that the principal sources of messages in the courtroom are the lawyers and witnesses. However, the witnesses' messages are controlled by the lawyer during direct examination and cross-examination.

For some time the language utilized by lawyers during the questioning of witnesses has been under attack by the legal profession and laymen alike. It has been said that lawyers use written words and sentences as if they were spoken orally. It is a truism to say that what is well spoken may have an abdominable written style and vice versa. Oral style involves two or more persons interacting. On the other hand, written style is what lawyers call an "ex parte proceeding"—only one side is presented. There is no opportunity in writing, as in talk, for instantaneous question and reply. When an address is in an oral-written style, particular words are presented one by one before the reader's eye and each must make its point or fail, for there is no chance for clarification when a misunderstanding arises.

Lavery (1921) pointed out that the written communication of the lawyer is "prolix and muddy in his literary style and is given to the overuse of words." In oral presentations lawyers usually multiply terms in order to express facts precisely. Precision consists in the use of many words rather than a few. The prolixity of lawyers may be caused by the inherent complexity of subject matter, and an impelling urge toward guarded and cautious language. Lawyers use circumlocution, rather than straight, blunt speech.

Despite the fact that the mass of language used by lawyers is ordinary English, laymen are certain that law language is not really English. In fact, the language lawyers utilize in oral presentations is different from the nonlawyer (laymen) oral language. Mellinkoff (1963) has listed nine obvious differences in language style that can lead to misunderstanding on the part of the jury.

1. Frequent use of common words with uncommon meanings. For example, prayer means a form of pleading request addressed to the court or action means a law suit.
2. Frequent use of old or middle English words once in use but now rare; for example, thence, aforesaid, forthwith.
3. Frequent use of Latin words and phrases; for example, *caram nobis*. Some of the Latin has become an accepted part of the English language, for example, affidavit, alibi.
4. The use of French words not in our general vocabulary.
5. The use of terms of art, that is, the use of a technical word with specific meaning.
6. The use of *argot* or a specialized legal vocabulary.
7. The frequent use of formal words; for example, I do solemnly swear that I . . .
8. Deliberate use of certain words and expressions with flexible meaning.
9. Attempts by the lawyer to have extreme precision in language usage.

In addition to these obvious differences in language use, the lawyer also has certain stylistic mannerisms that characterize his presentation before the court:

1. He is wordy.
2. He is generally unclear. The language of the law is full of long sentences, awkward constructions, and "fuzzy-wuzzy words."
3. His presentation is rather pompous. The language gives an air of importance out of proportion to the substance of what is said.
4. His presentations are usually quite dull. This is an effect of the wording, unclear presentation, and pomposity of the oral presentation.

The language and its manner of presentation share the imperfections of common language and language itself. While it can be more exacting, better used, more refined than common language, it can never become precise as long as it is used as an instrument for interpersonal communication (Mellinkoff 1964).

Let us move from our discussion of the language in the courtroom to the types of messages used and their possible effect upon the jury.

An individual who has personal knowledge of a case is not qualified to serve on a jury. In order to determine if jurors possess this information, they must be told to a limited degree the facts of the case. This information is provided partially by both prosecution (first) and defense (second) through a process known to the lawyers as *voir dire* examination. Thus, prior to their selection as members of the jury, jurors are given some factual information by both sides which may ultimately be used in their decision making.

After the jury is selected, the defense and prosecution make a second communication to the jury. This communication is known as the opening statement and once again the prosecution goes first, followed by the defense. These statements are in narrative form and describe the events leading to the litigation. Usually, the attorneys' opening statements attempt to outline the evidence that will be presented through the testimony of witnesses. The court does not permit either side to draw inference from facts, to present argumentation, or to attempt to persuade the jury to adopt its position on an issue.

After the opening statements are made, the attorneys begin to present the evidence through the testimony of witnesses. The prosecution does present its evidence first. The advantage of the prosecution's going first may be offset by the manner in which the witnesses are examined. In addition, the defense is permitted to cross-examine the witness immediately following the prosecution's examination of the witness. In courts allowing a broad scope of cross-examination—questioning on any matter relevant to the case, without regard to the intent of the witness's testimony on direct examination—the defense can elicit from the witness, through suggestive questions, his position on a particular point prior to the prosecution. After the prosecution has presented all its evidence under these conditions, the defense calls its witnesses and the trial proceeds in the same manner with the order of examination reversed. Lawson (1969) suggests that it is not until after this stage of the trial proceedings that either side has a substantial advantage of the first position.

If the testimony of a witness is false, cross-examination is the first step toward its destruction. The jury usually listens more attentively to cross-examination than direct examination. Some lawyers put too much of themselves and too little of the witness into the direct testimony. The lawyer who begins and ends by shouting may achieve the result of underscoring the important parts of testimony. A lawyer, by having the witness repeat the whole story from beginning to end, sometimes brings out the phonographic record quality of a coached witness. When the lawyer uses indignation, shouting, or belligerent hostility, a jury may regard the combat as unequal because of the skill and experience of the lawyer. Its sympathies may come to reside with the underdog or witness (Wellman 1936).

During the presentation of evidence by both sides, the attorneys are not permitted to ask argumentative questions or to address the jury in any manner. However, questions can be put to a witness under cross-examination, in argumentative form, and often have a greater effect upon the minds of the jury than the same line of reasoning where reserved for the summing up. The juror sees the point for himself, as if it were his own discovery, and clings to it all the more tenaciously. A lawyer should never ask a witness a question on cross-examination unless he knows the answer or doesn't care what the answer will be. This is the principle of a lawyer who claimed that the result of most trials depended upon which side perpetrated the greater blunders in cross-examination. Certainly no lawyer would ask a critical question unless he was reasonably sure of the answer (Wellman 1936).

During the examination of witnesses, jury members may be exposed to prejudicial, legally inadmissible testimony. It is generally assumed that such inadmissible testimony has an influence on juror decision making, even though the judge may order the jury to disregard it. Moreover, the general belief seems to be that the influence exerted is detrimental to the victim of the inadmissible testimony. For example, if a prosecuting attorney elicits from a witness a damaging inadmissible remark, it increases the likelihood of the jury's returning a guilty verdict.

In some instances, stricken testimony may indeed be injurious to its intended victim; inadmissible testimony that derogates the defendant may increase the probability of a guilty verdict, or stricken remarks against a prosecution witness may enhance the likelihood that the jury will return a verdict of not guilty. However, consider another possible outcome of the stricken testimony. The typical juror, while not highly conversant with the legal system, enters the courtroom with certain expectations about what will transpire. One of his expectations is that legal communication is highly rule-governed; in other words, there exist established standards which dictate the appropriate form and content of courtroom communication. The juror observes these standards being violated by the introduction of inadmissible testimony. Rather than strengthening the case of the attorney who elicits the testimony, the effect may be entirely the opposite. The juror may perceive that the eliciting attorney is incompetent, or ignorant of the appropriate communication rules, or unethical and deliberately violating established courtroom standards. To the extent that the attorney's credibility affects the juror's judgments of the case's merits, his elicitation of inadmissible testimony may be damaging to his client's case (Miller 1972). The jury may try the lawyer rather than his client. The jurors allow their opinions to be swayed in favor of the side represented by the lawyer they like rather than the testimony presented in the courtroom.

Through this stage of the trial, the attorneys have dealt with factual information. However, the presentation of information does not involve only the testimony of witnesses. Lawyers will present demonstrative evidence before the jury or judge, which is evidence imparted directly to the senses without the intervention of testimony. Demonstrative evidence may be used with witness testimony. For example, a medical doctor may use an X-ray as part of his testimony. However, the oral testimony must conform to the exhibit. Demonstrative evidence is used many times for reproduction. A jury is not present at an accident or homicide. He must be given the evidence second-hand. In criminal cases, the "deadly" weapon is a more dramatic piece of evidence than oral testimony. Knives, guns, blackjacks, saws, ice-picks, and every conceivable or usable instrument of death have been offered and received for jury inspection because, despite their emotional impact, they are factual. Belli (1954) suggests that a jury is more likely to vote in favor of factual proof rather than for personality, whether that of the litigant or lawyer.

Upon completion of the examination period, the attorney's communications turn from being primarily factual and informative to being argumentative and persuasive. The lawyers are permitted to draw inferences from the evidence to support their position. These communications—"closing arguments"—constitute the final presentations to the jury prior to deliberation. "It is at this stage of the proceedings that the order of presentation would seemingly have its greatest significance" (Lawson 1969).

In our courts, the accused is presumed to be innocent until proven guilty. Therefore, it is the prosecutor's role to persuade the jury that the accused is guilty "beyond all reasonable doubt." Thus, since the burden of proof rests with the prosecution, he is provided with the last word to the jury before their deliberations. The defense precedes the prosecution in presenting closing arguments. The law assumes that the last word to the jury is the best word (law of recency). The last argument is thought to be more effective because the prosecution can refute the arguments of the defense and the jury will remember the refutation at the time of making its decision.

We have already seen that the argument for primacy or recency is situationally specific. A primacy effect might result for the prosecution since he is first to present the information to the jurors, except that the facts are presented in an informational format, not an argumentative or persuasive style. The persuasive communication comes after the jury has been provided with background information on the issue. It is possible that this factual information operates against the primacy effect in the criminal trial.

However, Lana (1961) found that increased familiarity produces increased primacy effects. The communication presented first, whether pro or con, is more effective the more familiar the subject is with the topic. The situation in which Lana found the primacy effect is similar to the courtroom. There was an absence of predisposed opinion. The type of information provided before the persuasive communications was purely factual. The receiver knew that a controversy existed and that two communications would be heard. The decision makers made their decision immediately following the last communication. This would support the possibility of a primacy effect operating in the criminal trial. Thus, the defense has a definite advantage over the prosecution.

The messages are evaluated by the jury. This evaluation is governed by the jury's attitudes and determinations, the weight given to the testimony of witnesses, and the closing arguments of opposing lawyers. The weighing of messages is influenced by the character of witnesses, the credibility of the attorneys, the order of presentation, the amount of evidence retained or even understood, the method of presenting evidence (demonstrative or oral), and the reasonableness or unreasonableness of the "facts."

In the final analysis, successful courtroom persuasion is dependent upon the tactics of the lawyers, the evidence presented, understanding how to evaluate the messages, and the personalities of the jurors. Ideally, scientific or logical laws would exist for determining rationally the persuasive effect of the lawyer, judge, witnesses, or messages. However, no such laws exist. We can never be certain exactly what will happen in a specific courtroom. No set of rules has been developed to guarantee the lawyer's success in persuading a particular jury to a specific course of action.

Additional Readings

Marshall, J. "The Evidence: Do We See and Hear What Is? Or Do Our Senses Lie?" *Psychology Today* 2 (1969): 48-52. The article examines a number of problems which can lead to the inaccurate presentation of facts in the courtroom.

Mellinkoff, D. *The Language of the Law.* Boston: Little, Brown, and Company, 1963. The text tells what the language of the law is, how it got that way, and how it works in practice.

10

Persuasion and
the Classroom

We walk into a college classroom, look around at the room and the students in it, note the orderly arrangement of chairs, and notice the instructor standing behind a lectern. It is not an entirely new experience, because we have all had classes of one type or another before, and have all formed attitudes and opinions about them. In fact, our reaction to the entire class (students, subject matter, and teacher) will be influenced by our past school experiences. We try to fit course materials into cognitive patterns we have developed for prior classes. The language we use in school, the amount of information we have about the subject matter, and the opinions of others with whom we interact will all affect our reactions in a classroom environment. Our attitudes and behaviors toward the teacher and the classroom are influenced not only by all our past encounters but also by what the teacher appears to be or says and how we presently perceive the classroom. Past and present experiences and future expectations will all affect the potential influence of a classroom situation upon our attitudes and behaviors.

When we began our course in persuasion, our past experiences led us to a number of conclusions about what a "good class" or "good teacher" is. The atmosphere was informal and relaxed, students were free to express their opinions and criticize course materials. The teacher didn't lecture, he led discussions. He wasn't limited to his own "pet" theories. He wasn't pedantic about written assignments, class setting, or response formats. During the first class meeting, everything the teacher said, the language he used, the way he dressed, the method he used to conduct the class, and the way he responded to student questions all led to our own unique perception of the class. This perception affected the value we assigned to the class and the quality of the materials presented. If our evaluation was positive, we accepted and internalized the ideas presented by the teacher. If our evaluation was negative, we may have accepted the class structure and ideas to comply with class requirements merely in order to derive a high grade (reward). In both cases the teacher and classroom environment led to a change in our attitudes, opinions, and behaviors within the classroom.

The most powerful formal system of influence or persuasion in any society is education. And yet, until the student disturbances of the late sixties, most people failed to recognize the instructional system as an environment of persuasion. Unfortunately, only the overt acts of political persuasion were observed and reacted to by the general public. The inherent persuasive nature of the classroom environment continues to be recognized by only a few.

If we examine the educational policies of other countries, the persuasive nature of education is more apparent. For example, the British schools of the eighteenth and nineteenth centuries molded students into efficient administrators for exercising control over Britain's numerous colonies. However, the extent of educational persuasive efforts is more apparent in countries under authoritarian rule. In the USSR, schools espouse one common political and social philosophy preparing students for well-defined agricultural, technological, and managerial classes; Red Chinese students have intensive vocational training combined with Maoist doctrine and Marxist materialism.

Education also provides the vehicle for dissociating present events from past events. In Russia and China, present educational policies and philosophies separate the influences of pre-revolutionary from post-revolutionary practices. Prior events are reinterpreted or rewritten to reflect the existing political philosophies. In ancient Greece, the birthplace of democracy, the basic principles of education, being part of politics, were a function of the state. The Greek state trained its young for its own welfare. Aristotle viewed education as an art for shaping children to "love that which they ought to love and hate that which they ought to hate."

Early Americans believed that a fundamental prerequisite for democracy was education. Education was the tool for providing wise government. As the nineteenth century progressed, the need to provide merely an enlightened electorate became less important. It became obvious that voters did not need a formal educational background to nominate or elect superb governmental representatives. On the other hand, the technological revolution required the training of individuals with specialized skills. In the twentieth century, the character of education has changed to reflect the changing needs of society. In general, public education has served the socially acceptable purpose of preparing people for public health, social work, teaching, and government (Gordon 1971). The Sputnik challenge of the late fifties and early sixties provided the impetus for training thousands in the physical and engineering sciences. Educational reformers developed programs that clearly coincided with the growing materialism in America at large. As our society became more complex technologically and socially, the length of schooling necessary for coping with new jobs became longer and training became more specialized. The Educational Policies Commission (1961) stated:

> In any democracy education is closely bound to the wishes of the people, but the strength of this bond in America is unique. The American people have traditionally regarded education as a means for improving themselves and their society. Whenever an objective has been judged desirable for the individual or the society, it has tended to be accepted as a valid concern of the school. The American commitment to the free society—to individual dignity, to personal liberty, to equality of opportunity—has set the frame in which the American school grew. . . . The schools have been designed also to serve society's needs. The political order depends on responsible participation of individual citizens; hence schools are concerned with good citizenship; the economic order depends on ability and willingness to work; hence the schools have taught vocational skills. The general morality depends on choices made by individuals; hence the schools have cultivated moral habits and upright character. (pp. 1-2)

It is beyond the scope of this text to investigate educational philosophy in terms of its persuasive impact on society. Rather, we will explore in the remainder of this chapter the persuasive nature of the classroom.

The classroom process possesses all the elements of the persuasive model in chapter 1. The teacher is the primary source and students the secondary sources of messages. The receiver is either the student (primary) or teacher (secondary). The messages are transmitted reciprocally

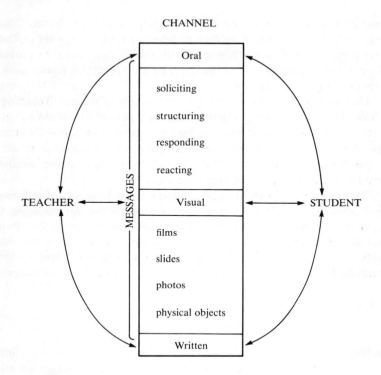

FIGURE 10-1.   The Classroom Persuasive Process

between teacher and student verbally or nonverbally. The principal channel of communication is oral. Visual aids, films, and slides are frequently utilized to support oral presentations. Most take-home assignments, on the other hand, are written responses to the teacher's instructional messages. We will be concerned with the verbal and nonverbal communication occurring within the classroom environment. Figure 10-1 depicts a model of the classroom process.

Teaching involves at least one teacher, at least one student, and the course subject matter. Teaching is, then, a triad of elements; it is not dyadic (teacher-student). It is impossible to teach persuasion theory to no one, or to teach students without subject matter. The type of subject matter can influence the methods of instruction utilized. If we examine the classroom model, we will notice a distinct difference between it and the courtroom model in the last chapter. The teacher and student are in a circular symbolic interaction process. When the teacher (source) transmits a message to the student (receiver), the student can become the source and transmit messages to the teacher (receiver). In the court-room, we have only a one-way flow of information from lawyer or judge to the jury. The jurors are never provided with the means to transmit oral or written messages to the lawyer. The only feedback from jurors to lawyers or judges is nonverbal.

How can we say that teaching is persuasive in nature? Teaching is a perfomance (by a teacher) that influences a person (student) to act in a certain way, deliberately specified by someone else (teacher). Further-more, the performance provides a means to enable the person to act in an appropriate manner on future occasions without being similarly prompted (eliciting of a specified response).

Sherif and Sherif (1956) suggest that it is the interplay of influences from within individuals and from social environments, for example, the classroom, which shapes any particular experience and behavior. Pupils adopt the standards of behavior and manners prescribed by the adult society and the teacher then becomes society's agent for enforcing these standards. The teacher plays a key role in formulating the experiences.

The Teacher

Teaching is a system of actions intended to induce learning (Smith 1961). It is a form of interpersonal influence aimed at changing the be-havior potential of another person (Gage 1962). Each behavior a teacher exhibits has a purpose (conscious and unconscious) which may be effec-tive in achieving its purpose to a greater or lesser degree. A teacher is usually judged as competent, however, only when his behavior achieves its intended effects.

The teacher establishes specific educational goals for his specific class of students dealing with a specified course content. He structures the method of instruction to direct and modify the students' conception of the course materials in order to reach the educational goal.

To fully comprehend the teacher's influence in the classroom we must understand the teacher-student interaction, and the specific condi-tions under which learning (change) is maximized (Flander 1963). A crucial element in maximizing learning is the *classroom climate*. Class-room climate refers to attitudes toward the teacher and class that stu-dents share in common despite individual differences. These attitudes are an outgrowth of classroom interaction. As a result of participating in classroom activities pupils develop expectations about how a teacher will act, what kind of person he is, and how they like a class. These expectations color all aspects of classroom behavior creating a social atmosphere or climate that becomes fairly stable, once established. The behavior of the teacher, more than any other individual, sets the climate of the class. A teacher's behavioral tendencies set a pattern generally followed by pupils even when the teacher is no longer present in the classroom. A domineering, authoritarian teacher incites further authoritarian behaviors by his students. A teacher who attempts more socially integrative behaviors, may have students who show more spontaneity and initiative, voluntary conclusions, and acts of problem solving. Teachers who use more dominative behaviors have students who show greater compliance to, as well as rejection of, teacher influence.

In the early school years, the teacher must use a good deal of direct, formalized persuasion to carry on the social reciprocity that is necessary to provide an effective learning environment. The failure of teachers to utilize this persuasion can result in their failure to create such a climate. Students who are not impressed by the precepts of their teachers may learn few of the facts and skills they are supposed to. They may not develop the desired social attitudes which they are expected to assimilate in school.

In the classroom, teacher-pupil interaction is essentially superior-subordinate in quality. The responsibility for classroom activities is with the teacher. Teachers and pupils generally expect the teacher to take charge, to initiate, and control the learning activities. The freedom to direct or not to direct the activities of students is initially given only to the teacher; whatever freedom the pupils have results from the actions of the teacher. While a student may ignore the authority of the teacher, it is difficult, if not impossible, for a student to escape the teacher's control.

The teacher possesses a high power position derived from several sources: age, society, and legally bestowed sanctions. Society expects that the teacher will do something to make the student learn. He has power to arrange the learning environment, to decide the content to which attention is to be given, what standards are to be maintained, and who is to do what. Also, the what and how of the distribution of rewards and punishments are teacher prerogatives. The teacher's acts in the interactive situation always have the latent power of punishment and even ultimate removal of students from the classroom. The teacher cannot act in the classroom without exercising influence. Getzels and Thelen (1960) state:

> If one thinks of authority, control, and leadership in political terms,
> it is clear that the classroom group, at least in its formal aspects,

is about as far from democracy as one can get. Not only do the students have no control over the selection of their leader, they normally also have no recourse from his leadership, no influence on his method of leadership beyond that granted by him, and no power over the tenure of his leadership. There are very few working groups in our society in which these essentially despotic conditions are legitimately so much the rule. (p. 56)

If the classroom interactive process is reciprocal in reality, logic requires that the student influences the classroom environment. However, student influence can only be known through the teacher's response to what the student says and does. For example, the teacher may respond by accepting, rejecting, or considering a student's statements or questions; by clarifying and elaborating the student verbalizations, and approving of or reproving the student. In effect, the teacher's control over the classroom environment is so pervasive that he or she alone can determine if a reciprocal system of interaction will be permitted within the classroom.

The teacher's actual influence may be related also to the pupils' perception of the learning goals and methods utilized in reaching that goal. We would assume that both teacher and student establish learning goals and work toward those goals. However, when the teacher's goals are unclear, the behavior of the student participating in identifying and clarifying the goals is determined by the real or imagined restraints of the teacher's control. When the goal is unclear, teacher influence increases, or at least maintains the dependence of the student on the teacher. The students' compliance behaviors are severely restricted. Compliance becomes less a matter of working on an interesting or uninteresting goal, and more a matter of the student's perception that he will receive approval or disapproval from the teacher who holds ultimate authority. If student goals differ from teacher goals (assuming the goals are clear), the student may behave in a manner contrary to that desired by the teacher. His behaviors may not comply with those that will gain teacher approval.

Gordon (1971) has differentiated between the teacher as educator (mediator of facts and skills) and the teacher as propagandist (agent of indoctrination). As a propagandist, the teacher may indoctrinate his students toward his subject matter and often society at large. The amount and necessity of propagandizing diminishes as the level of schooling becomes more advanced. In high school and college, it is expected that the need for propaganda decreases as students are competent in handling information and drawing relevant and logical conclusions from their inquiries. By graduate or professional school, the persuasion is usually limited to the precepts provided by the instructors (Gordon 1971). At the college level, it is assumed, perhaps erroneously, that students can recognize persuasive influences and evaluate their worth. This is particularly true of material presented by teachers that is not germane to the content of the course; for example, political philosophy. The inherent role relationship between teacher and student may negate the normal evaluation of ideas presented by the teacher in the classroom.

In the classroom, the college instructor is perceived as higher status than the college student. The role-status of the instructor will also function as a variant of the topic of conversation. Let's say that we are listening to a speech instructor discuss the effect of messages on persuasion. We would probably perceive him of high status and accept his ideas without much critical review. However, should he begin espousing the candidacy of a student for the student government, we are unlikely to give the teacher the same status or accept his views without carefully examining them.

The teacher's position in the communication setting is a major factor affecting how students perceive him. Since the teacher occupies the central position in the classroom communication network, the more he communicates, the more status and power should be attributed to him. The greater his power, the more communication he will initiate and the more power attempts he will not only try, but also complete successfully. Since a teacher realizes that his power is superior to that of the students, he will resist the influence attempts of the student.

We will now turn from our examination of the teacher as an agent of persuasion and look at the primary instrument used to activate an influence over the student in the classroom — messages.

The Message

Teaching cannot occur without the use of language. Teaching is above all a linguistic activity (Smith 1956). When we teach we use language. To perform many activities necessary to achieve the aims of teaching, the teacher needs the use of either oral or written language to communicate his ideas or feelings. This does not deny the presence or influence of nonverbal communication. Students, for example, raise their hands, nod their heads, smile, look drowsy, and appear puzzled. In addition to these behaviors, the teacher may point, snap a finger, or raise his eyebrows in order to communicate in the classroom. While nonverbal communication is a legitimate persuasive tool, the principal means of influence is oral and written language.

We realize from observations in elementary, secondary, and college classrooms that pedagogical methods are dependent upon verbal interaction between teacher and student. These interactions are of such a nature that they invite, encourage, or demand a response on the part of the individual addressed. Questions are asked to be answered; explanations are made to produce clarity; comments are made to indicate reactions to ideas presented. Since verbal interaction is a reciprocal process involving teacher and students, the communication by each can only be described in relation to the communication of the other.

The primary function of language is the communication of meaning. The meaning is determined by the situation in which the language is presented. Thus, the meaning of language in the classroom will differ from that of, for example, the courtroom. The adaptability of language allows it to function in various activities, environments, or "language games" (Wittgenstein 1958). Classroom discourse is a kind of language game within which one can identify how verbal expressions communicate various kinds of meanings.

Bellack (1966) has provided a descriptive model of what actually occurs verbally in the classroom. Figure 10-2 depicts this verbal interaction cycle. Structuring statements set the context for subsequent behavior by (1) launching or halting teacher-student interactions, and (2) indicating the time, agent, activity, topic and cognitive processes, regulations, reasons, and instructional aids. These statements may set the context for the entire classroom persuasive process. They indicate the interaction direction by launching classroom interaction in specified directions and by focusing topics, individuals, or problems to be discussed or procedures to be followed. They are established by the speaker's concept of what should be said or taught.

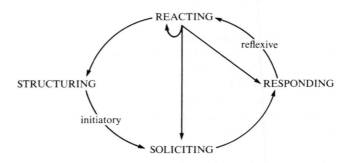

FIGURE 10-2.   Classroom Interaction Cycle

Soliciting verbal statements are intended to elicit (1) and active verbal response on the part of the person addressed; (2) a cognitive response; for example, encouraging individuals addressed to attend to something; or (3) a physical response. The statements are directive in intent, function, and crucial in any classroom interchange between teachers and students. In the classroom, the speaker of the solicitation is usually the teacher. The source expects a certain response from the receiver and he conveys the method of responding in the style of his solicitation. For example,

TEACHER: What affects attitude change?

Response occurs only in relationship to soliciting verbalizations. Their pedagogical function is to provide feedback on the desired solicitation and is, therefore, reflexive in nature. All solicitations are intended to elicit a response, and no response exists that has not been directly elicited by solicitation. For example,

TEACHER: What affects attitude change?
           (solicitation)
STUDENT: Source credibility.
           (response)

Reacting statements are *occasioned* by the structuring, soliciting, responding, or prior reacting statement, but are not elicited by them. Pedagogically, reacting statements serve to modify (clarify, synthesize, or expand) and/or to rate (positively or negatively) what was said to produce them. For example, a teacher's evaluation of a student's response is called reacting. His evaluation is occasioned by the student's response.

TEACHER: What affects attitude change?
STUDENT: Source credibility.
TEACHER: That's partly it. . . .
           (reacting)

The complete cycle begins with structuring followed by solicitation or solicitation without preceding structuring. The solicitation is usually followed by a response that provides occasion for reacting.

Bellack established five empirically based rules for teacher-student interaction:

1. The basic verbal interaction entails structuring and soliciting, which are initiatory moves; and responding and reacting which are reflexive moves. In terms of oral communication, reacting accounted for three-eighths of the comments and the remaining comments were equally distributed among the remaining three.

2. The teacher is the most active communicator in the classroom. He speaks most frequently and his comments are the longest (3:1 speaking ratio).

3. Teachers and students deviate from discussions of course content to tangential topics that are irrelevant to the subject material. The teacher usually initiates these discussions, sometimes for the purpose of introducing a substantive point. Students may introduce an irrelevant comment, but the frequency depends upon the reactions of the teacher. In general, discussion takes place within the substantive framework of the teacher's structuring.

4. The teacher and student generally use the empirical mode of thought (stating facts and explaining), rather than the analytic mode (defining terms and interpreting statements) when dealing with the materials under discussion. The amount of evaluative statements is also low in comparison to empirical statements. The teacher or student does, however, report opinions of others, such as public officials, or report arguments used by others to justify opinions.

5. In the classroom language game the teacher does not win while the student loses. Rather, there are degrees of winning and losing. The teacher's winnings are a function of the student's performance. While the teacher has greater power and freedom, he is ultimately dependent on his student for the success he achieves.

The soliciting-response pattern between teacher and student accounts for over three-fifths of the total verbal interaction. Typically, the pedagogical pattern of discourse consists of a teacher's solicitation followed by a student's response; this sequence is then followed by the teacher's reaction. The solicitation usually calls for the performance of a substantive task by one student at a time; a teacher rarely expects students to respond in unison (beyond the elementary levels). When he does ask for the performance of a multiple task, he may expect two similar information processes — but different logical processes, fact-finding and explaining. With instructional tasks, the teacher most often expects a form of oral recitation.

As the chief solicitor, the teacher normally attempts to provide cues regarding the appropriate verbal response from the student. Depending upon the student's initial response, the teacher may provide additional cues to either ask for the correction of statements, amplification of response, or to provide positive or negative reinforcements to their statements.

While the student's primary task is that of responding, he does at times solicit statements from the instructor. In most cases, the student is asking for the information which assigns truth to the teacher's statements. Frequently, he offers such cues as, "Don't you think that . . ." or "Is it true that . . .". A student will solicit a response from a teacher, rather than from a fellow student. This may be the result of the teacher's power in the classroom, his ability to reward or punish, his expertise, his high status, and his ability to increase a student's status within the class.

Let's apply our information on message variables from chapter 5 to the classroom environment. Keep in mind, however, that the research upon which we draw our hypotheses was not conducted in an educational context.

Teachers spend most of their time disseminating information to students. In most cases, the information is new to the student, and we might expect that the teacher will play a great role in creating many attitudes regarding subjects for which the student has no existing attitudes.

It is highly unlikely that a teacher will forewarn a student of his persuasive attempts, and thus he increases his chances for producing attitude and behavior change. Since students, at least on the college level, can be classified as intelligent, the teacher might influence his students more if he allows them to draw their own conclusions regarding his persuasive communication. If the conclusions are obvious, the student may feel the teacher is pampering him and resist the influence attempts. However, stating the conclusions might be successful if the teacher's message is highly complex.

Some teachers come to class well prepared, while others seem disorganized. We suggest that a disorganized teacher will produce less attitude change, but the lack of organization will probably not affect the students' comprehension of the communication. Students may lower the evaluation of the teacher if he appears to be disorganized, and thus diminish the teacher's persuasive efforts.

Teachers may attempt to present a more objective position during their persuasive attempt by providing more than one side of an issue. The issue placed first may be the most influential. A class session lasts from forty-five minutes to three hours. Since the attention span of students is rather limited, issues presented first might be attended to, whereas later issues will be disregarded. If, on the other hand, there is a time lag between the presentation of issues — for example, two class periods — the students may forget more of the first side and less of the second side presented. This particular effect may be tempered by note taking. In public speaking situations the audience rarely is prepared to transcribe the ideas of the speaker, however, in the classroom the student comes prepared to record the instructor's comments for later reference. This may negate any effect of time lag on the presentation of issues.

A teacher generally has the respect of the student, and thus the student will be influenced more when he presents the arguments for his position first followed by the arguments against his position. If a teacher has, over a semester, provided the students with acceptable ideas, the students may find themselves more responsive and less critical of the teacher's later views. If a teacher can establish the students' needs before his communciation and see that his communication satisfies those needs, his communication will be more acceptable to the student. Should students perceive the change as rewarding or satisfying or associated with something that is rewarding, they will tend to change in the desired direction. For example, a teacher gives a student an *A* for following his advice when writing a term paper (reward). The teacher then advises the student how to study for an exam. Since the student was rewarded the first time he followed the teacher's advice, he may be more accepting of the teacher's influence attempts the second time. We also suggest that the teacher has an advantage over the typical public speaker in ascertaining the needs of his receivers. The teacher generally spends some time counseling his students and can discover their specific needs.

The teacher must be as concerned with the information he uses as with how he orders that information. A teacher should be perceived to be a highly credible source and, therefore, does not profit as much from the use of evidence. However, the effect of including evidence may be topic related. A teacher attempting to influence students in his area of expertise may need little evidence to gain support, but when the teacher is dealing with subject matter outside his specialty, he may need the evidence before students will accept his influence attempt. In addition, should the teacher deliver the evidence poorly, his influence might be further lowered. We know that the educational level of the receiver plays a role in whether the source should use a one-sided or two-sided message. A college teacher, for example, should use a two-sided message to produce a change in attitudes since his receivers or students have a high level of education.

Classroom Control

The basic purpose of controlled learning is compliance; we are told that students need to be taught certain acceptable behaviors. The demand to comply is made upon students at all levels of education. Obviously, students have a predetermined notion of what is right and wrong. If a teacher feels his obligation in the classroom is to have students comply with what he believes, then the teacher may employ persuasive techniques when the student is reluctant to comply. Holt (1967) points out that teachers may employ coercion or punishment in the form of ridicule, sarcasm, physical punishment, withholding of approval and recognition, and withdrawal of affection and attention. He describes a variety of techniques teachers use to make students submit to their demands. For example, a student may be made to feel that survival in the classroom is predicated on acceptance and approval by the teacher. Unfortunately, the basic weapon for compliance is fear.

Let's apply our conclusions on the use of fear appeals in messages to the classroom environment. The research was not conducted in a classroom, but did involve an educational context. The effectiveness of fear appeals utilized by a teacher is related to a number of factors. If the teacher's communication is of little importance to the student— for example, participating in a student association—the use of a strong fear appeal will be more effective than a weak appeal in producing the desired behavior. Assuming that the teacher has high credibility, the use of high fear messages should be more effective than a low fear message. Since the teacher is generally regarded as high on the expertness dimension and relatively honest, the student would find it difficult to discredit the teacher's influence attempts. In addition, the student would have difficulty utilizing defense mechanisms to counter the teacher's fear appeals. For example, the teacher threatens to fail a student if he does not submit a paper. The student cannot rationalize away the failure. He must submit the paper or be penalized by the instructor.

The student's personality also affects the success of the teacher's fear appeals. A student who is confident in his own abilities would be more resistant to a teacher's use of fear appeals. On the other hand, a student who believes himself to be lacking in class abilities would be more affected by the teacher's appeals.

Unlike the speaking situation, the classroom environment may not provide any avenue for a student to avoid the consequences of a teacher's fear appeal. Thus, the degree of fear (high, medium, low) may not be important in the classroom. The use of fear appeals alone may produce student compliance.

While many educators believe that a predetermined set of conditions is necessary for subjects to learn and develop in a way valuable to themselves and society, control of the learning environment may be based on four erroneous assumptions (Lembo 1971).

1. Manipulation is needed for students to learn.
2. Adults know what students ought to learn.

3. There is a particular process of learning through which all students should be guided.
4. There is a particular level of learning and performance that all students need to achieve.

First is the assumption that students must be made to learn. Unless students are forced into specific behavioral patterns, they will not learn in the "correct" manner. As Lembo (1971) expresses it,

> The question is not "Is the management or arrangements of learning conditions a desirable practice?" Clearly, the arrangement of conditions is necessary for effective learning. Rather, the question is "How are conditions to be arranged?" More specifically, "Are conditions to be arranged for the purpose of helping the individual student learn and develop in personally satisfying ways, or are they to be arranged for the purpose of satisfying the needs of the instructor?"

When a student perceives the learning patterns to be irrelevant, he may devise strategies to avoid the learning activities. Coercion and punishment are needed to persuade students to perform activities that they perceive to be irrelevant. When the desired behavioral patterns are consonant with the student's predispositions to learn, the teacher's influence attempts will be successful, and coercion and punishment strategies will not be needed.

Second is the assumption that students are not experienced enough to realize what is important, useful, and of value. As we might guess, such an educational policy leads to a curriculum composed of facts, concepts, and issues which the teacher feels are necessary. The student may perceive the content of the learning process to have little relationship to his life. This usually means that the student will need more time and have difficulty in mastering difficult tasks. He may not learn what the teacher wants him to learn.

Third is the assumption that a single pattern of learning is appropriate for all learners. Research on individual differences indicates that no two students respond in the same manner to the identical influence attempt. Yet, many teachers are unwilling to give up old patterns of influence when they are inappropriate to their students' capabilities. Influence attempts will be more successful when the teacher plans and provides conditions in which each student can learn, and when he imposes a common set of objectives and procedures which compare that student's capabilities with those of other students.

Fourth is the assumption that a fixed standard of performance is applicable to all students regardless of individual differences in ability and motivation. Different rates and styles of students indicate that the use of a single criterion of achievement is unjustified.

As we have indicated, the educational system is a formidable persuasive tool. The classroom is an environment for initiating change and reinforcing previously held attitudes and behaviors.

Additional Readings

Bellack, A., et al. *The Language of the Classroom.* New York: Teachers College Press, 1966. The text presents the results of a three-year examination of classroom interaction.

Gordon, G. N. *Persuasion.* New York: Hastings House Publication, 1971. Pp. 152-70. A discussion of educational systems and policies as an agent for persuasion.

Bibliography

Abelson, R., and M. Rosenberg. "Symbolic Psycho-logic: A Model of Attitudinal Cognition." *Behavioral Science* 3(1958):1-13.

Abraham, H. J. *The Judicial Process.* New York: Oxford University Press, 1962.

Addington, D. W. "The Effects of Vocal Variations on Ratings of Source Credibility." *Speech Monographs* 38(1971):242-47.

Addis, B. "Media Credibility: An Experimental Comparison of the Effects of Film, Audio Tape and Written Communication on Beliefs in the Existence of Unusual Phenomena." Doctoral dissertation, University of Oklahoma, 1970.

Adorno, T., E. Frenkel-Brunswik, D. Levinson, and R. Sanford. *The Authoritarian Personality.* New York: Harper, 1950.

Allport, G. "Attitudes." In C. Murchison, ed. *Handbook of Social Psychology.* Worcester: Clark University Press, 1933. Pp. 798-844.

_____. *The Nature of Prejudice.* Cambridge: Addison-Wesley, 1954.

Allport, G. and H. Cantril. "Judging Personality from Voice." *Journal of Social Psychology* 5(1934): 37-54.

Allport, G. and L. Postman. "The Basic Psychology of Rumor." New York: Academy Science (Series 2) 8(1945): 61-81.

216

Allyn, J. and L. Festinger. "The Effectiveness of Unanticipated Persuasive Communications." *Journal of Abnormal and Social Psychology* 62 (1961):35-40.

Anast, P. "Personality Determinants of Mass Media Preferences." *Journalism Quarterly* 43(1966):729-32.

Anderson, D. C. "The Effect of Various Uses of Authoritarian Testimony in Persuasive Speaking." Master's thesis, Ohio State University, 1958.

Applbaum, R. L. and K. W. E. Anatol. "The Factor Structure of Source Credibility as a Function of Speaking Situation." *Speech Monographs* 39(1972):216-22.

Aronson, E. "Dissonance Theory: Progress and Problems." In R. Abelson, et al., eds. *Source Book on Cognitive Consistency.* New York: Rand McNally, 1968. Pp. 5-27.

Aronson, E. and B. W. Golden. "The Effect of Relevant and Irrelevant Aspects of Communicator Credibility on Opinion Change." *Journal of Personality* 30(1962):135-46.

Aronson, E., et al. "Communicator Credibility and Communication Discrepancy as Determinants of Opinion Change." *Journal of Abnormal and Social Psychology* 67(1963):31-36.

Back, K. "Influence through Social Communication." *Journal of Abnormal and Social Psychology* 46(1951):9-23.

Baker, E. B. "The Immediate Effects of Perceived Speaker Disorganization on Speaker Credibility and Audience Attitude Change in Persuasive Speaking." *Western Speech* 29(1965):148-61.

Barber, T., and D. Calverley. " 'Hypnotizability,' Suggestibility and Personality: IV. A Study with the Leary Interpersonal Checklist." *British Journal of Social and Clinical Psychology* 3(1964):149-50.

Bass, B. *Leadership, Psychology, and Organizational Behavior.* New York: Harper & Row, 1960.

Bass, B. and C. R. Wurster. "Effects of Company Rank of LGC Performance of Oil Refinery Supervisors." *Journal of Applied Psychology* 37(1953): 100-104.

Bastide, R. and P. Van Den Berghe. "Stereotypes, Norms and Interracial Behavior in Sao Paulo, Brazil." *American Sociological Review* 22(1957): 689-94.

Bauer, R. "The Obstinate Audience: The Influence Process from the Point of View of Social Communication." *American Psychologist* 19, May 1964.

————. "Personality, Perception of Source and Persuasibility." In W. H. Joseph, ed. *On Knowing the Consumer.* New York: John Wiley and Sons, 1966. Pp. 83-89.

Bauer, R., and D. Cox. "Rational Versus Emotional Communications: A New Approach." In L. Arons and M. May, eds. *Television and Human Behavior*. New York: Appleton-Century-Crofts, 1963.

Beighly, K. C. "An Experimental Study of the Effect of Four Speech Variables on Listener Comprehension." *Speech Monographs* 19(1952): 249-58.

Bell, W. "Consumer Innovators: A Unique Market for Newness." In S. Greyser, ed. *Proceedings of the American Marketing Association*, 1963, pp. 85-95.

Bellack, A., et al. *The Language of the Classroom*. New York: Teachers College Press, 1966.

Belli, M. *Modern Jury Trials*. Indianapolis: Bobbs-Merrill Company, Inc., 1954.

Belson, W. "Learning and Attitude Change from Viewing a Television Series,'Bon Voyage'." *British Journal of Educational Psychology* 26(1956):31-38.

Bem, D. J. "An Experimental Analysis of Self-persuasion." *Journal of Experimental Social Psychology* 1(1965):199-218.

_____. "Self-perception: An Alternative Interpretation of Cognitive Dissonance Phenomenon." *Psychological Review* 74(1967):183-200.

Bennis, W. G., et al. "Authority, Power, and the Ability to Influence." *Human Relations* 11(1958):143-55.

Berelson, B. "The Effects of Print upon Public Opinion." In D. Waples, ed. *Print, Radio, and Film in a Democracy*. Chicago: University of Chicago Press, 1942.

Berelson, B. and G. Steiner. *Human Behavior*. New York: Harcourt, Brace and World, 1964.

Berelson, B., P. Lazarsfeld, and W. McPhee. *Voting*. Chicago: University of Chicago Press, 1954.

Berkowitz, L. and D. Cottingham. "The Interest Value and Relevance of Fear-Arousing Communications." *Journal of Abnormal and Social Psychology* 60(1960):37-43.

Berkowitz, L. "Violence in the Mass Media." In *Studies in Communication*. Stanford: University of Paris and Stanford University, Institute for Communication Research, 1962. Pp. 117, 119.

Berkowitz, L. and D. R. Cottingham. "The Interest Value and Relevance of Fear-Arousing Communications." *Journal of Abnormal and Social Psychology* 60(1960):37-43.

Berkowitz, L. and R. Lundy. "Personality Characteristics Related to Susceptibility to Influence by Peers or Authority Figures." *Journal of Personality* 25(1957):306-16.

Berlo, D. K., J. B. Lemert, and R. J. Mertz. "Dimensions for Evaluating the Acceptability of Message Sources." *Public Opinion Quarterly* 33(1969-70):563-76.

Berscheid, E. "Opinion Change and Communicator-Communicatee Similarity and Dissimilarity." *Journal of Personality and Social Psychology* 4(1966):670-80.

Bettelheim, B. and M. Janowitz. *Dynamics of Prejudice: A Psychological and Sociological Study of Veterans.* New York: Harper, 1950.

Bettinghaus, E. P. "The Operation of Congruity in an Oral Communication Situation." *Speech Monographs* 28(1961):131-42.

————. *Persuasive Communication.* New York: Holt, Rinehart and Winston, 1968.

Bettinghaus, E. P. and J. R. Baseheart. "Some Specific Factors Affecting Attitude Change." *The Journal of Communication* 19(1969):227-38.

Bochner, B., A. Bochner, and D. Hilyard. "An Experimental Investigation of the Effect of Social Status and Social Dialect upon Listener Responses." Paper presented SCA convention San Francisco, 1971.

Bogart, L. *Strategy in Advertising.* New York: Harcourt, Brace & World, 1967.

Bostrum, R. N. and R. K. Tucker. "Evidence, Personality, and Attitude Change." *Speech Monographs* 36(1969):22-27.

Bowers, J. W. "Language Intensity, Social Introversion, and Attitude Change." *Speech Monographs* 30(1963):345-52.

————. "The Influence of Delivery on Attitudes toward Concepts and Speakers." *Speech Monographs* 32(1965):154-58.

Bowers, J. W. and W. A. Phillips. "A Note on the Generality of Source Credibility Scales." *Speech Monographs* 34(1967):185-86.

Boyd, H. and J. Newman. *Advertising Management.* Homewood, Ill.: Richard D. Irwin, 1965.

Brehm, J. and A. Cohen. *Explorations in Cognitive Dissonance.* New York: Wiley, 1962.

Brock, T. "Communicator-Recipient Similarity and Decision Change." *Journal of Personality and Social Psychology* 1(1965):650-54.

Browne, G. G. "A Study of Executive Leadership in Business: 1. The R, A, and O Scales." *Journal of Applied Psychology* 33(1949):521-26.

Bruner, J. "Social Psychology and Perception." In E. Macoby, T. Newcomb, and E. Hartley, eds. *Readings in Social Psychology.* New York: Holt, 1958. Pp. 85-94.

Buck, J. "The Effects of Negro and White Dialectal Variations upon Attitudes of College Students." *Speech Monographs* 35(1968):181-86.

Burgoon, M., G. Miller, and S. Tubbs. "Machiavellianism, Justification, and Attitude Change Following Counter-attitudinal Advocacy." *Journal of Personality and Social Psychology* 22(1972):366-71.

Burke, K. A. *A Rhetoric of Motives.* New York: Prentice-Hall, 1950.

Buss, L. "Motivational Variables and Information Seeking in the Mass Media." *Journalism Quarterly* 44(1967):130-33.

Byrne, D. "Interpersonal Attraction and Attitude Similarity." *Journal of Abnormal and Social Psychology* 62(1961):713-15.

Byrne, D., W. Gaiffitt, and C. Golightly. "Prestige as a Factor in Determining the Effect of Attitude Similarity-Dissimilarity on Attraction." *Journal of Personality* 34(1966):434-44.

Byrne, D. and C. McGray. "Interpersonal Attraction toward Negroes." *Human Relations* 17(1964):201-13.

Bryne, D., D. Nelson and K. Reeves. "Effects of Consensual Validation and Invalidation on Attraction as a Function of Verifiability." *Journal of Experimental Psychology* 2(1966):98-107.

Campbell, A., G. Gurin, and W. Miller. *The Voter Decides.* Evanston, Illinois: Row, Peterson, 1954.

Campbell, D. "The Generality of Social Attitudes." Doctoral dissertation, University of California, Berkeley, 1947.

Cannell, C. and J. MacDonald. "The Impact of Health News on Attitudes and Behavior." *Journalism Quarterly* 33(1956):315-23.

Cannan, G. *Satire.* London: G. H. Doran, 1914.

Caples, J. *Tested Advertising Methods.* New York: Harper and Row, 1961.

Carlson, E. "Attitude Change Through Modification of Attitude Structure." *Journal of Abnormal and Social Psychology* 52(1956):256-61.

Carment, D., C. Miles, and V. Cervin. "Persuasiveness and Persuasibility As Related to Intelligence and Extraversion." *British Journal of Social and Clinical Psychology* 4(1965):1-7.

Carmichael, C. and G. Cronkhite. "Frustration and Language Intensity." *Speech Monographs* 32(1965):107-11.

Carrigan, W. and J. Julian. "Sex and Birth-Order Differences in Conformity as a Function of Need Affiliation Arousal." *Journal of Personality and Social Psychology* 3(1966):479-83.

Carter, R. "Communication and Affective Relations." *Journalism Quarterly* 42(1965):203-12.

Carter, R. and B. Greenberg. "Newspapers or Television: Which Do You Believe?" *Journalism Quarterly* 42(1965):29-34.

Cartwright, D. "Some Principles of Mass Persuasion." In W. Vinacke, W. Wilson, and G. Meredity, eds. *Dimensions of Social Psychology.* Chicago: Scott, Foresman and Company, 1964.

Chapanis, N. and A. Chapanis. "Cognitive Dissonance: Five Years Later." *Psychological Bulletin* 61(1964):1-22.

Christie, R. "Some Consequences of Taking Machiavelli Seriously." In E. F. Borgatta and W. W. Lambert, eds. *Handbook of Personality Theory and Research*. Chicago: Rand McNally, 1968.

Christie, R. and F. Geis. *Studies in Machiavellianism*. New York: Academic Press, 1970.

Cohen, A. "Communication Discrepancy and Attitude Change: A Dissonance Theory Approach." *Journal of Personality* 27(1959):386-96.

————. *Attitude Change and Social Influence*. New York: Basic Books, 1964.

Cohen, J. "The Role of Personality in Consumer Decisions." In H. Kassarjian and T. Robertson, *Perspectives in Consumer Behavior*. Chicago: Scott, Foresman, 1968. Pp. 220-33.

Coleman, J., E. Katz, and H. Menzel. *Doctors and New Drugs*. New York: The Free Press of Glencoe, 1973.

Collins, G. and H. Guetzkow. *A Social Psychology of Group Processes for Decision-Making*. New York: John Wiley & Sons, 1964.

Cooper, E. and H. Dinerman. "Analysis of the Film 'Don't be a Sucker': A Study in Communication." *Public Opinion Quarterly* 15(1951):243-64.

Cooper, E. and M. Jahoda. "The Evasion of Propaganda: How Prejudiced People Respond to Anti-prejudice Propaganda." *Journal of Psychology* 23(1947):15-25.

Costanzo, P., H. Reitan, and M. E. Shaw. "Conformity as a Function of Experimentally Induced Minority and Majority Competence." *Psychonomic Science* 10(1968):329-30.

Countryman, V. and T. Finman. *The Lawyer in Modern Society*. Boston: Little, Brown, and Company, 1966.

Cox, D. "Clues for Advertising Strategists." *Harvard Business Review* 39 (Part I, Sept.-Oct. 1961) (Part II, Nov.-Dec. 1961).

————. "The Measurement of Information Value: A Study in Consumer Decision-making." In W. Decker, ed., *Emerging Concepts in Marketing*, Proceedings of the Winter Conference of the American Marketing Association, 1962, pp. 413-21.

Cox, D. and R. Bauer. "Self-Confidence and Persuasibility in Women." *Public Opinion Quarterly* 28(1964):453-66.

Crane, E. *Marketing Communications: A Behavioral Approach to Men, Messages, and Media*. New York: John Wiley and Sons, Inc., 1965.

Croft, R., et al. "Comparison of Attitude Changes Elicited by Live and Video-tape Classroom Presentation." *AV Communication Review* 17 (1969):315-21.

Cromwell, H. "The Relative Effect on Audience Attitude of the First versus the Second Argumentative Speech of a Series." *Speech Monographs* 17(1950):105-22.

Cronkhite, G. *Persuasion: Speech and Behavioral Change.* New York: Bobbs-Merrill, 1969. Pp. 184-85.

Daniels, D. "Humor in Advertising." In E. French, ed., *The Copywriter's Guide.* New York: Harper and Row, 1959.

Darnell, D. K. "The Relation Between Sentence Order and Comprehension." *Speech Monographs* 30(1963):97-100.

DeFleur, M. *Theories of Mass Communication.* New York: McKay, 1970.

Deutsch, M. and H. Gerard. "A Study of Normative and Informational Social Influences upon Individual Judgment." *Journal of Abnormal and Social Psychology* 51(1955):629-36.

Deutsch M. and R. M. Krauss. "The Effect of Threat upon Interpersonal Bargaining." *Journal of Abnormal and Social Psychology* 61(1960): 181-89.

_____. *Theories in Social Psychology.* New York: Basic Books, 1965.

Doob, L. *Propaganda: Its Psychology and Technique.* New York: Henry Holt and Company, 1935.

_____. *Public Opinion and Propaganda.* New York: Henry Holt and Company, 1948.

_____. *Public Opinion and Propaganda.* Hamden, Conn.: Archon Books, 1966.

Dresser, W. R. "Studies of the Effects of Satisfactory and Unsatisfactory Evidence in a Speech of Advocacy." Doctoral dissertation, Northwestern University, 1962.

_____. "Effects of 'Satisfactory' and 'Unsatisfactory' Evidence in a Speech of Advocacy." *Speech Monographs* 20(1963): 302-6.

Dunn, S. *Advertising Copy and Communication.* New York: McGraw-Hill, Inc., 1965.

_____. *Advertising: Its Role in Modern Marketing.* New York: Holt, Rinehart and Winston, 1969.

Educational Policies Commission. *The Central Purpose of American Education.* Washington, D. C.: N.E.A., 1961.

Ehrlichs, J. W. *A Reasonable Doubt.* Cleveland: World Publishing Co., 1964.

Eldersveld, S. "Experimental Propaganda Techniques and Voting Behavior." *American Political Science Review* 50(1956):154-65.

Elms, A. C. "Role Playing, Incentive, and Dissonance." *Psychological Bulletin* 68(1967):132-48.

Emery, F. and O. Oeser. *Information, Decision and Action.* New York: Cambridge University Press, 1958.

English, H. and A. English. *A Comprehensive Dictionary of Psychological and Psychoanalytical Terms.* New York: Longmans, Green and Company, 1958.

Epstein, G. "Machiavelli and the Devil's Advocate." *Journal of Personality and Social Psychology* 11(1969):38-41.

Erlich, D., I. Guttman, P. Schonbach, and J. Mills. "Postdecision Exposure to Relevant Information." *Journal of Abnormal and Social Psychology* 54(1957):98-102.

Evans, F. "Psychological and Objective Factors in the Prediction of Brand Choice: Ford versus Chevrolet." *Journal of Business* 32(October 1959): 340-69.

Feather, N. T. and D. J. Armstrong. "Effects of Variations in Source Attitude, Receiver Attitude, and Communication Stand on Reactions to Source and Content of Communications." *Journal of Personality* 35(1967):435-55.

Feiler, J. "Machiavellianism, Dissonance, and Attitude Change." Unpublished manuscript, New York University, 1967.

Feinberg, L. *Introduction to Satire.* Ames: Iowa University Press, 1967.

Feshbach, S. "Plan 6. The Effects of Aggressive Content in Television Programs upon the Aggressive Behavior of the Audience." In L. Arons and M. May, eds. *Television and Human Behavior.* New York: Appleton-Century-Crofts, 1963. Pp. 63-82.

Festinger, L. "Informal Social Communication." *Psychological Review* 57(1950):271-82.

_____*A Theory of Cognitive Dissonance.* Stanford: Stanford University Press, 1957.

Festinger, L., and J. Carlsmith. "Cognitive Consequences of Forced Compliance." *Journal of Abnormal and Social Psychology* 58(1959):203-10.

Festinger, L., et al. "The Influence Process in the Presence of Extreme Deviates." *Human Relations* 5(1952):327-46.

Festinger, L. and N. Maccoby. "On Resistance to Persuasive Communications." *Journal of Abnormal and Social Psychology* 68(1964):359-66.

Festinger, L., S. Schacter, and K. Back. *Social Pressure in Informal Groups.* New York: Harper, 1950.

Fishbein, M. "An Investigation of the Relationships between Beliefs about an Object and the Attitudes toward that Object." Technical Report No. 6. Los Angeles: University of California, 1961.

Fishbein, M., and B. Raven. "The AB Scales: An Operational Definition of Belief and Attitude." *Human Relations* 15(1962):35-44.

Flanders, N. A. "Teacher Influence in the Classroom." In Arno A. Bellack, ed., *Theory and Research in Teaching*. New York: Bureau of Publications, 1966. Pp. 37-52.

Forston, R. F. "Judge's Instructions: A Quantitative Analysis of Jurors' Listening Comprehension." *Today's Speech* 18(1970):34-38.

_____. "Does the Jury Understand? Usually Not." *Des Moines Sunday Register*, May 21, 1972, p. 15-C.

_____. "The Foreman Myth." *PAX Today*, No. 4, November 11, 1972.

Frank, J. *Courts on Trial*. New York: Atheneum, 1963.

Freedman, M. B. "Changes in Attitudes and Values over Six Decades." *Journal of Social Issues* 17(1961):19-28.

Gallup, G. "What Makes a Good Ad . . . on TV or in Print." *Printers' Ink*, November 6, 1953.

Gantt, V. W. "Attitude Change as a Function of Source Credibility and Levels of Involvement." Doctoral thesis, Ohio University, 1970.

Geis, F., E. Krupat, and D. Berger. "Taking Over in Group Discussion." Unpublished manuscript, New York University, 1965.

Gelfand, D. "The Influence of Self-Esteem on the Rate of Verbal Conditioning and Social Matching Behavior." *Journal of Abnormal and Social Psychology* 65(1962):259-65.

Gerard, H. B. "Conformity and Commitment to the Group." *Journal of Abnormal and Social Psychology* 68(1964):209-10.

Getzels, J. W. and H. A. Thelen. "The Classroom Group as a Unique Social System." In *The Dynamics of Instructional Groups*. Chicago: University of Chicago Press, 1960.

Gilkinson, H., S. F. Paulson, and D. E. Sikkink. "Effects of Order and Authority in an Argumentative Speech." *Quarterly Journal of Speech* 40(1954):183-92.

Gold, M. "Power in the Classroom." *Sociometry* 21(1958):50-60.

Gollob, H. and J. Dittes. "Different Effects of Manipulated Self-Esteem on Persuasibility Depending on the Threat and Complexity of the Situation." *Journal of Personality and Social Psychology* 2(1965):195-201.

Gordon, G. N. *Persuasion*. New York: Hastings House Publications, 1971.

Gottlieb, M. "Segmentation of Personality Types." In L. Stockman, ed., *Proceedings of the American Marketing Association*. American Marketing Association, 1959. Pp. 148-58.

Greenberg, B. "Media Use and Believability: Some Multiple Correlates." *Journalism Quarterly* 43(1966):665-70.

Greenberg, B., and J. Dominick. "Racial and Social Class Differences in Teenagers' Use of Television." *Journal of Broadcasting* 13(1969):331-44.

Greenberg, B. S. and G. R. Miller. "The Effects of Low-Credible Sources on Message Acceptance." *Speech Monographs* 33(1966):127-36.

Greenberg, B. S. and P. H. Tannenbaum. "The Effects of Bylines on Attitude Change." *Journalism Quarterly* 38(1961):535-37.

Gruner, C. R. "An Experimental Study of the Effectiveness of Oral Satire in Modifying Attitude." *Speech Monographs* 32(1965):149-54.

————. "A Further Experimental Study of Satire as Persuasion." *Speech Monographs* 33(1966):184-85.

————. "Satire As a Reinforcer of Attitude." Paper presented at SCA, Chicago, December, 1972.

Guterman, S. *The Machiavellians.* Lincoln: University of Nebraska Press, 1970.

Haaland, G. A. and M. Verbeatesan. "Resistance to Persuasive Communication: An Examination of the Distraction Hypothesis." *Journal of Personality and Social Psychology* 9(1968):167-70.

Hadley, H. "The Non-directive Approach in Advertising Appeals." *Journal of Applied Psychology* 37(December, 1953):496-98.

Haiman, F. "An Experimental Study of the Effects of Ethos in Public Speaking." *Speech Monographs* 16(1949):190-202.

Haines, H. D. "A Study of Why People Purchase New Products." In Raymond Haas, ed., *Science, Technology, and Marketing.* Fall Conference Proceedings of the American Marketing Association, 1966. Pp. 685-97.

Halloran, J. *Attitude Formation and Change.* Leicester, England: Leicester University Press, 1967.

Harris, T. "Machiavellianism, Judgment, Independence and Attitudes Toward Teammates in a Cooperative Judgment Task." Doctoral dissertation, Columbia University, 1966.

Hartmann, G. "A Field Experiment on the Comparative Effectiveness of Emotional and Rational Political Leaflets in Determining Election Results." *Journal of Abnormal and Social Psychology* 31(1936):99-114.

Harvey, O. "Personality Factors in Resolution of Conceptual Incongruities." *Sociometry* 26(1962):336-52.

Harvey, O. and Beverly, G. D. "Some Personality Correlates of Concept Change through Role-playing." *Journal of Abnormal and Social Psychology* 63(1961):125-30.

Harvey, O., D. Hunt, and H. Schroder. *Conceptual Systems and Personality Organization.* New York: Wiley, 1961.

Haskins, J. "Factual Recall as a Measure of Advertising Effectiveness." *Journal of Advertising Research* 6(1966):2-8.

Heider, F. "Attitudes and Cognitive Organization." *Journal of Psychology* 21(1946):107-12.

_____. *The Psychology of Interpersonal Relations.* New York: Wiley, 1958.

Heinberg, P. "Relationships of Content and Delivery to General Effectiveness." *Speech Monographs* 30(1963):105-7.

Hereford, C. *Changing Parental Attitudes through Group Discussion.* Austin: University of Texas Press, 1963.

Hewgill, M. A. and Miller, G. R. "Source Credibility and Response to Fear-Arousing Communication." *Speech Monographs* 32(1965):95-101.

Heyworth, D. "A Search for Facts on the Teaching of Public Speaking, IV." *Quarterly Journal of Speech* 28(1942):347-54.

Hochbaum, G. "The Relation between Group Members' Self-Confidence and Their Reactions to Group Pressures to Uniformity." *American Sociological Review* 19(1954):678-87.

Holt, J. *How Children Fail.* New York: Pitman, 1967.

Holtzman, P. *The Psychology of Speakers' Audiences.* Glenview, Ill.: Scott, Foresman, 1970.

Horney, K. *The Neurotic Personality of Our Time.* Norton, 1937.

Hovland, C. "Reconciling Conflicting Results Derived from Experimental and Survey Studies of Attitude Change." *American Psychologist* 14(1959):8-17.

Hovland, C. and I. Janis. *Personality and Persuasibility.* New Haven: Yale University Press, 1959.

Hovland, C., O. Harvey, and M. Sherif. "Assimilation and Contrast Effects in Reactions to Communication and Attitude Change." *Journal of Abnormal and Social Psychology* 55(1957):244-52.

Hovland, C., I. Janis, and H. Kelley. *Communication and Persuasion.* New Haven: Yale University Press, 1953.

Hovland, C., A. Lumsdaine, and F. Sheffield. *Experiments on Mass Communications.* Princeton: Princeton University Press, 1949. Pp. 201-27.

Hovland, C. I. and W. Mandell. "An Experimental Comparison of Conclusion Drawing by the Communicator and by the Audience." *Journal of Abnormal and Social Psychology* 47(1952):581-88.

Hovland, C. I. and H. Pritzker. "Effect of Opinion Change as a Function of Amount of Change Advocated." *Journal of Abnormal and Social Psychology* 54(1957):257-61.

Hovland, C. and M. Sherif. "Judgmental Phenomena and Scales of Attitude Measurement: Item Displacement in Thurstone Scales." *Journal of Abnormal and Social Psychology* 47(1952):822-32.

Hovland, C. I. and W. Weiss. "The Influence of Source Credibility on Communication Effectiveness." *Public Opinion Quarterly* 15(1951):635-50.

Howard, J. and J. Sheth. *The Theory of Buyer Behavior.* New York: John Wiley, 1969.

Hull, C. *Hypnosis and Suggestibility*. New York: Appleton-Century, 1933.

Insko, C. A. *Theories of Attitude Change*. New York: Appleton-Century-Crofts, 1967.

Insko, C. A., A. Arkoff, and V. Insko. "Effects of High Low Fear Arousing Communication Upon Opinions Toward Smoking." *Journal of Experimental and Social Psychology* 1(1965):256-66.

Janis, I. "Personality Correlates of Susceptibility to Persuasion." *Journal of Personality* 22(1954):504-18.

————. "Effects of Fear Arousal on Attitude Change: Recent Developments in Theory and Experimental Research." In L. Berkowitz, ed., *Advances in Experimental Social Psychology,* Vol. 3. New York: Academic Press, 1967. Pp. 166-224.

Janis, I. and S. Feshbach. "Effects of Fear-Arousing Communications." *Journal of Abnormal and Social Psychology* 48(1953):78-92.

Janis, I. and P. Field. "Sex Differences and Personality Factors Related to Persuasibility." In Janis et al., eds., *Personality and Persuasibility*. New Haven: Yale University Press, 1958.

Janis, I., D. Kaye, and P. Kirschner. "Facilitating Effects of 'Eating-While-Reading' on Responsiveness to Persuasive Communication." *Journal of Personality and Social Psychology* 1(1965):181-86.

Janis, I., and D. Rife. "Persuasibility and Emotional Disorder." In C. Hovland and I. Janis, eds., *Personality and Persuasibility*. New Haven: Yale University Press, 1958. Pp. 121-40.

Jecker, J., et al. "Teacher Accuracy in Assessing Cognitive Visual Feedback from Students." *Journal of Applied Psychology* 48(1964):393-97.

Jecker, J., N. Macoby, and H. Breitrose. "Improving Accuracy in Interpreting Nonverbal Cues of Comprehension." *Psychology in the Schools* 2(1965):239-44.

Johnson, A. "A Preliminary Investigation of the Relationship Between Message Organization and Listener Comprehension." *Central States Speech Journal* 21(1970):164-67.

Jones, E. and H. Gerard. *Foundations of Social Psychology*. New York: Wiley, 1967.

Jones, J. A. and G. R. Serlousky. "An Investigation of Listener Perception of Degrees of Speech Disorganization and the Effects on Attitude Change and Source Credibility." Paper presented at the ICA convention, Atlanta, Georgia, 1972.

Jones, S. C. and J. S. Shrauger. "Reputation and Self-Evaluation As Determinants of Attractiveness." *Sociometry* 33(1970):276-86.

Kaplan, A. *The Conduct of Inquiry*. San Francisco: Chandler, 1964.

Karlins, M. "Conceptual Complexity and Remote-Associative Proficiency as Creativity Variables in a Complex Problem-Solving Task." *Journal of Personality and Social Psychology* 6(1967):264-78.

Karlins, M. and H. Abelson. *Persuasion: How Attitudes and Opinions Are Changed.* New York: Springer Publishing Co., 1970.

Karlins, M. and H. Lamm. "Information Search as a Function of Conceptual Structure in a Complex Problem-Solving Task." *Journal of Personality and Social Psychology* 5(1967):456-59.

Katona, G. and E. Mueller. "A Study of Purchase Decisions." In L. Clark, ed., *Consumer Behavior: The Dynamics of Consumer Reaction.* New York: New York University Press, 1954. Pp. 30-87.

Katz, D. "The Functional Approach to the Study of Attitudes." *Public Opinion Quarterly* 24(1960):163-204.

Katz, D., I. Sarnoff, and C. McClintock. "Ego-Defense and Attitude Change." *Human Relations* 9(1956):27-45.

Katz, D. and E. Stotland. "A Preliminary Statement of a Theory of Attitude Structure and Change." In S. Koch, ed., *Psychology: Study of a Science,* Vol. 3. New York: McGraw-Hill, 1959. Pp. 423-75.

Katz, E. "The Social Itinerary of Technical Change: Two Studies on the Diffusion of Innovation." *Human Organization* 20(1961):70-82.

Katz, E., M. Gurevitch, and H. Haas. "On the Use of the Mass Media for Important Things." *American Sociological Review* 38(1973):164-81.

Katz, E. and P. Lazarsfeld. *Personal Influence: The Part Played by People in the Flow of Mass Communications.* Glencoe, Ill.: The Free Press, 1955.

Keilhacker, M. "Results of Recent Psychological and Pedagogical Research on the Protection of Youth and the Cinema (in German)." *Jugend und Film,* Munich, 1958, pp. 13-30. See also UNESCO (United Nations Educational, Scientific and Cultural Organization), Reports and Papers on Mass Communication, No. 31: *The Influence of the Cinema on Children and Adolescents: An Annotated International Bibliography.* Paris: UNESCO, 1961.

Kelley, H. "Two Functions of Reference Groups." In G. E. Swanson, T. M. Newcomb, and E. L. Hartley, eds., *Readings in Social Psychology.* 2d ed. New York: Holt, 1952. Pp. 410-14.

Kelman, H. "Effects of Success and Failure on 'Suggestibility' in the Auto-kinetic Situation." *Journal of Abnormal and Social Psychology* 45(1950): 267-85.

Kelman H. C. "Processes of Opinion Change." *Public Opinion Quarterly* 25(1961):57-78.

Kelman, H. C. and C. I. Hovland. "Reinstatement of the Communicator in Delayed Measurement of Opinion Change." *Journal of Abnormal Social Psychology* 48(1953):327-35.

Kendall, P. and K. Wolf. "The Analysis of Deviant Cases in Communications Research." In P. Lazarsfeld and Frank Stanton, eds. *Communications Research.* New York: Harper & Brothers, 1949. Pp. 152-79.

Kiesler, C. A., B. E. Collins, and N. Miller. *Attitude Change: A Critical Analysis of Theoretical Approaches.* New York: John Wiley & Sons, Inc., 1969.

Kimbrell, D. and R. Luckey. "Attitude Change Resulting from Open House Guided Tours in State Schools for Mental Retardates." *American Journal of Mental Deficiency* 69(1964):21-22.

King, B. "Relationships between Susceptibility to Opinion Change and Child Rearing Practices." In Janis, et al., eds., *Personality and Persuasibility.* New Haven: Yale University Press, 1954.

King, S. W. "An Experimental Analysis of the Effects of Message Type, Degree of Interpersonal Similarity, and Type of Interpersonal Similarity on Attitude Change and Ratings of Source Credibility." Doctoral dissertation, University of Southern California, August, 1971.

King, T. R. "An Experimental Study of the Effect of *Ethos* upon the Immediate and Delayed Recall of Information." *Central States Speech Journal* 17(1966):22-28.

Kipnis, D. M. "The Effects of Leadership Style and Leadership Power upon the Inducement of an Attitude Change." *Journal of Abnormal and Social Psychology* 57(1958):173-80.

Klapper, J. "What We Know About the Effects of Mass Communications: The Brink of Hope." *Public Opinion Quarterly* 21(1957-58):453-74.

_____. *The Effects of Mass Communication.* New York: The Free Press, 1960.

Kline, J. A. "Interaction of Evidence and Readers' Intelligence on the Effects of Short Messages." *Quarterly Journal of Speech* 55(1969):407-13.

Koponen, A. "Personality Characteristics of Purchasers." *Journal of Advertising Research* 1(1960):6-12.

Kraus, S., ed. *The Great Debate.* Bloomington: Indiana University Press, 1962.

Kraus, S., E. El-Assal, and M. DeFleur. "Fear-Threat Appeals in Mass Communication: An Apparent Contradiction." *Speech Monographs* 33(1966): 23-29.

Krech, D. and R. Crutchfield. *Theory and Problems in Social Psychology.* New York: McGraw-Hill, 1948.

Kretch, D. R., S. Crutchfield, and E. L. Ballachy. *Individual in Society.* New York: McGraw-Hill, 1962.

Lana, R. E. "Familiarity and Order of Presentation of Persuasive Communication." *Journal of Abnormal and Social Psychology* 62(1961): 573-77.

Lavery, U. A. "The Language of Law." In E. C. Gerhart, ed., *The Lawyer's Treasury.* Indianapolis: Bobbs-Merrill Co., Inc., 1956. Pp. 376-94.

Lawson, R. G. "The Law of Primacy in the Criminal Courtroom." *Journal of Social Psychology* 77(1969):121-31.

Lazarsfeld, P. *Radio and the Printed Page.* New York: Duell, Sloan and Pearce, 1940.

Lazarsfeld, P., B. Berelson, and H. Gaudet. *The People's Choice.* 2d ed. New York: Columbia University Press, 1948.

Lembo, J. M. *Why Teachers Fail.* Columbus, Ohio: Charles E. Merrill, 1971.

Lerbinger, O. *Designs for Persuasive Communication.* Englewood Cliffs, N. J.: Prentice-Hall, 1972.

Leventhal, H. "Fear Communications in the Acceptance of Preventive Health Practices." Department of Psychology, Yale University, January, 1965 (mimeographed).

Leventhal, H. and J. M. Dabbs. "Effects of Varying the Recommendations in a Fear-Arousing Communication." *Journal of Personality and Social Psychology* 4(1966):525-31.

Leventhal, H., S. Jones, and G. Trembly. "Sex Differences in Attitude and Behavior Change under Conditions of Fear and Specific Instructions." *Journal of Experimental Social Psychology* 2(1966):387-99.

Leventhal, H. and P. Niles. "A Field Experiment on Fear-Arousal with Data on the Validity of Questionnaire Measures." *Journal of Personality* 32(1964):459-79.

——————. "Persisting of Influence for Varying Durations of Exposure to Threat Stimuli." *Psychological Reports* 16(1965):223-33.

Leventhal, H. and S. Perloe. "A Relationship between Self-Esteem and Persuasibility." *Journal of Abnormal and Social Psychology* 64(1962): 385-88.

Leventhal, H. and R. P. Singer. "Affect Arousal and Positioning of Recommendations in Persuasive Communication." *Journal of Personality and Social Psychology* 4(1966):137-46.

Leventhal, H., R. Singer, and S. Jones. "Effects of Fear and Specificity of Recommendations upon Attitudes and Behavior." *Journal of Personality and Social Psychology* 2(1965):20-29.

Leventhal, H. and J. C. Watts. "Sources of Resistance to Fear-Arousing Communications on Smoking and Lung Cancer." *Journal of Personality* 34(1966):155-75.

Levy, S. "Symbolism and Life Style." In H. Boyd, Jr., and J. Newman, eds., *Advertising Management: Selected Readings.* Homewood, Ill.: Richard D. Irwin, Inc., 1965.

Lewin, K. "Studies in Group Decision." In D. Cartwright and A. Zander, *Group Dynamics.* Evanston: Row, Peterson, 1953.

Linder, D., J. Cooper, and E. Jones. "Decision Freedom as a Determinant of the Role of Incentive Magnitude in Attitude Change." *Journal of Personality and Social Psychology* 6(1967):245-54.

Lindesmith, A. and A. Strauss. *Social Psychology.* New York: Dryden Press, 1956.

Lionberger, H. *Adoption of New Ideas and Practices.* Ames: Iowa State University Press, 1960.

Lippitt, R. N., et al. "The Dynamic of Power." *Human Relations* 5(1952): 37-64.

Lippmann, W. *Public Opinion.* New York: The Macmillan Company, 1922.

Litcher, J. and D. W. Johnson. "Changes in Attitudes toward Negroes of White Elementary School Students after Use of Multi-Ethnic Readers." *Journal of Educational Psychology* 60(1969):148-52.

Lott, A. J. and B. E. Lott. "Group Cohesiveness, Communication Level, and Conformity." *Journal of Abnormal and Social Psychology* 62(1961): 408-12.

Lucas, D. and S. Britt. *Measuring Advertising Effectiveness.* New York: McGraw-Hill, 1963.

Lumsdaine, A. A. and I. L. Janis. "Resistance to 'Counter-Propaganda' Produced by One-sided and Two-sided 'Propaganda' Presentation." *Public Opinion Quarterly* 17(1953):311-18.

Lund, F. H. "The Psychology of Belief. IV. The Law of Primacy in Persuasion." *Journal of Abnormal and Social Psychology* 20(1925):183-91.

McCroskey, J. C. "A Summary of Experimental Research on the Effects of Evidence in Persuasive Communication." *Quarterly Journal of Speech* 55(1969):169-76.

————. "The Effects of Evidence as an Inhibitor of Counter-Persuasion." *Speech Monographs* 37(1970):188-94.

McCroskey, J. C. and R. E. Dunham. "Ethos: A Confounding Element in Communication Research." *Speech Monographs* 33(1966):456-63.

McCroskey, J. C. and R. S. Mehrley. "The Effects of Disorganization and Nonfluency on Attitude Change and Source Credibility." *Speech Monographs* 36(1969):13-21.

McCroskey, J. C. and D. W. Wright. "A Comparison of the Effects of Punishment-Oriented and Reward-Oriented Messages in Persuasive Communication." *Journal of Communication* 21(1971):83-93.

McCroskey, J. C., T. Jensen, and C. Todd. "The Generalizability of Source Credibility Scales for Public Figures." Paper presented at SCA convention, Chicago, Illinois, December, 1972.

McCroskey, J. C., T. Jensen, C. Todd, and J. K. Toomb. "Measurement of the Credibility of Organizational Sources." Paper presented at WSA Convention, Honolulu, Hawaii, November, 1972.

McCroskey, J. C., T. J. Young, and M. D. Scott. "The Dimensions of Source Credibility of Spouses and Peers." Paper presented at WSA Convention, Fresno, California, November, 1971.

McDavid, J. and H. Harari. *Social Psychology*. New York: Harper and Row, 1968.

McGinnes, E. "Studies in Persuasion: III. Reactions of Japanese Students to One-Sided and Two-Sided Communications." *Journal of Social Psychology* 70(1966):87-93.

McGuire, W. "The Effectiveness of Supportive and Refutational Defenses in Immunizing and Restoring Beliefs against Persuasion." *Sociometry* 24(1961):184-97.

_____. *Effectiveness of Fear Appeals in Advertising*. Advertising Research Foundation, August, 1963.

_____. "Inducing Resistance to Persuasion: Some Contemporary Approaches." In *Experimental Social Psychology*. Vol. 1 New York: Academic Press, 1964: 191-229.

_____. "The Nature of Attitudes and Attitude Change." In G. Lindzey and E. Aronson, eds. *The Handbook of Social Psychology*. Cambridge, Mass.: Addison-Wesley, 1969. Pp. 136-314.

McLuhan, M. *Understanding Media: The Extension of Man*. New York: McGraw-Hill, 1964.

McLuhan, M. and Q. Fiore. *The Medium Is the Massage*. New York: Bantam, 1967.

MacNeil, R. *The Influence of Television on American Politics*. New York: Harper & Row, 1968.

Maier, N. and R. Maier. "An Experimental Test of the Effects of 'Developmental' Versus 'Free' Discussions on the Quality of Group Decisions." *Journal of Applied Psychology* 41(1957):320-23.

Maloney, J. "Is Advertising Believability Really Important?" *Journal of Marketing* 27(1963):1-8.

_____. "Advertising Research and an Emerging Science of Mass Persuasion." *Journalism Quarterly* 41(1964).

Markel, L. "How Drastically Has Television Changed Our Politics?" *TV Guide,* October 22, 1966, p. 7.

_____. "A Program for Public-TV." *New York Times Magazine,* March 12, 1967.

Markiewicz, D. "The Effects of Humor on Persuasion." Doctoral dissertation, Ohio State University, 1972.

_____. "Can Humor Increase Persuasion, or Is It All a Joke?" Paper presented at SCA convention December, 1972, Chicago.

Maslow, A. "A Theory of Human Motivation." *Psychological Review* 50(1943):370-96.

Mausner, B. "Studies in Social Interaction: III. Effects of Variation in One Partner's Prestige on the Interaction of Observer Pairs." *Journal of Applied Psychology* 37(1953):391-93.

Mausner, B. and B. Bloch. "A Study of the Additivity of Variables Affecting Social Interaction." *Journal of Abnormal and Social Psychology* 54(1957):250-56.

Mellinkoff, D. *The Language of the Law*. Boston: Little, Brown, and Company, 1963.

Mendelsohn, H. "Broadcast Versus Personal Sources of Information in Emergent Public Crises: The Presidential Assassination." *Journal of Broadcasting* 8(1964):147-56.

_____. "Ballots and Broadcasts, Exposure to Election Broadcasts and Terminal Voting Decisions." *Public Opinion Quarterly* 29(1964):445-46.

Menzel, H. and E. Katz. "Social Relations and Innovation in the Medical Profession: The Epidemiology of a New Drug." *Public Opinion Quarterly* 19(1955):337-52.

Messerschmidt, R. "Response of Boys between the Ages of 5 and 16 years." *Journal of Genetic Psychology* 43(1933):422-27.

Meyer, V. H. and J. Gute. "The Effects of Channel Variation on Attitude Change and Source Credibility." Paper presented at the WSA convention, Honolulu, Hawaii, November, 1972.

Miller, G. R. and M. A. Hewgill. "The Effects of Variations in Nonfluency on Audience Ratings of Source Credibility." *Quarterly Journal of Speech* 50(1964):36-44.

Miller, G. R., et al. "Communication Variables in the Judicial Process." Paper presented at the SCA Convention, Chicago, December 1972.

Mills, J. and E. Aronson. "Opinion Change as a Function of the Communicator's Attractiveness and Desire to Influence." *Journal of Personality and Social Psychology* 1(1965):173-77.

Moe, J. D. "Listener Judgements of Status Cues in Speech: A Replication and Extension." *Speech Monographs* 39(1972):144-47.

Moore, J. "Status and Influence in Small Group Interactions." *Sociometry* 31(1968):47-63.

Murphy, G. *Personality, A Biosocial Approach to Origins and Structure*. New York: Harper and Row, 1947.

Myers, M. T. and A. A. Goldberg. "Group Credibility and Opinion Change." *Journal of Communication* 20(1970):174-79.

Niles, P. "The Relationship of Susceptibility and Anxiety to Acceptance of Fear-Arousing Communications." Doctoral dissertation, Yale University, 1964.

Nisbett, R. and A. Gordon. "Self-Esteem and Susceptibility to Social Influence." *Journal of Personality and Social Psychology* 5(1967):268-76.

Novak, D. W. and M. J. Lerner. "Rejection as a Consequence of Perceived Similarity." *Journal of Personality and Social Psychology* 9(1968): 147-52.

Nunnaly, J. and H. Bobren. "Variables Concerning the Willingness to Receive Communications on Mental Health." *Journal of Personality* 27(1959):38-46.

Osgood, C. F., G. J. Suci, and P. H. Tannenbaum. *The Measurement of Meaning*. Urbana: University of Illinois Press, 1957.

Osgood, C. and P. Tannenbaum. "The Principle of Congruity in the Prediction of Attitude Change." *Psychological Review* 62(1955):42-55.

Osterhouse, R. A. and T. C. Brock. "Distraction Increase Yielding to Propaganda by Inhibiting Counterarguing." *Journal of Personality and Social Psychology* 15(1970):344-58.

Ostermier, T. H. "The Effects of Type and Frequency of Reference upon Perceived Source Credibility and Attitude Change." *Speech Monographs* 34(1971):137-44.

Parker, E. "Changes in the Function of Radio with the Adoption of Television." *Journal of Broadcasting* 5(1960):39-48.

Peak, H. "Attitude and Motivation." In M. R. Jones, ed., *Nebraska Symposium on Motivation*. Lincoln: University of Nebraska Press, 1955. Pp. 149-88.

Pearce, W. B. and B. J. Brommel. "Vocalic Communication in Persuasion." *Quarterly Journal of Speech* 58(1972):298-306.

Pearce, W. B. and F. Conklin. "Nonverbal Vocalic Communication and Perceptions of a Speaker." *Speech Monographs* 38(1971):235-37.

Politz, A. "The Dilemma of Creative Advertising." In H. Boyd, Jr. and J. Newman, eds., *Advertising Management: Selected Readings*. Homewood, Ill.: Richard D. Irwin, Inc., 1965.

Powell, F. A. "The Effect of Anxiety-Arousing Messages When Related to Personal, Familial, and Impersonal Referents." *Speech Monographs* 32(1965):102.

Priest, R. F. and J. Abrahams. "Candidate Preferences and Hostile Humor in the 1968 Elections." *Psychological Reports* 26(1970):779-88.

Public Opinion Index for Industry. *Building Opposition to the Excess Profits Tax*. Princeton: Opinion Research Corporation, 1952.

Putnam, G. N. and E. M. O'Hern. "The Status Significance of an Isolated Urban Dialect." *Language* 31(1955):1-32.

Reitan, H. and M. Shaw. "Group Membership, Sex-Composition of the Group, and Conformity Behavior." *Journal of Social Psychology* 64(1964):45-51.

Reymert, M. and H. Kohn. "An Objective Investigation of Suggestibility." *Character and Personality* 9(1940):44-48.

Reynolds, W. "More Sense about Market Segmentation." *Harvard Business Review* 43(1965):107-14.

Riecken, H. W. "The Effect of Talkativeness on Ability to Influence Group Solutions of Problems." *Sociometry* 21(1958):309-21.

Riestra, M. and C. Johnson. "Change in Attitudes of Elementary School Pupils Toward Foreign Speaking Peoples Resulting from a Study of a Foreign Language." *Journal of Experimental Education* 33(1964):65-72.

Rim, Y. "Machiavellianism and Decisions Involving Risks." *British Journal of Social and Clinical Psychology* 5(1966):50-56.

Robertson, T. S. *Consumer Behavior.* Glenview, Ill.: Scott, Foresman, 1970.

Rogers, E. *Diffusion of Innovations.* Glencoe, Ill.: Free Press, 1962.

Rohrer, J. and M. Sherif, eds. *Social Psychology at the Crossroads.* New York: Harper, 1951.

Rokeach, M. *Open and Closed Mind.* New York: Basic Books, 1960.

————. *Beliefs, Attitudes, and Values.* San Francisco: Jossey-Bass Inc., 1968.

Rokeach, M. and L. Mezel. "Race and Shared Belief as Factors in Social Choice." *Science* 151(1966):167-72.

Rokeach, M., P. Smith, and R. I. Evans. "Two Kinds of Prejudice or One?" In M. Rokeach, *The Open and Closed Mind.* New York: Basic Books, 1960.

Rose, A. "The Study of the Influence of the Mass Media on Public Opinion." *Kyklos* 15(1962):465-82.

Rosenberg, M. "The Experimental Investigation of a Value Theory of Attitude Structure." Doctoral dissertation, University of Michigan, 1953.

————. "Cognitive Structure and Attitudinal Effect." *Journal of Abnormal and Social Psychology* 53(1956):367-72.

————. "An Analysis of Effective-Cognitive Consistency." In C. Hovland and M. Rosenberg, eds., *Attitude Organization and Change.* New Haven: Yale University Press, 1960 a.

————. "Cognitive Reorganization in Response to the Hypnotic Reversal of Attitudinal Affect." *Journal of Personality* 28(1960b):39-63.

————. "A Structural Theory of Attitude Dynamics." *Public Opinion Quarterly* 24(1960c):319-40.

Rosenberg, M. and R. Abelson. "An Analysis of Cognitive Balancing." In C. Hovland and M. Rosenberg, eds., *Attitude Organization and Change.* New Haven: Yale University Press, 1960. Pp. 112-63.

Rosenthal, P. I. "The Concept of Ethos and the Structure of Persuasion." *Speech Monographs* 33(1966):114-26.

Rosenthal, R. "Covert Communication in the Psychological Experiment." *Psychological Bulletin* 67(1967):356-67.

Rosnow, R. and Robinson, E., eds. *Experiments in Persuasion*. New York: Academic Press, 1967.

Rubin, I. "Increased Self-Acceptance: A Means of Reducing Prejudice." *Journal of Personality and Social Psychology* 5(1967):233-38.

Samelson, F. "Conforming Behavior under Two Conditions of Conflict in the Cognitive Field." *Journal of Abnormal and Social Psychology* 55(1957):181-87.

Samuelson, M., R. Carter, and L. Ruggels. "Education, Available Time, and Uses of Mass Media." *Journalism Quarterly* 40(1963):491-96.

Sandage, C. and V. Fryburger. *Advertising Theory and Practice*. Homewood, Ill.: Richard D. Irwin, 1971.

Sargent, L. "Communicator Image and News Reception." *Journalism Quarterly* 42(1965):35-42.

Schacter, S., N. Ellertson, D. McBride, and D. Gregory. "An Experimental Study of Cohesiveness and Productivity." *Human Relations* 4(1951): 229-38.

Scheidel, T. "Sex and Persuasibility." *Speech Monographs* 30(1963):353-58.

Schliesser, H. F. "Information Transmission and Ethos of a Speaker Using Normal and Defective Speech." *Central States Speech Journal* 19(1968): 169-74.

Schramm, W. "The Nature of News." In W. Schramm, ed., *Mass Communications*. Urbana: University of Illinois Press, 1949.

_____. *The Process and Effects of Mass Communications*. Urbana: University of Illinois Press, 1954.

_____. "How Communication Works." In W. Schramm, ed., *The Process and Effects of Mass Communication*. Urbana: University of Illinois Press, 1961.

Schramm, W. and D. Roberts, eds. *The Process and Effects of Mass Communication*. Chicago: University of Illinois Press, 1971.

Schroder, H., M. Driver, and S. Streufert. *Human Information Processing: Individuals and Groups in Complex Social Situations*. New York: Holt, 1967.

Schulman, G. I. and C. Worrall. "Salience Patterns, Source Credibility, and the Sleeper Effect." *Public Opinion Quarterly* 34(1970/71):371-82.

Scott, W. "Attitude Change through Reward of Verbal Behavior." *Journal of Abnormal and Social Psychology* 55(1957):72-75. ,

_____. "Attitude Change by Response Reinforcement: Replication and Extension." *Sociometry* 22(1959):328-35.

Schweitzer, D. A. "The Effect of Presentation on Source Evaluation." *Quarterly Journal of Speech* 56(1970):33-39.

Schweitzer, D. A. and G. P. Ginsburg. "Factors of Communicator Credibility." In C. W. Backman and P. T. Secord, eds., *Problems in Social Psychology*. New York: McGraw-Hill, 1966. Pp. 94-102.

Secord, P. F. and C. W. Backman. *Social Psychology*. New York: McGraw-Hill Book Company, 1964.

Seibert, J. *Concepts of Marketing Management*. New York: Harper & Row, 1973.

Seiler, W. J. "The Conjunctive Influence of Source Credibility and the Use of Visual Materials on Communicative Effectiveness." *Southern Speech Journal* 32(1971):174-85.

_____. "The Effects of Visual Materials on Attitudes, Credibility and Retention." *Speech Monographs* 38(1971):331-34.

Selock, D. "Political Perception at a Midwestern University." Study completed for honors social psychology seminar, University of Illinois, 1967.

Sereno, K. K. "Ego Involvement, High Source Credibility and Response to a Belief-Discrepant Communication." *Speech Monographs* 35(1968): 476-81.

_____. "Ego-Involvement: A Neglected Variable in Speech Communication Research." *Quarterly Journal of Speech* 55(1969):69-77.

Sereno, K. and G. J. Hawkins. "The Effects of Variations in Speakers Nonfluency upon Audience Ratings of Attitude toward the Speech Topic and Speaker's Credibility." *Speech Monographs* 34(1974):58-64.

Shapiro, J. G. "Responsivity to Facial and Linguistic Cues." *Journal of Communication* 18(1968):11-17.

Sharp, H. and T. McClung. "Effects of Organization on the Speaker's Ethos." *Speech Monographs* 33(1966):182-83.

Shaw, M. "A Serial Position Effect in Social Influence on Group Decisions." *Journal of Social Psychology* 54(1961):83-91.

_____. *Group Dynamics: The Psychology of Small Group Behavior*. New York: McGraw-Hill, 1971.

Sherif, C., M. Sherif, and R. Nebergall. *Attitude and Attitude Change: The Social Judgment-Involvement Approach*. Philadelphia: Saunders, 1965.

Sherif, M. "Reference Groups in Human Relations." In Coser and Rosenberg, eds., *Sociological Theory* IX. New York: Macmillan, 1957.

Sherif, M. and C. W. Sherif. *An Outline of Social Psychology*. Revised edition. New York: Harper and Brothers, 1956.

_____. "Attitude as the Individual's Own Categories: The Social Judgmental Approach to Attitude and Attitude Change." In Carolyn W. Sherif and M. Sherif, eds., *Attitude, Ego-Involvement and Change*. New York: Wiley, 1967. Pp. 105-39.

Shibutani, T. "Reference Groups as Perspectives." *American Journal of Sociology* 60(1955):562-69.

Silverman, I. "Differential Effects of Ego-Threat upon Persuasibility for High and Low Self-Esteem Subjects." *Journal of Abnormal and Social Psychology* 69(1964):567-72.

Silverman, I., L. Ford, and B. Morganti. "Inter-related Effects of Social Desirability, Sex, Self-Esteem and Complexity of Argument on Persuasibility." *Journal of Personality* 34(1966):555-68.

Simons, H. W., N. N. Berkowitz, R. J. Mayer. "Similarity, Credibility, and Attitude Change: A Review and Theory." *Psychological Bulletin* 73(1970):1-15.

Simonson, N. R. and R. M. Lundy. "The Effectiveness of Persuasive Communication Presented under Conditions of Irrelevant Fear." *Journal of Communication* 16(1966):32-37.

Singer, R. "The Effects of Fear-Arousing Communication on Attitude Change and Behavior." Doctoral dissertation, University of Connecticut, 1965.

Skornia, H. *Television and Society: An Inquest and Agenda for Improvement.* New York: McGraw-Hill, 1965.

Smart, G. "Content and Readership of Fear Magazines." *Journalism Quarterly* 41(1964):580-83.

Smith, B. O. "A Concept of Teaching." *Teachers College Record* 61(1960): 229-41.

_____. "A Conceptual Analysis of Instructional Behavior." *Journal of Teacher Education* 14(1963):294-98.

Smith, R. G. "'An Experimental Study of the Effects of Speech Organization upon Attitudes of College Students." *Speech Monographs* 18(1951): 292-301.

Sponberg, H. "A Study of the Relative Effectiveness of Climax and Anti-Climax Order in an Argumentative Speech." *Speech Monographs* 13(1946):35-44.

Staats, A. "An Outline of an Integrated Learning Theory of Attitude Formation and Function." In M. Fishbein, ed., *Readings in Attitude Theory and Measurement.* New York: Wiley, 1967.

_____. *Learning, Language, and Cognition.* New York: Holt, Rinehart and Winston, 1968.

Staats, A., C. Staats, and H. Crawford. "First-Order Conditioning of Meaning and the Parallel Conditioning of a GSR." *Journal of General Psychology.* 67(1962):159-67.

Stampel, G. and R. Kleisch. "Which Readers Are Reached if Paper Expands Coverage." *Journalism Quarterly* 43(1966):335-36.

Star, S. and H. Hughes. "Report of an Educational Campaign: The Cincinnati Plan for the United Nations." *American Journal of Sociology* 55(1950): 389-400.

Steiner, I. and H. Johnson. "Authoritarianism and Conformity." *Sociometry* 26(1963):21-34.

Stone, V. A. and H. S. Eswara. "The Likeability and Self-Interest of the Source in Attitude Change." *Journalism Quarterly* 46(1969):61-68.

Stukat, K. *Suggestibility: A Factorial and Experimental Study.* Stockholm: Almqvist and Wiksell, 1958.

Suedfeld, P. and J. Vernon. "Attitude Manipulation in Restricted Environments: II. Conceptual Structure and the Internalization of Propaganda Received as a Reward for Compliance." *Journal of Personality and Social Psychology* 3(1966):586-89.

Tannenbaum, P. "Effect of Serial Position on Recall of Radio News Stories." *Journalism Quarterly* 31(1954):319-23.

Thistlethwaite, D. L. and J. Kamenetsky. "Attitude Change Through Refutation and Elaboration of Audience Counter-Arguments." *Journal of Abnormal and Social Psychology* 51(1955):3-12.

Thistlethwaite, D. L., et al. "The Effects of 'Directive' and 'Nondirective' Communication Procedures on Attitudes." *Journal of Abnormal and Social Psychology* 51(1955):107-13.

Thompson, E. "An Experimental Investigation of the Relative Effectiveness of Organization Structure in Oral Communication." *Southern Speech Journal* 26(1960):59-69.

Tillman, R. and C. Kirkpatrick. *Promotion: Persuasive Communication in Marketing.* Homewood, Ill.: Richard D. Irwin, Inc., 1972.

Tompkins, P. K. and L. A. Samovar. "An Experimental Study of the Effects of Credibility on the Comprehension of Content." *Speech Monographs* 31(1964):120-23.

Torrance, E. P. "Some Consequences of Power Differences on Decision-Making in Permanent and Temporary Three-Man Groups," In A. P. Hare, E. F. Borgatta and R. F. Bales, eds., *Small Groups.* New York: Alfred A. Knopf, 1965. Pp. 600-609.

Triandis, H. C. *Attitude and Attitude Change.* New York: John Wiley and Sons, Inc., 1971.

Triandis, H. C. and L. Triandis. "A Cross-Cultural Study of Social Distance." *Psychological Monographs* 76(1962):No. 21 (whole No. 549).

Triandis, H. C., V. Vassilou, and M. Nassiakou. "The Cross-Cultural Studies of Subjective Culture." *Journal of Personality and Social Psychology, Monograph Supplement* No. 48(1968):1-42.

Tucker, R. K. "On the McCroskey Scales for the Measurement of Ethos." *Central States Speech Journal* 12(1971):127-29.

Tucker, W. and J. Painter. "Personality and Product Use." *Journal of Applied Psychology* 45(1961):325-39.

Wahrman, R. "High Status, Deviance and Sanctions." *Sociometry* 33(1970): 485-504.

Warren, I. D. "The Effect of Credibility in Sources of Testimony on Audience Attitudes Toward Speaker and Message." *Speech Monographs* 36(1969): 456-58.

Watson, G. and D. Johnson. *Social Psychology: Issues and Insights.* New York: J. B. Lippincott and Company, 1972.

Watson, J. D. *Behaviorism.* Chicago: W. W. Norton and Co., 1925.

Watts, W. "Relative Persistance of Opinion Change Induced by Active Compared to Passive Participation." *Journal of Personality and Social Psychology* 5(1967):4-15.

Wegrocki, H. "The Effect of Prestige Suggestibility on Emotional Attitudes." *Journal of Social Psychology* 5(1934):384-94. Cited by Hovland in G. Lindsey, ed., *Handbook of Social Psychology,* Vol. II. Cambridge: Addison-Wesley, 1954.

Weiss, W. "Emotional Arousal and Attitude Change." *Psychological Reports* 6(1960):267-80.

_____. "Effects of the Mass Media of Communication." In G. Lindzey and E. Aronson, eds., *The Handbook of Social Psychology,* Vol. V. Reading, Mass.: Addison-Wesley, 1969.

Weiss, W. and B. Lieberman. "The Effects of 'Emotional' Language on the Induction and Change of Opinions." *Journal of Social Psychology* 50(1959):129-41.

Weiss, W. and S. Steenbock. "The Influence of Communication Effectiveness of Explicitly Urging Action and Policy Consequences." *Journal of Experimental Social Psychology* 1(1965):396-406.

Weitzenhoffer, A. *Hypnotism: An Objective Study in Suggestibility.* New York: Wiley and Sons, 1953.

Weld, H. P. and M. Roff. "A Study in the Formation of Opinion Based on Legal Evidence." *Journal of Psychology* 51(1938):609-28.

Wellman, F. L. *The Art of Cross-Examination.* New York: Collier Books, 1936.

Westfall, R. "Psychological Factors in Predicting Product Choice." *Journal of Marketing* 26(1962):34-40.

Westley, B. H. and W. J. Severin. "A Profile of the Daily Newspaper Non-Reader." *Journalism Quarterly* 41(1964):45-50, 156.

Wheatley, J., ed. *Measuring Advertising Effectiveness.* Homewood, Ill.: Richard D. Irwin, 1969.

Whitehead, J. L. "Factors of Source Credibility." *Quarterly Journal of Speech* 54(1968):59-63.

_____. "Effects of Authority-Based Assertion on Attitude and Credibility." *Speech Monographs* 38(1971):311-15.

Whittaker, J. "Sex Differences and Susceptibility to Interpersonal Persuasion." *Journal of Social Psychology* 66(1965):91-94.

Widgery, R. and S. Tubbs. "Machiavellianism and Religiosity as Determinants of Cognitive Dissonance in a Counterattitudinal Situation." Paper presented to the International Communication Association, Atlanta, Georgia, April, 1972.

Wigmore, J. H. *The Principles of Judicial Proof.* Boston: Little, Brown, and Company, 1913.

Wittgenstein, Ludwig. *Philosophical Investigations.* Oxford: Basil Blackwell, 1958.

Zaltman, G. *Contributions from the Behavioral Sciences.* New York: Harcourt, Brace and World, Inc., 1965.

Zimbardo, P., E. Ebbesen, and S. Fraser. "Emotional Persuasion: Arousal State as a Distraction." Unpublished manuscript, Stanford University, 1968.

Zimbardo, P. and E. Ebbesen. *Influencing Attitudes and Changing Behavior.* Reading, Mass.: Addison-Wesley Publishing Company, 1969.

Zimbardo, P., et al. "Modifying the Impact of Persuasive Communication with External Distraction." *Journal of Personality and Social Psychology* 16(1970):669-80.

Author Index

243

Subject Index